# The Library Renovation, Maintenance, and Construction Handbook

Donald A. Barclay and Eric D. Scott

Neal-Schuman Publishers, Inc.
New York                    London

Published by Neal-Schuman Publishers, Inc.
100 William St., Suite 2004
New York, NY 10038

Copyright © 2011 Neal-Schuman Publishers, Inc.

Printed and bound in the United States of America.

The paper used in this publication meets the minimum requirements of American National Standard for Information Sciences—Permanence of Paper for Printed Library Materials, ANSI Z39.48-1992.

Library of Congress Cataloging-in-Publication Data

Barclay, Donald A.
    The library renovation, maintenance, and construction handbook / Donald A. Barclay, Eric D. Scott.
        p. cm.
    Includes bibliographical references and index.
    ISBN 978-1-55570-717-0 (alk. paper)
    1. Library buildings—United States—Design and construction. 2. Library buildings—Remodeling—United States. I. Scott, Eric D., 1965- II. Title.

Z679.2.U54B37 2011
022'.3—dc22

                                                                            2011000446

# Contents

## Part II: Library-Specific Construction and Renovation

# List of Illustrations

**FIGURES**

## TABLES

# Preface

Whether they are as small as reading-room spruce-up projects or as big as the ground-up construction of steel-and-concrete megalibraries, building projects come with the territory if you work in a library, be it public, academic, school, or special. In fiscal year 2009, for example, more than $1 billion was spent in the United States alone to build, renovate, remodel, and expand library buildings (Fox, 2009). Library building projects involve big money, and with them comes big responsibility for using all that money to the very best advantage. At the same time, the day-in, day-out responsibility of maintaining existing library buildings, while certainly less glamorous than undertaking major building projects, also involves big expenditures. The cost of adequately maintaining a building for 50 years adds up to a sum greater than the cost of constructing the building in the first place. Coincidentally, 50 years is the expected useful life span of most modern buildings (Hahn, 1990). Perhaps because they are not trained in it, perhaps because it seems tangential to the mission of filling the information needs of the people whom libraries serve, those who manage and work in libraries are too often unfamiliar with the art and science that goes into constructing, renovating, and maintaining library buildings. But, as noted, the high stakes involved demonstrate that those in the library profession have an obligation to become familiar with all that goes into putting—and keeping—a roof over their professional heads.

## Purpose

Reading *The Library Renovation, Maintenance, and Construction Handbook* will not transform a reference librarian into a general contractor, a circulation supervisor into an architect, or a desktop support technician into a building inspector. Instead, *The Library Renovation, Maintenance, and Construction Handbook* is offered as a practical familiarization manual for those facing the enormous challenges presented by either the construction of a new library building or a major remodeling of, renovation of, or addition to an existing library building. Such projects are costly and disruptive; worse, for most people who work in libraries, they are largely unfamiliar phenomena. Library staff typically have no education or training in the area of construction, and what practical knowledge exists among a library staff is usually acquired piecemeal during the course of miscellaneous library building projects and is, therefore, inevitably out-of-date. While there is nothing intrinsically wrong with learning on the job or with the passing down of lore from gray heads to greenhorns, when dealing with something as costly as a building project, and when such projects offer only one chance to get things right, a measure of advanced learning is worth a lot. That measure of learning is a big part of what *The Library Renovation, Maintenance, and Construction Handbook* was written to provide. In addition, as the title implies, this book gives library employees a solid background in the important, if not always appreciated, art of maintaining a building.

In any library project, the role any given library employee plays in that project will vary a great deal. On the low-end scale there is the library employee who is, in effect, a passive observer of a building project, having no input on the overall design, exchanging not so much as a single word with a construction professional of any sort, and contributing to the project chiefly by staying out of the way. Such sidelined individuals will, nonetheless, benefit from this book in that reading it prepares them for what to expect and, if they are by nature curious, answers many questions they might have about the mysterious construction processes unfolding around them. On the other end of the active-involvement scale are those library employees who are tapped to serve as the library's chief liaison to a project's architects and builders and who may, for the duration of a major project, spend more time in construction trailers and on the worksite than in their assigned library offices. For those placed in such exalted, occasionally overwhelming, positions, *The Library Renovation, Maintenance, and Construction Handbook* provides a detailed overview of the construction process while equipping the reader with the basic knowledge and vocabulary necessary to communicate effectively with construction professionals.

## Organization of This Book

### Part I: The Basics of Construction and Renovation

The first three chapters of *The Library Renovation, Maintenance, and Construction Handbook* provide an overview of the construction process and of how modern buildings work. Chapter 1, "Getting Familiar with the Process: The Stages of a Building Project" divides a building project into three main stages:

1. The Design Process
2. Construction
3. Commissioning

The section on the design process focuses on the importance of getting useful, realistic input from stakeholders during the programming of a building project and describes techniques for achieving this goal. While no construction process is ever typical, the construction section of Chapter 1 takes readers through the stages of a hypothetical construction process as a way of introducing such concepts as the roles of executive architects, project managers, general contractors, library project liaisons, and other key players. This section also covers such topics as the bidding process, value engineering, and worksite tours. The final section of Chapter 1, commissioning, calls out the importance of an often overlooked part of any building project by discussing such concepts as beneficial occupancy, punch lists, and final handoff from general contractor to building owner.

Chapter 2, "Overview of Building System Basics," introduces readers to the essential mechanical and structural systems that underpin modern buildings. Other topics covered include building-classification systems, steel-and-concrete construction, framed construction, site preparation, foundations, electrical and data networking systems, heating, ventilation, and cooling (HVAC) systems, plumbing systems, and lighting.

Chapter 3, "Going into Detail: Plans, Codes, and Construction Professions," picks up and expands on the theme of Chapter 2. The first part of Chapter 3 focuses on building plans and explains the major types of plans encountered during a library building project. This is supplemented by sample plans available on the accompanying CD-ROM. The second part introduces readers to the concept of building codes by covering their history as well as the current state of building codes and standards. The final part looks at the building trades, providing a listing of the major trades and describing the work typically performed by each.

### Part II: Interior Design, Maintenance, and Construction

The second part, Interior Design, Maintenance, and Construction, focuses on library interiors. Chapter 4, "How Libraries Function," surveys and generally describes the attributes of functional libraries. Divided into sections covering public and staff areas, the chapter considers library entrances and exits, book stack areas, reading areas, auditoriums, computer areas, service points, meeting rooms, children's and teenagers' rooms, restrooms, cafés, staff break rooms, workrooms, server rooms, and more.

As the title of Chapter 5, "Library Interiors," makes clear, this chapter delves into the specifics of how to creating functional and attractive interior spaces. Topics covered include working with interior designers, purchasing processes, choosing furniture, furnishings, paint, floor coverings, and lighting design.

Chapter 6, "Library Wayfinding," looks at the importance of library design as a tool for enhancing the success of library users in the simple but crucial task of finding their way around a library building. Library designs that ignore wayfinding frustrate users and impose long-term public-service burdens on library staff, so integrating wayfinding into library design is essential. This chapter goes into considerable detail on the subject of signage, in particular its use and misuse as a wayfinding tool.

### Part III: Maintaining an Existing Library Building

The final part of the book, which consists of Chapters 7 through 10, is less thematically unified than the first two sections but nonetheless covers topics of importance and interest.

Chapter 7, "Library Security and Safety in Building Design and Construction," examines a variety of threats to safety and security and describes how building design, coupled with staff training, can be used to ameliorate threats to library users, staff, collections, and equipment.

Chapter 8, "Green Libraries," treats a subject of increasing interest to librarians by looking at not only how design and construction can ease a library building's impact on the environment but also how library operations can be made greener.

Chapter 9, "Running a Library during an Addition, Renovation, or Remodeling," is concerned with the tricky balancing act of maintaining library services while the roof may be, quite literally, coming down on your head. The chapter outlines techniques for preparing library staff and users for the inconveniences of a major building project, methods for protecting library collections and equipment from worksite hazards, and options for continuing to provide library service in the midst of the chaos of construction.

Chapter 10, "Building Maintenance," covers a topic of immediate importance to underfunded libraries faced with the task of making their existing buildings last as long as possible, often well beyond those buildings' intended service lives. Topics covered include routine building maintenance; maintenance frequency and scheduling; and preventive, condition-based, and emergency maintenance.

The book ends with, Chapter 11, "The End of the Job: Building for the Future," which sums up the main concepts presented and highlights the important take-away points for readers, and an appendix on the art of crafting a request for proposal.

## CD-ROM Contents

*The Library Renovation, Maintenance, and Construction Handbook* includes a CD-ROM of supplemental materials:

1. **Glossary of Building Terms**
   A searchable glossary in HTML format defining around 800 terms likely to be encountered in the course of a library building project.

2. **Common Blueprint Symbols**
   A set of slides in PDF format showing symbols commonly used in construction blueprints. See page 2 of the PDF for an index to specific elements illustrated in the slides.

3. **Annotated Photographs to Illustrate Construction Techniques**
   A set of 160 photographs in PDF format illustrating both exterior and interior construction techniques. See p. 2 of each PDF for an index to specific elements illustrated in the photographs.

4. **List of Websites for State and Provincial Code Authorities**
   Table 3.1 provided in HTML format with live links to the different websites.

5. **Sample Building Plans**
   A set of 22 images of building plans in PDF format, including Figures 3.1–3.14, to help librarians increase their understanding of building plans.

- Sample Detail Drawing 1
- Sample Detail Drawing 2 (Figure 3.10)
- Sample Drawing Index 1 (Figure 3.2)
- Sample Drawing Index 2 (Figure 3.13)
- Sample Egress Diagram (Figure 3.12)
- Sample Elevation (Figure 3.7)
- Sample Floor Plan (Figure 3.4)
- Sample Generic Blueprint (Figure 3.1)
- Sample HVAC Plan
- Sample Interior Finish Plan (Figure 3.11)
- Sample IT Floor Plan
- Sample Lighting Plan
- Sample Partial Elevation (Figure 3.9)
- Sample Plumbing Plan
- Sample Power & Signal Plan
- Sample Reflected Ceiling Plan (Figure 3.5)
- Sample Roof Plan (Figure 3.6)
- Sample Section Elevation (Figure 3.8)
- Sample Security Plan 1 (Figure 3.14)
- Sample Security Plan 2
- Sample Site Plan 1
- Sample Site Plan 2 (Figure 3.3)

Like anyone (including library employees) who is part of a specialized profession, architects and builders will throw around the jargon of their trades without considering that outsiders do not understand it; at times, it sometimes seems they use jargon precisely *because* outsiders do not understand it. Even though construction-related jargon words may seem incomprehensible, they often have simple, easily understood definitions if one knows where to look. That is where the searchable glossary on this CD-ROM comes in. Using it will allow library workers to look up construction jargon they read or hear during a project in order to understand what is being said as well as to communicate their desires to architects and builders.

The building plans and blueprint symbols included on the CD-ROM may be used to familiarize oneself with the symbols, layout, and purpose of building plans without the confusing distraction of an entire set of plans that one is supposed to read through and fully understand, often in a very short time. The construction photos serve a similar purpose by illustrating various construction methods so that the reader knows either what to expect from a coming project or how to identify what is happening during an ongoing project.

## Audience

Whether it is managing an existing library building, surviving a remodeling job, or being party to a major construction project, the people who actually work in libraries should have a voice in decisions about the design and function of their workplaces. This is especially true in an era when the importance of the library as a place is recognized as key to the long-term survival of libraries and the library profession. Too often, however, those who work in libraries find that decisions about the design and function of library buildings are made without their input because, in part, they do not have enough knowledge about how library facilities are constructed and maintained to know when they should be part of the decision-making process or how to make their voices heard when they do choose to speak up. With this in mind, the primary audience for *The Library Renovation, Maintenance, and Construction Handbook* includes anyone who works in a library, whether that person is a library administrator, an MLS-holding librarian, or a nondegreed library staff member. For those who have been through a building project or two, this book provides a comprehensive review and perhaps a new idea or two; for those new to building projects, it provides an excellent preparation for embarking on such an adventure for the first time.

Among the secondary audiences for this book are those who, while not actually employed by a library, work closely with libraries. This group includes high-level non-librarian administrators (such as city, school district, or campus administrators) with some authority over a library operation, library board members, or members of the public who have been invited to participate in planning a library building project. Library school students make up another secondary audience. While library schools do not teach construction management, *The Library Renovation, Maintenance, and Construction Handbook* could be used as a library school management course because the management issues raised by building projects—budgeting, human resources, planning, prioritizing, crisis management—are the core issues with which any manager must contend. Finally, this book may also find an audience among architects and construction management professionals working on library building projects.

No, this book will not teach such professionals anything they do not already know about building design or construction techniques; it will, however, teach them a lot about how library professionals see the buildings in which they work and how they would like those buildings to function.

## References

Fox, Bette-Lee. 2009. "The Constant Library." *Library Journal* 134, no. 20 (December 15): 26–40.

Hahn, Arthur P. 1990. "Facility Performance and Serviceability from a Facility Manager's Viewpoint." In *ASTM STP 1029, Performance of Buildings and Serviceability of Facilities*, edited by Gerald Davis, Francis T. Ventre, ASTM Committee E-6 on Performance of Building Constructions, 37–44. Philadelphia: American Society for Testing Materials.

# Acknowledgments

The authors would like to thank their many University of California, Merced, colleagues, both inside and outside the library, who experienced (or maybe endured) with us the once-in-a-lifetime experience of simultaneously building a brand-new library and a brand-new campus. We extend our special thanks to UC Merced University Librarian Bruce Miller, who generously shared his thoughts and experience as he read our draft chapters; to Sandy Wood, our wise and patient (did we mention patient?) editor; and to the indispensable Charles Harmon and the rest of the outstanding Neal-Schuman team.

For graciously sharing their excellent photographs, we also thank professional photographer Hans Marsden; Min Jiang-Kolb and the entire staff of UC Merced Physical Planning, Design, and Construction; Arnie Maurins (System Director), Corinne Dickman, and Elizabeth A. Williams of the Washoe County Library System. We also thank Helen Henry of UC Davis Library for providing us with data about the UC Davis Library's successful energy-saving program.

Donald Barclay especially thanks his daughter, Tess, who patiently puts up with her dad's annoying habit of writing books without any wizards or magic in them.

Eric Scott particularly thanks his wife, Claudia Lange, who tolerated his many weekend days spent in the office while writing this book... and for doing his share of cleaning the cat box. He also wishes to thank William C. (Bill) Scott, a retired building inspector who generously provided both his knowledge and photographs.

# I

# The Basics of Construction
# and Renovation

# 1

# Getting Familiar with the Process: The Stages of a Building Project

A rule of thumb for project-management timelines holds that, of the total time spent on a project, project managers should allocate:

- one-third for design,
- one-third for doing, and
- one-third for testing.

For a building project (which, throughout this book, signifies any project involving renovation, remodeling, expansion, or new-building construction) the middle third of the triad tends to bulge out in both directions, so the formula may end up closer to:

- one-quarter for design,
- one-half for doing (aka "construction"), and
- one-quarter for testing (aka "commissioning").

Even though construction may take the biggest bite out of the timeline, both the design and commissioning stages are essential to a successful building project. This chapter examines all three elements of the project-management triad in order to provide an outline of the stages of the building-project process and to suggest possible roles for library staff in each stage. Although this chapter discusses the most common methods and practices for designing, constructing, and commissioning a building project, there is always the chance for deviations from the norm. When embarking on a building project, it pays to be both informed and ready for surprises.

## Stage 1: The Design Process

Here is the worst-case scenario for designing any library building project:

*Some authority (library board, city council, library director, school board) announces to great fanfare that a library building project is in the works. And, ta-da, here is the architect's model along with the completed plans.*

Just one problem. With the possible exception of a few senior library managers far removed from the day-to-day operations of the library, nobody who actually works in or uses the library has been consulted in any way.

Could such a disaster really befall an innocent library? Possibly. Maybe the authorities, as devoted fans of *The Fountainhead*, granted some uncompromising architectural genius artistic license to freely create whatever they desired without being burdened by such mundane realities as the needs of everyday people. Maybe the big donor who gave the money for the project went to the trouble of specifying every project detail down to the color of the shag carpet in the public restrooms. (Wait a minute. Anyone who works in a library knows you can't... Exactly the point.) However it happens, top-down design is a recipe for disaster.

But doesn't someone have to take charge of a design project? If you try to involve everyone, you end up dragging your best creative minds down to the lowest common denominator. The result will be design by committee at its mediocre worst.

Obviously, there must be a balance between designs imposed from the top and mob rule. The way to achieve such a balance is to employ effective group processes in order to constructively involve stakeholders (library staff, local authorities, architects, builders, library users, etc.) in the design process. The goal is not to get everyone involved in the entire design process—much of which is far too technical and specialized for group input to be anything other than a hindrance—but specifically to get stakeholders involved in the early part of the design process known as *programming*. In a nutshell, programming is the part of the design process during which the stakeholders communicate to the design team their needs and desired outcomes for a building project. (The design team almost certainly includes architects but may also include surveyors, interior designers, and various types of engineers—civil, mechanical, electrical, structural, etc.)

## *Programming*

Designing a building project is in some ways like making a movie. While a movie may begin with a single individual's concept, and while it is possible for a single individual to write the initial screenplay that fleshes out that concept, by the time the screenplay has been interpreted by script doctors, the director, cinematographers, actors, film and sound editors, studio executives, the legal department, and marketing experts, the final result may not look all that much like the original concept. So too, by the time an initial concept for a building project has been through the hands of stakeholders, design architects, executive architects, engineers, lawyers, budget managers, project mangers, and construction workers, the final result may not look all that much like the original concept. Given the many hands involved in a building project, using group processes to involve multiple stakeholders is integral to a successful outcome rather than merely being a feel-good exercise. At the same time, it is important to remember that employing group process does not mean everyone connected in any way to the library gets a seat at the drafting table. Far from it. It means only that during the programming phase of the design process, the interests of all the stakeholders are (or should be) given fair consideration, though in the end nobody—not library staff, not library users, not the financers, not the architects, not the contractors—gets everything his or her way.

---

### Programming a Multiple-Use Building

Even more than with a stand-alone library building project, good group process is crucial when programming a multiple-use building. With a multiple-use building, the stakeholder group is expanded to include multiple tenants (architectural jargon for the people who will eventually occupy the completed project, regardless of whether they actually pay rent for the privilege). Even the most magnanimous, team-oriented co-tenants are, like it or not, in competition for limited space, and so the interest of one tenant must not be allowed to run roughshod over the interests of co-tenants. Suppose, for example, firefighters, sheriff's deputies, county clerks, and librarians are slated to share a multiple-use county building. A group process that brings together representatives of these groups so that they can learn about and appreciate one another's needs is much preferable to a situation in which co-tenants who mistrust one another approach the design process as a battle to see who can lay claim to the most usable square feet regardless of actual needs.

---

While the many techniques for carrying out effective group processes are beyond the scope of this book, the most common of these techniques—surveys, brainstorming sessions, focus groups, interviews—are likely familiar to anyone who has worked for long in the library profession. One group process technique which is often used in architecture and urban planning but which may be unfamiliar to many in the library profession is the charrette. A charrette typically involves a varied group of stakeholders intensively working under a rigid time constraint to resolve specific design issues. While the charrette can take many forms, in most cases a group of stakeholders meets and, for a set period of time, works exclusively to define the design issues and determine the basic requirements for a building project. As the process unfolds, iterative feedback loops are created, ideas are revised and refined, and, in the end, a draft plan emerges. One of the greatest strengths of the charrette process is that the rigid timeline ensures that there will, in fact, be an end to the process. When conducted properly—under the guidance of a well-trained and experienced facilitator—a charrette will save time and money, represent the interests of a wide swath of stakeholders, build trust among stakeholders, and result in the adoption of the best possible design.

Whatever group process is used during programming, it is important for participants to express themselves freely, secure in the knowledge that none of their ideas will be killed at birth. It is equally important, however, to recognize that not all ideas are good ideas and that most ideas—even those with some merit—will never make it into the final construction documents. The reason for allowing ideas, no matter how absurd, to fly freely in the early stages of the design process is partly to generate creative new ideas and partly to put enough ideas on the table for the purpose of comparison. Since no idea is perfect, it is only by comparing ideas to one another that programmers can decide which ideas rate as good/workable and which rate as bad/unworkable. Yes, there is, in the end, such a thing as a bad idea.

---

**Don't Forget the Drawing Board**

Possibly because librarians are highly oriented to the written word, the profession tends to rely more on speech and writing than on images. In programming a building project, images can be the most powerful tools for conveying ideas. To encourage the use of images in the programming process, it is necessary both to supply participants with the tools to create images (paper, pencils, flip charts, whiteboards, markers, etc.) and to reassure everyone involved that even crude images are an acceptable means for communicating ideas. The purpose of images in early design stages is to communicate ideas, not win first prize at an art exhibition.

Because they allow images to be saved as digital files, interactive whiteboards are great tools for such group processes as design charrettes and brainstorming sessions. If interactive whiteboards are not available but ordinary whiteboards are, participants or facilitators can use digital cameras to record sketched-out images before a board is erased and reused.

---

## Data for Programming

Any programming process is going to be more effective if everyone involved is supplied with the best, most complete data on the library and its users, both current and potential. Important point: Anecdote is not data. Collecting good data requires hard work. It also requires money to design objective data-collection instruments, collect the data, and then process and accurately interpret the meaning of the data. While data may be collected and processed using in-house resources, and while in-house data collection and analysis is better than nothing at all, the do-it-yourself approach is perilous at best. To begin with, it is amazingly easy to (quite unintentionally) skew homemade data-collection instruments to produce the result the data gatherer sought in the first place. Then there are such pitfalls as insufficient sample sizes, nonrandom samples, statistical errors, and misinterpretation of the results. Data collection is not a job for amateurs when the stakes are as high as they are for building projects. Employing outside assistance to collect and analyze data is an up-front financial burden that is temptingly avoidable; however, the payoffs to be gained from basing design decisions on good data, as opposed to basing them on guess-work or bad data, dwarf even steep up-front costs. Finally, if library managers know that planning for a building project is in the pipeline—even if it is a year or more in the future—it is not too soon to start collecting the best possible data to inform that planning process.

Data about things other than library use and users is valuable to those involved in a programming exercise. Budget information, for example, is key to good decision making. It is one thing to know you are planning a $100,000 remodeling job, quite another to know that there is $15 million available for a major expansion. Information about the mission and history of both the library and its parent institution is valuable, especially for those stakeholders who are not members of the library's staff. Such key facts as the amount of land available for building, major zoning limitations, and specific building requirements (e.g., the exterior must be red brick to fit in with the rest of the campus architecture; the building may not be more than three stories high) are all examples of information that will help participants produce realistic outcomes that actually can be implemented rather than fantasy castles on which ground will never be broken.

A final point about basing programming decisions on data is that there are times when it is perfectly reasonable to go against what the data say. For example, suppose that data on students at a commuter college show that 90 percent of the students own laptop computers but that, overwhelmingly, these students report they do not like carrying their laptops to campus. One legitimate decision path would be to incorporate large computer labs into the library design to accommodate the students' preference. However, an equally legitimate decision path would be to develop a laptop-oriented design under the reasoning that the expense of computer labs is not justified simply to accommodate the students' preference for not carrying their laptops.

### Group Process Outcomes

On the one hand, a good design team wants to know what its clients (in effect, the stakeholders) need and want from a building project. Phrases like "client involvement," "client focus," and "client centered" are part of the rhetoric of contemporary design architects because, by and large, today's practicing architects accept the idea that creating a successful design requires involving the client in the process. By this standard, a project that pleases the design team while failing to meet the needs of the client is not considered a success. When group processes work as they should, the outcomes clearly communicate client needs and wants so that the design team can apply its talents and knowledge to deliver a successful project.

On the other hand, design teams are not comprised of obedient robots. So when stakeholders involved in programming a building project produce what they consider outstanding outcomes, those outcomes should not be considered rigid specifications. Even if a design team was willing to slavishly follow a set of outcomes put together by a group of stakeholders, to do so would be impossible given all the limitations around which design teams must work: project budgets, building codes, environmental regulations, engineering requirements, topography, aesthetic concerns, and the laws of physics. The outcomes of a programming exercise comprise a sketch map, not a set of marching orders.

To foster communication between stakeholders and design teams, what form should programming outcomes take so they can they be successfully incorporated into an architectural plan? In fact, there is no single form for the simple reason that programming outcomes vary according to the group process followed. Even very similar group processes may use different labels to identify their outcomes. Whatever the group process, and whatever labels are attached to the final products of the process, the end result should produce a vision statement and a prioritized list of outcomes.

### Vision Statement

A vision statement is a high-level expression of what the stakeholders hope a building project will achieve. A vision statement should look to the future, provide inspiration, and contain enough specificity for decision making. Two sample vision statements follow:

The Normal State University Library renovation and expansion will enhance access to information by students, faculty, and staff by expanding physical space, enhancing access to electronic information resources, and facilitating both group and individual study.

The Bower Creek Public Library remodeling project will empower library users by enhancing wayfinding, relocating the most popular information resources and services near the entrance of the building, and improving sight lines between staffed service points and the most heavily used areas in the building.

While the second vision is more specific than the first, both are acceptable because they strike a balance by being specific enough to express ideas on which to base decisions ("facilitating both group and individual study," "enhancing wayfinding,") but not so specific as to be dogmatic or inflexible. For an existing organization, vision statements may take cues from the organization's mission statement. For a building project undertaken by a new organization, a vision statement can come before the mission statement. In the case where a building project will fundamentally transform an organization, an existing mission statement may need to be rewritten to encompass that transformation.

### Outcomes: Communicating Needs and Wants

Besides providing a vision statement, the programming process should produce a set of outcomes that spell out what the library needs and wants from the building project. While these outcomes are more specific than what is called out in a vision statement, they are still general enough to allow for creative solutions from the architectural team. Whether these outcomes are labeled "requirements," "desirables," "needs," "project goals," or something else entirely, they work best when they are about what is needed or wanted rather than about the exact means for meeting a particular need. For example, an outcome might state:

*Usage and survey data show that the students of Normal State University need library spaces to accommodate group study, typically involving groups of from four to eight students. The redesign of the library should accommodate this need.*

Some things worth noting about this outcome:

1. It is based on data.
2. It states a need but does not state a specific solution. That is, it does not say, "The NSU Library redesign must include eleven 8-foot by 10-foot group study rooms." Stating the need rather than dictating the details opens the door for the design team to come back with innovative solutions that perhaps never occurred to the stakeholders. At the same time, it also leaves room for the design team to come back with a design that calls for eleven 8-foot by 10-foot group study rooms, if that turns out to be the best solution. Knowing all of the options and staying current with new trends and solutions is a big part of what designers are paid to do. Rigid stakeholder demands that do not allow the hired design-team experts to bring all their knowledge to the table are a waste of resources.

3. The open-endedness of this outcome implicitly recognizes that each need must be balanced against every other need. Group study space is needed, but it must be balanced against equally valid needs for individual study space, stack areas, and library office spaces. In fact, prioritizing needs is a necessary part of any group process. Coming up with a laundry list of needs is rather easy and enjoyable; prioritizing such a list is where the hard work begins.

---

### Useful Resources for the Programming Process

A copy of *Time-Saver Standards for Interior Design and Space Planning*, 2nd Edition, by Joseph De Chiara, Julius Panero, and Martin Zelnik (New York: McGraw-Hill, 2001) is a great investment for librarians involved in programming a building project. Something of a *CliffsNotes* for architects, *Time-Saver Standards for Interior Design and Space Planning* contains data and drawings for such features as furniture, architectural details, and interior spaces. Have no idea how big a public restroom should be or how it should be laid out? There is a drawing of one, with dimensions, in *Time-Saver Standards*. Want to know how to create a layout for classroom space, an in-house café, or an office suite? *Time-Saver Standards* can help with those, too. *Time-Saver Standards for Interior Design and Space Planning* is not the only book in the *Time-Saver Standards* family, but it is the most useful for nonexperts. That said, other books in the *Time-Saver Standards* family may be worth considering, depending on the level of need and amount of librarian involvement in a building project.

Other useful planning resources include the following:

- Sannwald, William W. 2009. *Checklist of Library Building Design Considerations*, 5th edition. Chicago: American Library Association. Published in true checklist format, Sannwald's *Checklist of Library Building Design Considerations* consists of something in the neighborhood of 2,000 questions designed to help library building programmers make sure that nothing is overlooked in the programming process.
- Lushington, Nolan. 2002. *Libraries Designed for Users: A 21st Century Guide*. New York: Neal-Schuman Publishers. Focused on library users, this book provides a thorough guide for planning and designing a new library or remodeling an existing one.

---

## Designing for the Future; Designing for Flexibility

Before prioritizing any programming outcomes, it is the job of the stakeholders involved in the process to closely examine and critically analyze each proposed outcome. When proposed outcomes are analyzed it is very likely that, before the process is through, each one is going to end up changed, if not entirely discarded.

Both of the revised outcomes in the Sample Outcomes sidebar point out the importance of programming to meet future needs rather than present or, even worse, past needs. In most cases, once a building project is completed, the library is not going to see another such project for many years, perhaps many decades. If a completed building project is going to function well over the span of all those years and decades, programmers must work with an eye on the future, not on the present or past. Although data that show

---

### Sample Outcomes

**Proposed Outcome #1**

Collection data show that in the past ten years the library has added an average of 5,000 volumes per year to the collection. In order to get through the next 20 years, the library will need additional stack space to accommodate 100,000 new volumes.

**Analysis of Outcome #1**

- The library is rapidly canceling print-format journals in favor of online journals and rarely acquires indexes or book series in print format any longer. From all appearances, the volume of print-format materials will decline over the next 20 years.
- The library could easily send 10,000 low-use books to its off-site storage facility instead of keeping them in the library.
- The library has not carried out a systematic weeding in over 20 years. Doing so could remove an estimated 5,000 to 10,000 unneeded and unwanted books from the library stacks.
- Erecting excess stacks that will not be needed for many years takes away space that could be used for other purposes right now.

**Revised Outcome #1**

Although collection data show that in the past ten years the library has added an average of 5,000 volumes per year to the stacks, our prediction is that electronic information will reduce this rate of growth; in addition, the library plans to send 10,000 low-use volumes to its off-site storage facility and weed 5,000 to 10,000 books from the collection. In order to get through the next 20 years, the library will need additional stack space to accommodate 25,000 new volumes.

**Proposed Outcome #2**

The library currently has ten microfilm/microfiche readers. The redesigned library will need space to accommodate this equipment.

**Analysis of Outcome #2**

- The rise of online newspapers, magazines, and government documents has sharply reduced the use of this equipment.
- Eliminating all but one or two readers would allow the library to meet the need for access to microfilm/microfiche-format information while opening up space for other uses.

**Revised Outcome #2**

Although the library currently has ten microfilm/microfiche readers, changes in information technology have reduced the need for these readers. The redesigned library need include space for only two readers.

---

how a library is being used in the present day is, as stated, valuable for informing the planning process, data about today does not necessarily predict future use; in fact, such data can actually send planners down the wrong path. In 1995, library-use data from almost any academic research library would have pointed out the necessity of providing a large current-periodicals reading room equipped with multiple copiers to support access to scholarly journals; by 2005, that model of accessing information had been rendered largely obsolete by the advent of electronic journals.

Another path that leads to designs overly focused on the present instead of the future is to make decisions based to a large extent on the idiosyncratic likes and dislikes of the people who happen to be working in the library during the design process. The fact that the outspoken and influential head of circulation has a prejudice against windows in staff offices is not, by itself, a good reason to eliminate office windows from a design plan if the presence of those windows is a better long-term choice for the library. A related error is to rigidly plan around a very specific workflow or job duty:

> The interlibrary loan (ILL) office must have both an entrance and exit door for circular patron flow; a stand-up service counter exactly ten feet long; and a courtroom-gate-style entrance for access to the staff area behind the service counter. No other design is acceptable because this is how ILL is done.

And always will be done. Until there is a change to how ILL is done, thereby rendering such a rigid design more of a hindrance than a help.

Even when library stakeholders consciously program with the future in mind, doing so successfully is not easy, especially in a world where technology changes constantly. If planners guess wrong about the future, the result can be as bad as, or worse than, not having planned for the future at all. Imagine library building-project planners circa 1985 calling for thousands of linear feet of purpose-built shelving to house and display all the tens of thousands of VHS (or, worse, Betamax) tapes the library anticipated acquiring over the next 30 years. A second hazard in planning for the future is planning so far in advance that present-day library users end up excessively shortchanged. Not providing power outlets in public study spaces because all electronic devices are predicted to have (in ten years) batteries that last 48 hours on a single charge is getting too far ahead of the curve.

The best way to accommodate the needs of the future without shortchanging the needs of the present is to plan, as much as possible, for flexibility. Conservators of rare books and manuscripts live by one golden rule: "Don't do anything to a book or manuscript that cannot be undone at a later date." While "Don't do anything to a building that cannot be undone at a later date" may be a little too extreme for building-project planners, it is not a bad goal to keep in mind. After all, every design element—computer lab, study rooms, office spaces, book stacks—is a temporary arrangement that will, sooner or later, be converted to some other purpose or used in some dramatically different way. And with that in mind, it pays to think about how to design spaces so they can be most easily reconfigured for some unanticipated use. A rather simple example is acquiring computer-lab furniture that meets today's need for desktop computing but is not so purpose-built that it could not someday be used for other purposes. Of course there is no magic formula for flexibility, and some spaces must be designed to meet a present need without regard for what may come five or ten or more years in the future; that said, designing in flexibility wherever possible is still worth the effort and expense. Except in the case of a major remodeling project, the funds available for repurposing spaces piecemeal are almost always much less than what is available during a building project. Spending a little more in the course of a building project in order to reduce the cost of repurposing at a later date is an investment in the future that adds to the overall value and usefulness of a project.

### The Building Project as Catalyst for Change

Although it may be silently understood by those programming a building project, the following idea is worth stating:

*Building projects are the best opportunities libraries have to make rapid, significant changes to their operations and institutional cultures.*

In many ways, the changes to operations and institutional cultures that can result from building projects are more important than any changes wrought on the built environment itself. A building-project programming process is the ideal opportunity to evaluate the big picture of what a library does, ask what the library could become, and take bold steps in a new direction. Even the simple disruptiveness of a building project—normal work routines broken; a sacrosanct "vital" service interrupted without the world ceasing to spin; staff displaced and forced to figure out creative new, sometimes better, ways to do their jobs—can open up staff and library users to the possibility of changes that they would oppose with all possibly mulishness under normal circumstances. However, if substantial change is going to occur, it must be intentionally and thoughtfully programmed into the project; coming up with a design and hoping that it will make things change is not enough. If the only outcome a building project achieves is to let a library do what it has always done in bigger/newer surroundings, the programmers have allowed a rare opportunity to slip through their fingers.

*If a building project does not substantially change the way a library operates, if it fails to change what the library does and how it does it, that project is a failure.*

### The End of the Programming Phase

After the programming phase, the design team will likely produce rough schematic drawings to give some substance to the ideas that have been put forward. Schematic drawings include rough floor plans with dimensions, materials, colors, and so on. It is common for all the outcomes that result from a programming process to exceed the budget, so downward adjustments (smaller, fewer, cheaper) may kick in as early as the schematic drawing stage. While there should be feedback from the stakeholders to the design team during the schematic drawing stage, the feedback loop must inevitably tighten as the design team produces increasingly detailed architectural drawings. The cost of constantly redoing detailed drawings at the whim of the stakeholders is prohibitive, and the more detailed the drawings get, the more costly changes become. This is why it is important for stakeholders to be fully involved and to communicate their needs as clearly as possible during the programming portion of the design phase before big changes to the design become a financial impossibility.

After the schematics come the working drawings detailing the specific requirements of the building project, including electrical and mechanical systems. In their final form, working documents become contract documents (though the terms "working documents" and "contract documents" are sometimes used interchangeably). Once all parties sign off on the contract documents, they become part of the legal contract that binds the owner, architect, and contractor. (The owner is the person or, more often in the case of a library, the corporate body [library board, local government entity, school board, university regents, etc.] that funds the building project and has legal ownership of it. In practice, the owner is usually represented by a designated individual, such as the project manager, or a team comprised of various individuals—project manager, library director, vice president for administration, school district architect, etc.) Changes to finalized contract documents are considered change orders and may (though not inevitably) generate extra charges from contractors.

---

**Basic Functions of Architectural Drawings**

1. Bring coherence to a set of ideas.
2. Convince the client that a design meets the client's needs.
3. Define the contractual obligations of all parties involved.
4. Give contractors a set of plans from which to carry out the actual construction work.
5. Create a record of the completed work.

---

### Executive Architects

When most people think of architects, they think of design architects like Frank Lloyd Wright or I.M. Pei, artistic geniuses whose brilliant creations are as much a part of the cultural heritage as the greatest paintings, novels, or symphonies. However, design architects do only a relatively small part of the work on building projects. It is the executive architects (also know as "architects of record") who will create up to 90 percent of the contract documents; deal with code, zoning, environmental, and other legal compliances; manage site preparation; and work directly with contractors to move a building project from design to reality. It is possible for executive architects to come from the same firm as the design architects, but they may just as easily come from an entirely different firm. Executive architects will spend far more time on the worksite than the design architects (who, in fact, need never set foot on the worksite) and are the architects who respond to the routine crises and road bumps that are part of every building project. Executive architects do not carry the glamorous cachet of design architects, but they are vital to the success of a building project.

## Stage 2: Construction

The most visible and visceral stage of any building project, construction is an exciting time. It can also be a disruptive, stressful, and frustrating time. During construction it is important for all involved to understand their roles in the building project and to prepare themselves so that the uncontrollables that occur in every construction job do not become overwhelming. Construction schedules fall behind; architects and contractors make mistakes; things that seemed wonderful on paper turn out to be disappointments in the cold light of three-dimensional reality. Working intimately on a building project makes disappointments seem all the worse because the eyes tend to focus on everything that goes wrong while becoming blind to everything that goes right. The best defense is to enter the construction stage understanding that there will be disappointments and remaining aware that every battle cannot be fought. Be prepared to live with the disappointments you can live with and save your energy for the battles that really matter. There will be enough of the latter to keep you plenty busy.

### Project Manager

Except for very small building projects, during the construction phase of the project the owner (the library or its parent organization) will likely employ a trained construction professional whose primary job is to look out for the owner's interest. This person is commonly called the *project manager* and may come from inside or outside the owner's organization. Project managers spend much of their time physically present on the worksite making sure that the work is being done correctly and up to the standards called for in the construction documents. The job of the project manger can be full time or more, and on larger projects there may be a team that includes a project manager as well as any number of assistants charged with overseeing and inspecting various aspects of the building project.

### The Library Building-Project Team

Because the job of project manager is a highly specialized role requiring substantial knowledge of construction theory and practice, it is unlikely that anyone from the library staff will serve as project manager except on the smallest of building projects. That said, it is not unusual for someone from the library staff to take on a project-liaison role that involves making sure the library's interests are represented during the construction phase. The project liaison works closely with the project manager and may also have direct dealings with contractors and executive architects. On big building projects, the project-liaison role can be a full-time job, with someone from the library staff issued a hard hat and relieved of other library duties in order to spend all of his or her time focusing on the building project. The project liaison may also work with a small building-project team composed of handpicked library staff who provide advice, assist in communicating construction-related news to the rest of the library staff, and otherwise pitch in as needed.

### Bidding Process

With the finalization of the contract documents comes the bidding process in which contracts for all or, on large projects, parcels of the building project are awarded. The most common type of bidding process is design-build-bid, in which the following process occurs:

1. Architects create construction documents.
2. These documents are made available to general contractors who calculate the cost of the project (including the hiring of subcontractors) and submit bids.

3. The general contractor with the winning bid is awarded the contract and can begin work on the project.

Other bidding methods include design-build (the designer and contractor are a single entity) and construction-manager-as-contractor (a construction manager is hired during the design phase and then becomes the contractor during the construction phase). The intricacies of bidding processes are managed by groups of experts (architects, construction consultants, and financial managers) that normally do not include librarians. This makes sense given the complexity of construction bidding, but it is useful if at least the library building-project liaison and key library managers are kept informed of the major ups and downs of the bidding process. Even if they do not play an active role in the bidding process, it is useful for librarians to understand some of the terminology of that process.

---

### Construction Bidding Terminology

**bid bond**: Bond posted by each contractor to ensure that, should the contractor who is awarded the bid prove unable to carry out the work, the owner can award the bid to the next highest bidder with the bid surety picking up the cost difference between the two bids.

**bid solicitation**: The process of making potential bidders aware of a bid opportunity and providing access to contract documents.

**competitive bidding**: A system under which the contractor who proposes to do the work at the lowest price is awarded the contract. At its best, competitive bidding keeps prices low, prevents fraud and favoritism, and stimulates innovation as contractors are pushed to find ways of doing things as efficiently as possible. While it is possible (if foolhardy) to award competitive contracts strictly on the basis of the lowest bid, it is more common to award competitive bids based on a combination of price, bidder qualifications, and estimated value of the end product.

**open bidding**: Under open bidding, a project is advertised in newspapers and trade publications with all qualified contractors allowed to bid. Open bidding is often required on projects funded with public monies. The opposite of open bidding is *closed bidding*, under which an owner can limit the contractors allowed to bid. Closed bidding is normally used only on private projects.

**payment bond**: Bond posted by each contractor to safeguard suppliers and subcontractors, should the contractor fail to pay for materials or labor.

**performance bond**: Bond posted by each contractor to safeguard the owner if the contractor is unable to complete the work as called for in the contract documents.

**prequalification**: A process in which potential bidders are screened to ensure that they are fundamentally qualified to do the work on which they are bidding.

**responsive bid**: A bid that is deemed to meet the requirements called for in the solicitation for bids.

---

## Value Engineering

When someone uses the phrase *value engineering*, he or she may be referring to a legitimate engineering specialty that focuses on getting the most value out of projects.

On the other hand, the phrase may also be meant as a euphemism for the process of cutting features out of a building project that is running over budget, typically by finding less expensive substitutes or removing discrete parts of the project. An extreme example of the euphemistic kind of value engineering would be reducing the cost of a building project by reducing the total square footage by 25 percent; obviously, such a drastic change would have to take place during the design stage rather than after construction has begun. A less extreme example might be replacing wood-and-chrome stair banisters with less expensive painted-metal banisters.

Value engineering becomes a dangerous game when someone in authority who does not fully understand the library's needs practices a little midnight value engineering on some "expendable" feature that is, from the library's point of view, in no way expendable. Just because most librarians would give up those lovely wood-and-chrome banisters long before they would give up, say, the circulation desk, this does not guarantee that a nonlibrarian with the power to make value-engineering decisions is going to make the same choice. It is important that an advocate of the library's interest (typically the library's building-project liaison) stay informed on value-engineering decisions and be prepared to head off unacceptable decisions before it is too late. Because value-engineering decisions can happen quickly, it requires considerable vigilance on the part of the library's advocate to stay on top of the situation.

### Worksite Tours

During the construction phase, especially when construction involves a new building or major expansion, everyone on the library staff is naturally curious to see what the project looks like from the inside. This natural curiosity grows more intense as the project starts taking form. However, there are good reasons to keep library staff away from the worksite:

- Worksites are dangerous places.
- Site visitors hinder the progress of the building project.
- A partially completed project can make an overly negative impression on worksite visitors who do not fully understand what they are seeing.

On the other hand, there are some excellent reasons to allow library staff to tour a worksite:

- It builds morale by making staff feel part of a project that may well be causing major disruptions in their work lives as well as anxiety about their future roles in the library.
- Seeing their future workspaces in advance helps staff start thinking about how they will function in their new spaces once they have moved in.
- Visiting staff may spot construction errors (e.g., "Hey, there's not supposed to be a toilet drainpipe in the middle of this doorway.") before it is too late to rectify them. (The previous example is from a real-life project in which both authors were involved. Believe it or not, major mistakes are made on construction projects

without anybody realizing it. Just as with mistakes made in written documents or on webpages, a pair of fresh eyes is often the best way to catch errors that have gone unnoticed by those most involved in the actual work.)

The best solution is to arrange strategically timed worksite tours that safely keep staff in the loop without slowing down the building project. For example, if construction workers are planning to take off a Friday afternoon before a three-day weekend, this creates an ideal opportunity to provide staff tours. In hot weather, construction crews often start and finish the workday very early, making unobtrusive late afternoon tours possible (if somewhat sweaty). Well-timed tours targeted at small groups can be effective without being overly disruptive; for example, it might be possible to bring in just the technical services crew for a tour of the spaces they will occupy once those spaces have been roughed out enough to give a feel of what the final result will be like. In any case, all tours must be coordinated with the contractors because they control the worksite during construction and face significant liability issues if anyone is injured while onsite. Those touring the site can expect to be required to wear a hard hat, appropriate footwear (often boots, at minimum closed-toed shoes), and long pants. While on the worksite visitors must carefully follow the instructions of those leading the tour, usually a contractor or a project manager. It is important for everyone to remember that during construction the space belongs to the general contractor, not the library or the library staff.

Everything that applies to tours for library staff also applies to tours for the general public, with the caveat that public tours are likely to cause even more disruption and headache than staff tours. As with staff tours, public tours can be a morale booster; even more, they can help spur potential library donors into providing financial support to the library. In the end, it is up to the leadership of the organization to decide whether public tours are worth the trouble and to ensure that such tours are conducted to minimize disruption and maximize safety.

Besides providing tours for the public, it is quite common for libraries to continue providing service to the public during a major building project. This topic is covered in depth in Chapter 9, "Running a Library during an Addition, Renovation, or Remodeling."

### As-Built Drawings

During the construction process, the executive architects will render a new set of documents called *as-built drawings*. There is always some variance between what the original drawings for a building project call for and what is actually done on the worksite. For example, the original contract drawings might have put network cable trays on the north side of a particular room, but when it comes time to do the work the contractor, project manager, and executive architects agree that it would be better to put those cable trays on the south side of the room. The "as-builts," as they are familiarly known, will reflect this change. As-built drawings create a permanent record of the building project as it really is as opposed to as it was conceived prior to construction. This record becomes a vital source of information for anyone who, at some later date, needs to make repairs or alterations to the building.

## *Managing Yourself through the Construction Process*

Except for the library's project liaison and perhaps the members of the library's building-project team, the construction stage is more a time of watching and anticipation rather than of activity. It can be difficult to watch and wait, and it is all too easy to come down with hard-hat fever when so much frenzied activity is taking place on the worksite. While the temptation may exist to play amateur construction foreman, the best thing library staff can do during the construction stage is focus on their assigned jobs, remaining always ready to help further the building project when called upon but never interfering or inserting themselves where they are not needed or wanted. And to repeat something mentioned previously, it is important not to go to war over every disappointment that surfaces during the construction stage. Someone who gets a reputation for pitching a fit over every little thing that goes wrong during construction is not going to be welcome on the worksite and is likely to make things worse, not better. Librarians understand that, in all honesty, they do a lot more to assist reasonable patrons than they do for problem patrons who complain about everything and are generally unpleasant. It should be no surprise, then, that those who work in the construction industry behave in the same way when working with their clients.

Another element of managing yourself through the construction process is to prepare for the all-but-inevitable postconstruction letdown. After the excitement and upheaval of construction followed by occupying a new space, returning to the routine of working in the library can seem dull. At the same time, the reality of the newly built environment can fall short of what was conceived of in the imagination. The final result may be very nice—but not as nice as it could have been. Not everything that could have been included in the final project made it off the drawing board. Library users are not as impressed as you had hoped they would be; some even say—and not in a polite way—that they don't like the colors, the furniture, the carpet... the list of complaints goes on and on. Not much can be done about the postconstruction letdown except to be prepared for it and to keep in mind the good outcomes of the project instead of focusing entirely on the disappointments.

## Stage 3: Commissioning

Commissioning is the process by which a building's systems and components are tested to ensure that they are working properly before the handover from contractor to owner. Building systems include everything from elevators to electrical outlets; components include everything from doorstops to book drops. Commissioning a complex building project requires a whole team rather than one or two individuals. Testing a doorstop is not necessarily a job for specialists, but testing an air-conditioning system takes real expertise. Commissioning an elevator requires not only expertise; in most states, it requires a licensed state inspector who checks out the entire elevator system and issues a certificate of worthiness before the elevator can convey passengers. Thoroughly testing every system and component is crucial. If the owner accepts delivery of a system or component that is not functioning or in good repair, getting the contractor to repair or replace it after the fact becomes difficult, if not impossible.

Commissioning is also the time to verify that contractors have lived up to their contractual obligations to clean up after themselves and haul away all trash for which they are responsible. The expense of postconstruction cleanup can be considerable, so this is not a trivial part of the commissioning process.

Another important part of the commissioning process involves training employees of the owner in the operation of building systems. Heating, ventilation, and air-conditioning (HVAC) systems, lighting, automatic door locks, and other complex systems require training, and providing this training is typically part of the general contractor's contractual obligation.

### Beneficial Occupancy

One of the key dates for wrapping up a building project is the date for *beneficial occupancy*, the point before final completion at which tenants can occupy the building to use it for the purpose for which it is intended. Ideally, taking beneficial occupancy of a building occurs after commissioning has been fully completed. However, it does happen that when construction schedules fall behind a building simply must be occupied, commissioned or not. Occupancy prior to commissioning can create major problems, mostly because contactors can claim that breakage or damage was caused by the tenants postoccupancy and is therefore not their responsibility to make right.

### Punch List

A part of the commissioning process, which might well involve library staff to one extent or another, is the *punch list*. At some point near the end of the building project, the contractor will declare that the building has reached a state of *substantial completion* and ask for a preinspection. A representative of the owner, often the project manager, will inspect the building project and make a list of things that have not been completed as called for in the contract documents or which are in need of repair. A window that does not open, a ding in an area of drywall, a missing thermostat—anything and everything that is wrong ends up on the punch list. Once the punch list has been completed, the contractor either makes each item right or convinces the project manager that an item does not belong on the punch list. After the contractor declares that everything on the punch list has been made right, representatives of the owner inspect each item to verify the contractor's claim or to ask that further work be done. In the past, a hole was literally punched next to each item to verify it had been completed, thus the name *punch list*; today, items are typically checked off and initialed. Punch list management software is available for complex building projects.

Members of the library staff may be called on to sign off on certain punch list items, especially those relating specifically to their assigned workspaces. For example, a librarian might be handed a punch list for her office and asked to sign off on items such as repairs to a light switch that was not working, touch-up to marred wall paint, replacement of a window shade torn during installation, and so on. That same librarian should not, however, be asked to sign off that the air return in her office is moving the called-for cubic feet of air per hour, something that only an expert with the proper equipment can determine.

## Commissioning Impasses

A commissioning process can end in an impasse that leaves the owner, the general contractor, or both parties feeling that the terms of the contract have not been fulfilled. These impasses may be settled by negotiation between the parties or through more formal arbitration processes. One possible outcome of negotiation or arbitration is for the owner to accept the building as is on the condition that the general contractor leave some specified amount of money "on the table." In effect, the owner pays less than the building project's contractually mandated price in exchange for relieving the general contractor of any further contractual obligations. The owner then uses (or should use) the money left on the table to remedy any unresolved problems with the building project. When arbitration fails, the parties may end up resolving the impasse through civil lawsuits.

## Handoff

With commissioning and the punch list completed and all the contractual obligations fulfilled, the building can be handed off from the general contractor to the owner. The handoff is a formal process defined by the terms of the contract. During the handoff the general contractor is required to provide the owner (usually represented by the project manager) with specific documents, typically including the following:

- As-built drawings
- Warranties
- Operation and maintenance manuals
- Building users' guide
- Utility management plan

The handoff is also the time when the contractor hands over keys and access cards. (A note about keys: During a building project, doors to which contractors need access are typically keyed to a "contractor core." This arrangement allows contactors to get where they need to be with just a single key. At some point near the end of the project the doors are rekeyed so that they can be opened only by keys in possession of tenants and owners.) Once the handoff has been completed, the building at last belongs to the owner.

Is the building project over? Ideally, yes. In reality, problems will likely crop up as the library staff and users settle into the new surroundings and give the system a real-world stress test. Keep those warranties handy; they will likely be needed.

## Conclusion

When embarking on a major library building project, it is helpful to think of it as having the three stages outlined in this chapter:

1. Design
2. Construction
3. Commissioning

## The Beat(down) Goes On

The following anonymous article appeared on page nine of the *New York Times* on February 7, 1892:

The mayor [of Boston, Massachusetts] is supposed to be hard at work upon a personal investigation of the real condition of affairs relating to the new Public Library on Copley Square before authorizing the issue of any portion of the new library loan. Everybody who has anything to say in regard to this matter is invited to report to the commission which consists of Mayor Matthews, the Corporation Counsel, and the City Architect. Almost everybody has something to say, even to the topical singers behind the footlights, for the big white library lingers in the building stage while an overwhelming sum total of expenses rolls up.

This great granite elephant was planned on a much less magnificent scale than was finally adopted in its elaboration. In 1887 it was estimated that the finished building in all its details would cost $892,253. This estimate has gradually been raised to a sum three times as great. A loan has already been authorized outside the debt limit for $1,000,000, and now another large loan is imperative.

Such changes as could consistently be made in the main design have been effected, with a view to reducing expense. The courtyard has been changed from the original granite of the design to brick and marble; the height of the building has been reduced nine feet, and changes have been made here and there wherever practicable, resulting in a saving of not less than a quarter of a million, yet the lowest estimate now made places the cost of the completed building at $2,218,865, including shelving, but no other furniture.

The building is planned to accommodate 2,000,000 volumes and the statistically inclined estimated the cost of housing each book at $1.00. The great proportion of these volumes, by the bye, remains to be acquired, the recent collection in the old library numbering something over 540,000 books.

The new building gives rise to the most diverse expression of opinion, some authorities pronouncing it one of the most noble and aesthetic examples of architecture in the United States. Its majestic simplicity and classical correctness are exalted in the sounding words, and the public taste is called upon to rise to its appreciation. It is useless to deny that the general public fails to rise to the occasion. The irreverent compare the great square pile to a bonded warehouse or a huge cake-box, and find it barren of beauty. The convenience of patrons has been made subordinate to architectural effect, and now the structure proves to be lacking in that important respect also.

As one plain-spoken critic affirms, the whole business has been bungled from the beginning, and there is every reason to fear that the new Public Library building, upon which the city has staked so much, will prove a huge and irremediable failure. But all this depends upon the point of view. When Copley Square has been made over to fit the library, as the hopeful believe it will be, the grand effect may be all that the architects fondly dreamed. ("The Past Week in Boston," 1892: 9)

The building so chastised in the quoted article was designed by noted American architect Charles Follen McKim and has stood a major Boston landmark, and focus of civic pride, for generations. The reason for reproducing the *New York Times* article here is to drive home the point that every library project is going to attract critics unhappy about the project's cost, its aesthetics, its usability, or all three. There is no way to curtail the critics, but being prepared for their slings and arrows will help soften the inevitable blows. So, too, does the fact that attractive and usable library buildings will always outlast their critics.

Remember that each stage is vital to the success of the overall project and that failing to put sufficient energy and thought into any one stage will sink a project regardless of how well the other phases may have been done. For each of the three phases, there is a corresponding key strategy:

1. Design: Getting stakeholders constructively integrated into the programming process.
2. Construction: Keeping the building tenant (i.e., the library) actively but appropriately involved in the construction process.
3. Commissioning: Following through to the very end of the building handoff.

# Reference

"The Past Week in Boston; the Coming and Going of the State Veterans. Silver Anniversary of the Massachusetts Grand Army Department—the City Hall Site, and the Public Library Building." 1892. *New York Times*, February 7: 9.

# 2

# Overview of Building System Basics

## Introduction

Anyone embarking on a major library building project will benefit from a working knowledge of the basic concepts and vocabulary related to buildings and construction. This chapter provides readers with enough basic information to effectively participate in a library project planning exercise and to interact smoothly and intelligently with architects, engineers, project and construction managers, and tradespersons. This chapter should also make clear the enormity of the scope of building types, construction processes, and code interpretation—subjects that this chapter cannot deal with in great depth. While other chapters in this book will add to the basic information provided here, neither this chapter nor this book is intended to provide a complete education in the art and science of building design and construction.

Modern institutional and commercial buildings, including libraries, are complex constructions consisting of various systems that, when integrated, create a habitable structure. Building systems are typically divided into structural and mechanical systems. Structural systems are the fundamental elements that create a framework to support the intended use of a building and the mechanical systems within it, much as a skeleton supports a body and the organs within it. Some examples of structural building elements include columns, beams, arches, trusses, and plates. Structural engineering, a major specialty field within civil engineering, focuses primarily on the analysis and design of structures that support or resist loads.

Mechanical systems, on the other hand, represent a separate discipline of engineering that, like structural engineering, involves the application of physics and materials science. Just as structural systems can be seen to perform the work of the skeleton, mechanical systems can be seen to perform the work of the body's internal organs. In modern buildings, mechanical systems include electrical, lighting, plumbing, and heating, ventilating, and air-conditioning (HVAC) systems.

Library buildings come in nearly every shape and size, ranging from converted Victorian homes to portable modular buildings to multistory institutional structures. Libraries integrated into nontraditional spaces such as commercial malls and business high-rises are becoming much more common as well. It is difficult to discuss all of these different type of structures in a common context. For example, multistory concrete-and-steel institutional structures are nothing like wood-framed residential or light-commercial buildings in terms of the materials used, the construction methods, and, ultimately, cost. To address these different types of buildings effectively, this chapter discusses small buildings separately from larger institutional buildings. On the other hand, many of the internal mechanical systems found in both small and large structures are essentially similar, varying only in scale and, to some extent, complexity.

## Building Basics

Buildings contain several distinct systems that together create the internal environment of the building. Many of these systems are interdependent and are found, in one form or another, in virtually all buildings. These types of systems include:

- Structural
  - Site preparation
  - Foundation
  - Construction
- Mechanical
  - Electrical
  - Data networking
  - Lighting
  - Plumbing

This chapter discusses each of these systems. An important consideration in planning, design, and construction is the life span of building systems. Industry standards predict that the estimated useful life for a permanent structure is 50 years in service for its original design purpose. For example, a firehouse is expected to serve as a firehouse for 50 years; after that, it might continue to serve as something else: a retail space, a restaurant, an apartment building, and so on. Obviously, some buildings exceed their expected life spans, with many continuing to serve in their original design function well beyond the 50-year mark (e.g., a 75-year-old library building that still serves as a library). However, it is rare to find a building of substantial age that has not undergone one or more (sometimes many more) major renovations and upgrades. Table 2.1 provides some general standards for renovations and upgrades. Changes in building functionality and emerging technologies are just two examples of factors that might influence changes to these estimates.

Just as many buildings last much longer than 50 years, their integral systems can last longer than the periods listed in Table 2.1. However, the fact that systems are still functioning does not necessarily mean that they adhere to current building codes and specifications. For example, consider the Empire State Building in New York City. Originally completed in 1931, it stood as the world's tallest building for more than 40 years. During its existence, this landmark building has received numerous upgrades and retrofits to keep up with changing needs and technologies. Obviously, twenty-first-century occupants of the Empire State Building are not routing every phone call through human switchboard operators or riding in elevators controlled by uniformed attendants; the reason they are not is because the building has been regularly updated over the years. The most recent, ambitious, and comprehensive renovation project in the Empire

### Table 2.1
### Building Renovation and Upgrade Timeline

| Expected Life Span (Years) | Systems or Components |
| --- | --- |
| 5 | Carpeting |
| 10 | Ceiling finish |
| 15 | Custom flooring<br>Interior renovation |
| 20 | Electrical<br>Elevators<br>HVAC<br>Plumbing |
| 25 | Fire system<br>Portable structures |
| 50 | Excavation<br>Exterior walls<br>Floor structure<br>Foundation<br>Frame<br>Permanent structures |

State Building's history is a $500 million effort, scheduled for completion in 2013, that will include upgrading and retrofitting many of the building's systems, particularly its HVAC system, to make them greener and less costly to operate by reducing their energy consumption.

### *Building Classification*

Construction and buildings in the United States are classified according to a complex matrix that is contained in both the older *Uniform Building Code* and the newer *International Building Code*. (See Chapter 3 for more detailed information on building codes.) This matrix classifies buildings into one or more of five types (I through V), four of which include two subtypes (A and B). Other factors considered in building typing include fire rating of construction materials, occupancy, and the size of the building (i.e., number of square feet and number of stories). A Type I building is a modern building constructed primarily of concrete and fire-resistant steel. Most large library buildings fall into this category. With a Type II building, the structural members are of a noncombustible material but have no fire resistance; in fact, the hallmark of a Type II building is the presence of unprotected steel structural members. The Type III (also known as *ordinary construction*) designation covers a wide variety of buildings; typically, in a Type III building the exterior load-bearing walls are some type of masonry (brick, stone, concrete block, terra cotta tile, adobe, or cast-in-place concrete) while all or some of the structural components are wood. The sort of four- and five-story buildings that one might find in an older downtown area—typically having retail space and plate-glass windows on the first floor; apartments or offices with operable windows on the upper floors—is a classic example of a Type III building. Type IV (also know as *mill construction*) buildings employ heavy wooden timbers which are, surprisingly, more fire resistant than steel beams. The exterior of a heavy timber will scorch in a fire yet still retain its structural integrity; in contrast, the same fire conditions can cause steel beams to become so soft that they bend and collapse under their load, as happened in the World Trade Center towers on September 11, 2001. A residential home or light-commercial building constructed of wood framing and siding is normally classified as a Type V building, though such structures may be classified as Type III if sufficient fire-resistant materials are used in their construction. This brief list gives only the barest coverage of the very complicated subject of building classification. As with all code issues, referring to the *International Building Code* and other authoritative sources is a good practice.

For simplicity, this chapter divides buildings into two general categories based on the type of structure and primary building materials. These categories are concrete buildings, which are constructed primarily of concrete and steel, and framed buildings, constructed of wood, steel, and other materials. Most library buildings fall into one of these two types.

## Concrete Buildings

The retired *RMS Queen Mary*, once one of the world's largest and most luxurious cruise ships, is today permanently anchored in Long Beach, California, where, still afloat though with most of her nautical propulsive equipment removed, she is officially designated as a building and serves as a hotel and maritime museum. While it may seem odd to think of a ship as a building, the fact is ships are so similar to medium and large concrete buildings that it is not uncommon to find trained maritime engineers employed as building mechanical engineers. Both ships and concrete buildings require strong external skeletons and complicated internal mechanical systems. Buildings even go through the equivalent of a shakedown cruise in the form of the commissioning process to get the bugs out before the building "puts out to sea." (See Chapter 1 for more details on the commissioning process.)

### Site Preparation

Unlike ships that spend most of their serviceable lives afloat in water, buildings are fixed to a particular piece of real estate commonly referred to as the *site*. The site must be properly prepared in advance of any construction or the building will not be stable, with larger, heavier buildings, such as concrete buildings, requiring more substantial site preparation than smaller, lighter buildings, such as framed single-family residences. The Leaning Tower of Pisa is certainly the most widely known example of a building with foundation problems, but there are many examples of buildings where the ground was not properly prepared or the foundation was flawed. Rather than the entire building leaning, typically only parts of the structure settle, creating problems that usually require costly mitigation.

Site preparation generally begins with a site plan developed through surveying and engineering evaluation. Site plans are architectural plans that show the engineering and development of a plot of land where a building will be constructed. The site plan usually includes the building footprint (the area of land the base of the building covers), walkways, parking, water lines, drainage, lighting, and landscaping. The site plan will specify whatever subsurface preparation is required. For many concrete buildings, site preparation begins by removing the earth on a building site down to a level specified in the site plan and replacing it with a precise fill mixture that helps ensure the stability of the building foundation. In other cases, the plan may call only for soil compacting to ensure stability. A major factor in site stability is soil moisture. The moisture content of the soil must fall within a fairly small range, usually measured as a percentage, in order to retain pliability and stability over time.

## Foundations

A building's foundation is the part of the structure below the lowest floor. The function of the foundation is to connect the structure to the earth and support the structure against downward, horizontal, and upward forces. Both large and small structures (including residential homes) are most commonly supported by concrete foundations. The two main types of foundations are shallow foundations and deep foundations. Whether a structure rests on a shallow or deep foundation depends on a number of factors, including soil type, building footprint, building height, and environmental factors such as the local propensity for earthquakes or flooding.

Shallow foundations are routinely used for residential homes and light commercial buildings. Types of shallow foundations include spread footing foundations, mat-slab foundations, slab-on-grade foundations, rubble trench foundations, and earthbag foundations.

Deep foundations, which are commonly used for large structures or where soil conditions are extremely unstable, consist almost exclusively of piles—pipes, poles, or columns that penetrate deeply into the ground beneath and around the structure. In some instances, premade piles are driven deeply into the soil like giant tent pegs, while in other instances machines drill deep holes that are then filled with various mixtures of concrete and steel. Piles are used where the soil is unstable. In some cases, a building may have a combination of different foundations types based on conditions and goals.

Raised-floor foundations, which are often shallow but may rest upon deeply driven piles, employ footings (usually piers, abutments, or small slabs) to lift a structure above grade, creating a crawl space under the structure. Raised-floor foundations have the advantages of providing easy access to utilities and providing protection from damp conditions and flooding.

## Structural Systems

Modern medium and large buildings are typically constructed with a basic framework or skeleton that supports the other building systems and everything else that may be required for occupancy (partition walls, flooring, furniture, equipment, and, most of all, people). The three most common contemporary structural materials are steel, concrete, and wood. Steel-reinforced concrete is almost exclusively the material of choice for large institutional structures. The combination of concrete with steel rods (known as *rebar*) running through it has proved to be an exceptionally strong building material that can withstand great loads and stresses compared with unreinforced concrete and other building materials such as brick or wood. This provides obvious advantages in areas prone to earthquakes and other severe natural phenomena such as hurricanes and heavy snowfall.

---

### Concrete and Concrete Reinforcement

Concrete is an amazing material with several unique qualities. It can be poured, molded, or spread on both horizontal and vertical surfaces. Once cured, concrete becomes one of the strongest and most stable materials available for building construction. It can be engineered and accurately mixed to specifications for withstanding just the right amount of stress and possessing the necessary tolerances and elasticity for a given application. Concrete holds the distinction of being the most widely used man-made material in the world.

Traditional concrete is composed of several parts: cement, water, fly or volcanic ash, aggregate, and other materials that enhance its strength and aesthetics. The Roman Empire made the first widespread use of concrete in structures, accounting for the survival of many Roman structures to this day. Architectural historians refer to this period as the Concrete Revolution. After the fall of Rome, the technology of concrete was lost until the mid-eighteenth century when a British engineer combined hydraulic lime with pebbles and powdered brick as aggregate. Several incremental developments ultimately led to a patent granted to a British bricklayer in 1824 for a process to produce what he called Portland cement. The name is derived from its similarity to Portland stone quarried on the Isle of Portland in Dorset, England.

Portland cement, a mixture of limestone and clay or shale, is the basic ingredient in most concrete, mortar, stucco, plaster, and grout. The precise combination of constituents varies depending upon the desired results. When the constituents are heated in giant kilns, several complex chemical reactions occur as the mixture reaches the optimal temperature of 1450°F. The resulting substance, known as clinker, emerges from the heating process in small lumps no bigger than pebbles. Clinker is relatively stable and can be stored for long periods of time. It is a major commodity that is traded heavily on commodities exchanges. When clinker is ground to a fine powder and combined with calcium sulfate, a setting agent, it is called cement. In construction applications, cement is reinforced through combination with various types of aggregate—a combination of pebbles, crushed rock, gravel, sand, or other materials—depending upon the application and codes or standards in use.

Unreinforced concrete is able to withstand great compressive loads (i.e., it is highly resistant to being crushed), but it is not as strong as reinforced concrete when exposed to tensile forces (i.e., it will deform under localized high pressure). This can be illustrated in a structure with simple column-and-beam construction. The individual columns are able to support great weight loads, but the beams are relatively weak, particularly near the middle of their spans. Estimates of the relative strength of concrete rate its tensile strength to be 10 to 15 percent of its compressive strength. Reinforcement (either primary or secondary) compensates for this shortcoming. The most common types of primary reinforcement consist of lattices of steel bars, wire, and wire meshes. However, steel fiber and other synthetic materials, such as fiber-reinforced plastic (FRP), are being increasingly adopted as economical replacements for traditional primary reinforcement materials. Secondary reinforcement through such means as the addition of alkaline-resistant glass fibers to the concrete mixture will increase concrete's strength and prevent surface cracking, especially due to exposure to frost. Frost protection is a serious concern in cold climates because water will condense and accumulate on concrete and find its way into exposed surface cracks. When the moisture freezes and expands it can cause severe cracking that may expose the reinforcing steel to rust and corrosion.

## Framed Buildings

Framed buildings, whether they are built of studs made of wood or steel, are commonly referred to among construction professionals as "sticks and bricks" buildings. Framed buildings offer many advantages over heavy concrete-and-steel structures. They are usually much cheaper to build, require less site preparation, and take less time to build. Framed buildings also readily lend themselves to renovations, remodels, and expansions. Examples of framed buildings include most residential buildings and light commercial structures, including the type of retail strip mall in which branch libraries may occupy leased storefront space. Small- and medium-sized freestanding library buildings, especially those located in suburban and rural areas, are more often framed buildings rather than concrete structures. While wood is still widely used in residential framed buildings, steel is becoming more common in commercial and public framed buildings. Steel is insect proof as well as more readily recyclable than wood. Unlike wood, steel studs will not burn, though they will soften and collapse if exposed to the high temperatures produced by a structure fire.

### Site Preparation

Because framed buildings tend to have substantially less mass and smaller footprints than large concrete-and-steel buildings, they usually require much less site preparation. Even so, soil must be tested and analyzed as part of the site planning process for a framed building. As with larger concrete structures, framed buildings may require soil treatment and compacting, but in most cases only to a depth of approximately 12 inches below surface level. Soil problems, however, could result in a need to go much deeper. In some instances, such as areas with very moist soil, the soil may need to be removed, dried, replaced, and compacted, although it is unusual for such soil to require total removal and replacement with entirely new material. Once the soil is stable, it is leveled and compacted to densities specified in applicable building codes. The resulting level plot is known as the grade. During or immediately after this process, underground services—including water and sewer lines, electrical power supply, and natural gas lines—are installed.

### Foundations for Framed Buildings

Though framed buildings require much less subsurface structural support than do large concrete buildings, strong foundations are no less important for framed buildings than they are for larger structures; in fact, the engineering concepts and foundations options are the same for both types of building. The two most common types of foundations in framed buildings are slab-on-grade and raised-floor foundations. Both of these types usually include a subsurface stem wall around the perimeter of the foundation. This will usually consist of a four- to eight-inch-wide wall of concrete or open-cell cinder blocks around the entire perimeter of the structure. In slab-on-grade foundations, the stem wall will be poured (or filled when using cinder blocks) at the same time that the concrete slab is poured; connective reinforcing serves to make the slab and stem wall essentially a single structure. In a raised-floor foundation, this stem wall will extend 12 to 18 inches above the grade. Concrete piers will be placed within the stem wall at equally spaced intervals. These piers will support floor joists and, at some points, internal load-bearing walls.

### Structural Systems

Most of us have seen homes and light commercial buildings under construction and, even if we didn't pay close attention, we have a rough idea of what a framed building looks like. Knowing some of the details of framed construction, however, will be of value if you become involved in the construction of a framed library building. Inside the stem wall that lies on top of the foundation of a framed building are piers to support large beams or joists that comprise the subfloor. The floor itself is constructed on top of the floor joists and is usually made with relatively heavy plywood or pressboard. A properly constructed raised floor will support a phenomenal amount of weight.

The stem wall also supports the exterior walls of the building, and these walls in turn provide the main load-bearing support for the structure and the roof. The exterior walls consist of a sill plate that sits atop the stem wall, vertical studs, and a top plate. Sill plates made of wood will usually be chemically treated to resist moisture and pests and then bolted or otherwise affixed to the stem wall by bolts cast in the stem wall when it is poured. In most framed buildings at least some interior walls will also be load-bearing walls that help support the structure. While non-load-bearing walls (aka *curtain walls*) in a framed building can be knocked out during remodeling, knocking out a load-bearing wall is courting disaster. No interior walls should be removed from a framed building without first consulting a knowledgeable professional who can determine whether the wall is load bearing.

The roof of a framed building is made up of trusses that are usually prefabricated off-site for the specific building. Roof trusses sit directly on the top cap (the horizontal timber that sits on top of and connects the vertical studs) of the walls. Once the roof trusses are installed the structural portion of the building is mostly complete and the building is considered "framed up." It is important to note that partly finished framed buildings are susceptible to shear (or sideways) forces. The interior and exterior finish materials (sheetrock, siding, stucco) help stabilize framed buildings against shear forces. Roofing materials serve the same support function across the roof trusses of framed buildings.

As mentioned earlier, framed buildings can be built with either wooden dimensional lumber (2x4s, 2x6s, etc.) or with steel members. The techniques of wood versus steel framing vary in certain details, but the overall processes are identical.

## Mechanical Systems

Most modern buildings incorporate some sort of building management system (BMS) that maintains the environment within the building by serving as the primary control for temperature, humidity, and $CO_2$ levels in the building. Many BMSs also control lighting, alarm, and other systems.

The term most often used when discussing building mechanical systems is HVAC (heating, ventilating, and air conditioning), most commonly pronounced "H-V-A-C" or "h-vac." Arguably the most important system in any medium- or large-sized buildings, HVAC systems regulate the temperature and humidity inside the building as well as maintain a flow of fresh air. The specifications and performance standards for HVAC (and other mechanical systems) are governed by the *International Mechanical Code*, one volume of the set of code books published by the International Code Council.

HVAC systems include a number of subsystems but can be generally divided into heating systems, cooling systems, and ventilation systems. In most large buildings air is delivered from a central plant location within or near the structure itself via a complex system of ducting and/or plumbing. This has become the standard and preferred method of climate control for most buildings, including residential homes, and is commonly known as *central air conditioning/heating*, or just *central air*. In some specialized cases, these systems also control humidity, odors, dust, and, airborne bacteria. The invention of central heating is often credited to the Romans, who installed in the floors and walls of private villas and public baths systems of air ducts that allowed distribution of heated air throughout a structure.

Very simply, HVAC systems pull outside air into the building, treat the air for temperature (heating or cooling), control for one or more of the other factors mentioned, and then circulate the air through ductwork to each habitable space within the building. The workhorses of this process are fan units that are typically referred to as *air handling units* or sometimes simply as *blowers*. These units vary in size from about one meter to several meters in diameter, and very large buildings may have several banks of blowers with multiple units in each bank. The two most common types of blowers are axial (suited for lower air volumes and pressures) and centrifugal (suited for higher air volumes and pressures). The flow of air is governed by systems of dampers and variable air volume (VAV) systems controlled locally by thermostats or centrally by computers that monitor thermostats and other sensors throughout the building. Sophisticated centrally controlled systems that balance the airflow throughout the building to maintain specified parameters are the most energy-efficient HVAC systems. Many buildings have integrated systems that allow some local control (from within offices, meeting rooms, etc.) while managing most of the system centrally.

Steam has been the most common method for heating large buildings for more than a century and continues to be the most energy-efficient method for heating most large structures, though in some regions natural gas, petroleum, or electrical systems are more practical. In all cases, the air is circulated over a system of heated coils or through a heated chamber before being moved through the ducting to each part of the building.

Cooling is usually accomplished by circulating air over a set of coils or pipes that contain coolant. While water is the most common coolant, many other compounds are used for cooling, some in combination with water. Most nonwater compounds, such as ammonia and Freon, require pressurization by a compressor. The two primary types of building cooling systems can be illustrated through comparison to two common residential cooling systems: swamp coolers and home air conditioners. The oldest method of air cooling for medium- to large-sized buildings is nothing more than a large-scale version of the home swamp cooler. These systems pump cool water so that it cascades over a screen of some sort. Fans move air past or through these screens, cooling the air before it enters the building duct system. A newer method for cooling buildings is comparable to the air conditioners (more accurately coolers or chillers) found on most modern homes. The major components of such systems consist of a compressor, coils, and a fan. The compressor pressurizes a gas (typically Freon) contained in coils so that the gas becomes very cold; the fan blows outside air over these coils, resulting in chilled air entering the structure.

The conditioning of air, either by heating or cooling, is vital for making a library structure habitable. These systems must be designed to provide the greatest control possible—in both large and small spaces—so that library users and workers can function at their best. Reading a book or article, designing a webpage, or searching a database is nearly impossible when one is either shivering from cold or perspiring from just sitting at a desk. When a building is commissioned, one of the most difficult and complex tasks is balancing the air handling systems to maintain comfortable temperatures throughout the building. Airflow is measured in cubic feet per minute (CFM). HVAC technicians endeavor to maintain an airflow through the duct system that keeps temperatures consistent within a given space. In large spaces, this may require increasing or decreasing the CFM in various locations to achieve a balanced temperature throughout the space. The goal is usually a one- to two-degree temperature range—typically 70 to 72°F in large buildings.

One problem that is often overlooked in heating and cooling large spaces is the human factor. Many people find too much airflow or lower temperatures uncomfortable. Frequently this results in the use of individual space heaters. These can be a fire hazard because they strain the electrical system. If a space heater is located near a thermostat, it can trick central controlled systems into thinking that particular space is too hot, causing the system to compensate by pumping more cool air into that space. The result can be a vicious cycle of heating and cooling that wastes energy and leads to uncomfortable, unhappy, and potentially unproductive employees.

### Electrical System

It is hard to imagine a life without electricity and all the electrical and electronic conveniences that we take for granted nearly every day of our lives. A modern workplace, particularly an information-dependent workplace like a library, requires substantial amounts of electricity not only for lighting, heating, air conditioning, and other mechanical systems but also to power multiple computers, copiers, printers, scanners, and innumerable other office devices.

---

**Electricity and Wiring**

Electricity is a term that describes a number of different phenomena such as lightning, static electricity, and electromagnetism. Entire books written by engineers and physicists are devoted to the physical characteristics and properties of electricity. Simply put, however, electricity is the movement or flow of electrically charged particles—electrons and protons—in a current. Electrical current is measured in amperes (amps); however, most people are accustomed to referring to

*(Continued)*

---

## Electricity and Wiring *(Continued)*

electricity by voltage as a unit of measurement. Amperes is a measurement of the intensity of the current, while voltage is a measurement of the capacity or the potential of the electricity to do work. Ohms, on the other hand, is the measure of resistance—the extent to which the material conducting the current resists the flow of electrons. The waterfall analogy is often used to explain electric current. If the flow of electricity were a waterfall:

- voltage represents the height of the falls (the higher the falls, the more energy the water possesses when it hits bottom);
- amperes represents the amount of water going over the falls each second; and
- ohms represents rocks, islands, and other obstructions impeding the flow of water.

In most building applications electrical current originates from a power source and moves to a receptacle or device via a metal wire that functions as the conductor of the current. The electricity is then routed back to its source via a second wire. These two wires are referred to respectively as the "hot" wire and the "cold" wire. Copper wire is the most common conductor due to its conductive qualities, cost, and availability. Other materials may be used in special applications or in cases where copper is difficult to obtain or prohibitively expensive. Copper wire is found in two common types: stranded and solid (also known as *single strand*). Each of these types has advantages in different applications, with one type or the other sometimes specified by building codes for particular applications. Solid wire is cheaper to manufacture and is more rugged than stranded wire. Stranded wire is more expensive to manufacture than solid wire but has the advantage of being more flexible and less prone to breaking and kinking.

Modern electrical wiring is insulated with a plastic sheath or coating to prevent electrocution and arcing or shorting (when the current jumps from one wire to another), which can cause fires. In North America, current-carrying wires are commonly called *live* or *hot* wires and insulated coatings are color-coded as follows:

Hot = black red
Neutral = gray
Ground = green

Building wiring usually consists of sets of three or four insulated wires for each circuit. Two wires will be the positive and negative (neutral) current-carrying wires while the third will be the ground wire. A fourth wire is usually an additional positive wire. Ground wires are intended to provide an escape path for excessive voltage and usually end with a rod or device that is buried in the earth, hence the term *ground wire*. Most commercial and institutional applications contain electrical wiring within a metal conduit (a tube or duct for enclosing wiring). However, in other applications, such as residential and light commercial construction, wiring will consist of two insulated wires and an exposed ground wire bundled together within a protective plastic sheath. The type of wiring and the required protection will be determined by applicable building codes.

The current-carrying capacity of electrical wire is determined by the diameter, or gauge, of the wire. In North America, American wire gauge (AWG) is the unit of measurement. In other parts of the world, such as Europe, wire sizes are determined by International Electrotechnical Commission (IEC) standards. AWG gauge numbers range from 0 to 36, where 0 is the largest diameter and 36 is the smallest diameter. Larger gauge (smaller diameter) wires are used for low voltage, while smaller gauge (larger diameter) wires are used for higher voltage. For example, Category 5 network cable uses AWG 24 gauge wire, while a 220 volt (V) circuit will probably be wired with AWG 10 or 8 gauge wire. Wire insulation often has letters printed on it in various colors. These markings tell the electrician what amperage the wire is rated for and, in some instances, whether the wire is rated for interior or exterior use.

Electricity is supplied to most buildings from a central public or private utility network via a complex network or grid. Electricity is generated and transmitted from a power-generation facility (gas, coal, or nuclear power plants; hydroelectric facilities; and solar or wind farms are the most common types). In much of North America, power is managed via regional grid systems that distribute power on a large scale. Power is initially generated at a very high voltage and then stepped down during the transmission process as it moves through various types of intermediary facilities known as substations. A catchall term, *substation* encompasses a variety of types of electrical stations, each with its own specific purpose or function. Most contemporary substations include, at a minimum, switching, protection, and control equipment; many also include transformers that step up or step down the transmission voltage depending upon the ultimate destination of the electricity. The regional grid systems feed electricity to local and municipal grid systems that further distribute the electricity to customers and end users. At each step in this process the voltage is usually stepped down incrementally. In the United States and Canada, the two most common end-user voltages are 110 V and 220 V. Common household and office devices—televisions, toasters, computers, electric pencil sharpeners—operate on 110 V. In the home, clothes dryers are a typical example of a 220 V appliance; in the office, special equipment, such as a large photocopier, routinely operates on 220 V. On the other hand, very large mechanical systems, such as elevators and whole-building HVAC systems, may require 440 V or greater.

Most large buildings receive power from the local grid at a still relatively high voltage and contain their own transformers and switching equipment to reduce the power to levels appropriate to the needs of the end user. This equipment is usually located within the building itself but may instead be located nearby, as is sometimes the case on college campuses. In addition to transformers and switching gear, most large buildings have devices known as an *uninterruptible power supply* (UPS). UPS devices used in buildings are similar in concept to the smaller UPS devices found in offices and used for protecting the valuable electronic equipment of individual workers. UPS devices are important for buildings because they not only ensure that power supply is not interrupted but also work with other electrical devices to ensure that the power supply remains constant, eliminating potentially damaging spikes and drop-offs that occur naturally in the flow of electricity.

From the building's UPS, a main distribution device sends power to a network of smaller distribution cabinets and boxes located throughout the structure. All of these boxes contain circuit breakers of varying sizes or capacities and are typically referred to as *switchgear* or simply *boxes*. Relatively simply devices, circuit breakers are essentially automatic power switches that protect an electrical circuit from short circuits or overloads that can occur as the flow of power fluctuates. Circuit breakers are rated for the maximum amperage that they are capable of carrying. Common building breakers are rated for 20 amps (A), 25 A, 32 A, and so on.

Generally, each circuit breaker controls one electrical circuit. Electrical engineers design a building's electrical plan to anticipate and distribute the electrical load in a way that minimizes the possibility of overloads and short circuits. For instance, one circuit may include all the lighting fixtures in a large room or several smaller rooms, while another circuit may include all the outlets or receptacles in the same area. Where there is a special device, such as a photocopier, or where there is an extraordinary need, such as in a computer lab, the electrical design will call for a dedicated circuit to serve that particular device or meet that specific need. In some cases the specifications of a particular device may drive the circuit load design. This is particularly common in modifications of existing buildings and renovations.

### Data Networking

Data networks and their components (cabling and devices) are commonly referred to as *Ethernet*. In simple construction terms, data cabling is very similar to electrical wiring and, in fact, electricians frequently install data cables right alongside electrical wiring. Data cabling, however, is low-voltage and subject to different code requirements than electrical writing. For example, unlike electrical wiring, data cabling is usually not required to be housed in metal conduits, as the risk of fire is very small because the voltage is low.

Beginning in the 1980s, telephone communications were converted to digital transmission and today use the same communication technology as standard desktop computers do. This is why some of the largest commercial Internet providers are the same companies that provide telephone service. Because the telephone and data networks are virtually one and the same in most institutional buildings, there is no need to provide dedicated telephone wiring separate from the data network when erecting a new building or renovating an existing building to contemporary standards.

Data transmission enters the building from the larger external telecommunications network. In a city, this will most likely be a metropolitan area network (MAN). In a campus setting, the institutional information technology (IT) organization probably maintains its own network that connects with a larger external network. Within a building, the data equivalent of the electrical switching room is the building data facility (BDF). This room houses switches, routers, and other devices that manage the flow of data into and out of the building. The devices in the BDF communicate data to other devices located in intermediate data facilities (IDF) that are the final distribution point before data is distributed to individual receptacles (known as jacks) throughout the building. This system is very similar to the electrical distribution system, albeit the distribution devices for data are somewhat more sophisticated.

### Lighting

Lighting is a key aspect of a building's interior environment. The two main types of lighting in a modern building are environmental lighting and emergency lighting. Environmental lighting includes both artificial and natural light. Building artificial light must, at a minimum, allow normal functioning within the structure when natural light is absent, as at night. There is a bewildering variety of fixtures and installation options available for environmental lighting, and these are discussed in detail in Chapter 5. Emergency lighting is critical for the safety of a building's occupants and is discussed in

Chapter 7. In terms of construction, however, emergency lighting is largely governed by building and fire/emergency codes. At a minimum, emergency lighting must be sufficient to allow occupants to exit the structure safely. In most cases, emergency lighting systems have their own independent electrical circuits that are powered by emergency generators or batteries. Batteries may be located centrally in a plant facility or locally in the device itself. A centrally controlled and powered emergency lighting system is the most reliable and requires the least maintenance.

## Plumbing

Plumbing systems are essential for any modern structure occupied by human beings. The larger the structure, the more important the systems become and the more reliable they must be to make the building habitable. There are essentially five functions of plumbing in modern buildings, including:

- delivery of clean potable water for human consumption,
- provision of water for human waste drainage,
- provision of water for temperature control (cooling and heating),
- provision of water for fire suppression systems, and
- removal of water from rain, snow, ice, etc., or runoff drainage.

Each of these functions is provided by its own independent system.

Water is usually routed into the building via a central pump room, though in some cases different plumbing systems such as fire sprinkler systems require a separate pump. Pumps are necessary because few locations possess adequate water pressure to move water throughout a medium-sized structure, let alone a high-rise or skyscraper. When water leaves the pump and charges the system, flow is controlled by valves throughout the structure. One of the most important types of valves in any building is the isolation valve. Isolation valves are installed so that a portion of a particular system can be isolated while still allowing plumbing to operate normally in the rest of the building. This is critical when repairs are required or when a portion of the building is being renovated. If isolation valves must be installed after initial construction, the cost and disruption can be substantial.

### Potable Water Supply and Venting Systems

Two essential plumbing systems in any inhabited building are the potable water supply and the drain-waste-vent (DWV) systems. The potable water supply provides water to areas of the building where water is needed for restrooms, drinking fountains, and utilities. The DWV system removes sewage and gray water (used water uncontaminated with human waste) from the building and also vents gases produced by waste. In most instances drainage for toilets, sinks, showers, etc., includes a trap—a U-shaped section of pipe in which a small amount of water is always present. This arrangement prevents gases from backing up and venting back into the structure. When these traps are allowed to dry through evaporation, unpleasant-smelling gases will infiltrate back into the structure. This is common during construction projects and periods during which plumbing systems are not in regular use. Pouring a gallon or so of water into a drain and airing out the space will usually solve such problems.

### Sprinkler Systems

In the United States, building codes generally require sprinkler systems for any structure with an occupancy rating over 100 persons. There are two types of fire sprinkler systems: wet and dry. Wet systems are preferred because the water is already in the overhead pipes so that when an individual sprinkler head is activated the water flows immediately. Wet pipe systems are also less likely to corrode and leak than dry systems. For most systems, sprinklers activate individually or in predetermined zones so that setting off one sprinkler or zone does not cause the entire system to go off, soaking areas where there is no fire. In dry systems the pipes must be charged before water is actually emitted from sprinkler heads. Dry systems are generally used only in unheated buildings or areas where there is concern about water freezing and bursting the pipes. Dry systems are occasionally used over book stacks in libraries, but the reliability of modern wet systems makes this precaution unnecessary.

Fire sprinkler heads are designed to activate only when they are heated to a predetermined temperature. There are several different types of activations systems, but the most common are activation by a glass bulb that shatters when heated or by a fused metal link that separates when heated. Sprinklers activate immediately and typically discharge between 20 and 40 gallons of water per minute for one to four minutes. Because a typical fire department hose stream discharges 250 gallons per minute and may take as long as 15 to 20 minutes to reach the fire area, sprinklers provide better fire suppression with considerably less water damage than do hose systems.

Many buildings are designed with plumbing overhead as opposed to having it contained in floors and walls. The purpose of overhead installation is to take advantage of gravity in water flow and to make plumbing more accessible for inspection and repairs. The disadvantage, particularly in libraries, is that water—possibly a lot of it—could potentially leak (or flood) down onto materials and equipment. If librarians can communicate to designers in the early planning stages of a building project their concerns about overhead plumbing, it is usually possible to route overhead plumbing so that it avoids the most vulnerable areas, like book stacks, special collections, server rooms, etc.

## Conclusion

This chapter has provided a very brief overview of what goes into constructing a functional building. Each of the systems described fits together to create a livable, workable space. In Chapter 3, we will discuss building codes, reading building plans, and understanding the building trades. Taken together, Chapters 2 and 3 will provide anyone who is not a construction professional with a reasonable understanding of what's what and who's who in the construction world.

# 3

# Going into Detail: Plans, Codes, and Construction Professions

Aworking ability to read building plans, a basic knowledge of building codes, and familiarity with the roles of the various construction professionals who turn plans into code-compliant finished buildings will equip a library employee to better follow the progress of, and contribute to the success of, a building project.

## Plans (aka Blueprints)

The words *plans* and *blueprints* are used somewhat interchangeably (though, in the strictest sense, not always correctly) to describe the architectural drawings from which new buildings and major renovation and remodeling projects spring. Although the word *blueprints* is still commonly heard, in the twenty-first century blueprints are rarely blue and, in cases when hard copies are not necessary, may exist primarily in electronic form. Dating from the mid-nineteenth century, blueprints were originally used for shipbuilding and constructing railroad equipment (locomotives, freight and passenger cars), with their application to large building projects following not long after their initial introduction. The blueprint process of copying building plans relied on specially made paper coated with a photosensitive solution of ferric ammonium citrate and potassium ferricyanide. Over this blueprint paper the original building plans, hand drawn in black ink or graphite on thin tracing paper, would be laid and exposed to very bright light. On the blueprint paper the underexposed lines and text of the original drawing would then show as white or light blue while the fully exposed remainder of the blueprint paper would turn a rich Prussian blue. While not particularly toxic, when combined the two chemicals used in the original process produce a strong ammonia odor and will turn blue the fingers of anyone handling genuine blueprints for any length of time. Because it involved neither reduction nor enlargement, the original blueprint process eliminated distortion if performed under the correct conditions. By the early twentieth century, improved copying machines allowed for the mass production of original drawings as blueprints (see Figure 3.1).

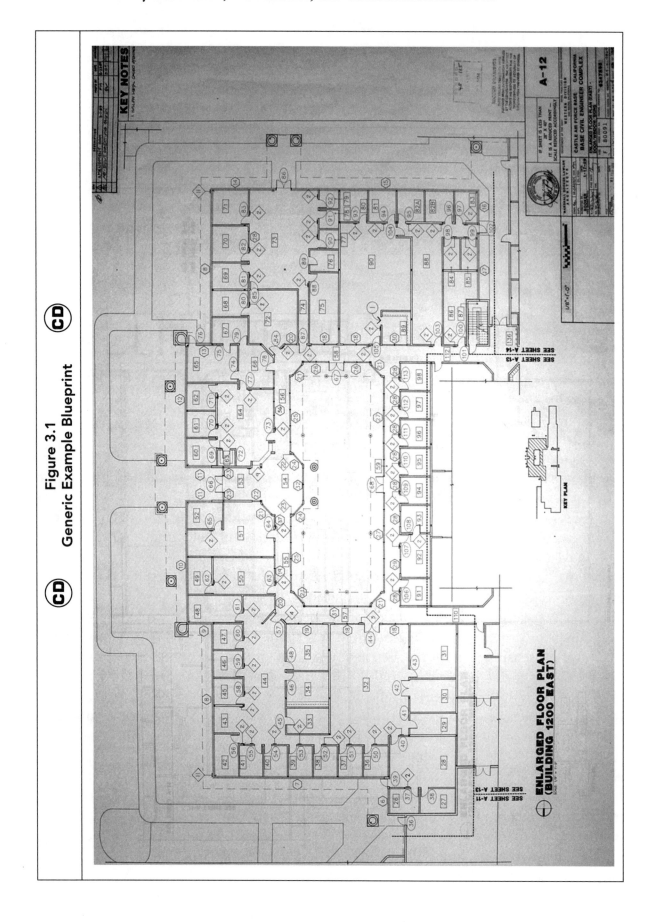

**Figure 3.1**
**Generic Example Blueprint**

By the mid-twentieth century, traditional cyanotype blueprints were supplanted by diazo prints on which drawings appear as blue lines on a white or light-colored background. Contemporary blueprints, created on computers using sophisticated drawing software, are generally printed on inkjet or laser plotter/printers. Even with these changes in technology, *blueprints* remains a common term for any sort of architectural or engineering drawing and is used interchangeably with the word *plans*.

During any planning and construction process, several consecutive sets of plans are produced as architects make changes to the original design, and these changes can lead to confusion. For example, room numbers can change from one version of the plans to the next, and there will obviously be confusion if a library project liaison working from old plans with superseded room numbers tries to communicate with architects and builders working from a newer set of plans with different room numbers. Because it is critical to work from the most up-to-date set of plans, the library's representatives on a building project—typically the project manager and the library project liaison—must have copies of the most recent version of the plans and also be in the loop to receive updated drawings as they are produced.

Each set of plans for a large project will include several sections, each of which contains drawings showing the entire structure (or large portions thereof) on a single sheet as well as many sheets depicting specific areas or features in greater detail. For an institutional structure of 50,000 square feet or larger, it is common for a set of building plans to consist of several hundred individual sheets.

Every plan set will always have at least a cover sheet containing an index to the sheets within the set, while very large plan sets will have separate index sheets (see Figure 3.2). Because each set of plans contains several subsets that act very much like the chapters of a book, finding your way around a large set of plans without an index is almost impossible, especially if you are not used to working with building plans. The subsets that comprise a full set of plans cover such essential elements as building architecture, electrical systems, mechanical systems, fire protection, plumbing, structural support, security, and technology. Additional subsets covering specialized building features—for example, telecommunications facilities, research laboratories, or special-needs classrooms—may also be part of a set of plans. Plans may include separate interior-design drawings that detail such features as floor and wall finishes and fixtures. Plans may also provide theoretical arrangements of interior furnishings but are unlikely to go into detail on this topic; any detailed treatment of furnishing will appear on separate plans created by an interior designer, assuming that project employs someone in this role.

### Architectural Plans

Within a full set of building plans, the architectural plans will prove to be the most useful subset for library staffers involved in a building project. This set of two-dimensional drawings shows the basic layout of a building without the clutter of mechanical, electrical, or plumbing systems to confuse the eye. Anyone wishing to get a feel for a new building or major remodeling will want to spend time with the architectural plans before turning to any of the more detailed, highly specialized subsets. Besides providing a sense of

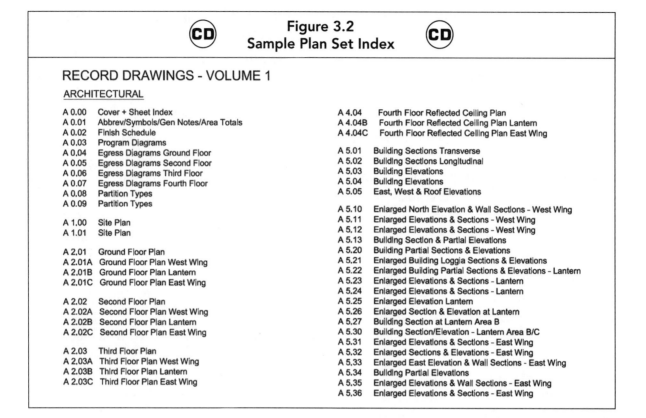

**Figure 3.2**
**Sample Plan Set Index**

RECORD DRAWINGS - VOLUME 1

ARCHITECTURAL

| | | | |
|---|---|---|---|
| A 0.00 | Cover + Sheet Index | A 4.04 | Fourth Floor Reflected Ceiling Plan |
| A 0.01 | Abbrev/Symbols/Gen Notes/Area Totals | A 4.04B | Fourth Floor Reflected Ceiling Plan Lantern |
| A 0.02 | Finish Schedule | A 4.04C | Fourth Floor Reflected Ceiling Plan East Wing |
| A 0.03 | Program Diagrams | | |
| A 0.04 | Egress Diagrams Ground Floor | A 5.01 | Building Sections Transverse |
| A 0.05 | Egress Diagrams Second Floor | A 5.02 | Building Sections Longitudinal |
| A 0.06 | Egress Diagrams Third Floor | A 5.03 | Building Elevations |
| A 0.07 | Egress Diagrams Fourth Floor | A 5.04 | Building Elevations |
| A 0.08 | Partition Types | A 5.05 | East, West & Roof Elevations |
| A 0.09 | Partition Types | | |
| | | A 5.10 | Enlarged North Elevation & Wall Sections - West Wing |
| A 1.00 | Site Plan | A 5.11 | Enlarged Elevations & Sections - West Wing |
| A 1.01 | Site Plan | A 5.12 | Enlarged Elevations & Sections - West Wing |
| | | A 5.13 | Building Section & Partial Elevations |
| A 2.01 | Ground Floor Plan | A 5.20 | Building Partial Sections & Elevations |
| A 2.01A | Ground Floor Plan West Wing | A 5.21 | Enlarged Building Loggia Sections & Elevations |
| A 2.01B | Ground Floor Plan Lantern | A 5.22 | Enlarged Building Partial Sections & Elevations - Lantern |
| A 2.01C | Ground Floor Plan East Wing | A 5.23 | Enlarged Elevations & Sections - Lantern |
| | | A 5.24 | Enlarged Elevations & Sections - Lantern |
| A 2.02 | Second Floor Plan | A 5.25 | Enlarged Elevation Lantern |
| A 2.02A | Second Floor Plan West Wing | A 5.26 | Enlarged Section & Elevation at Lantern |
| A 2.02B | Second Floor Plan Lantern | A 5.27 | Building Section at Lantern Area B |
| A 2.02C | Second Floor Plan East Wing | A 5.30 | Building Section/Elevation - Lantern Area B/C |
| | | A 5.31 | Enlarged Elevations & Sections - East Wing |
| A 2.03 | Third Floor Plan | A 5.32 | Enlarged Sections & Elevations - East Wing |
| A 2.03A | Third Floor Plan West Wing | A 5.33 | Enlarged East Elevation & Wall Sections - East Wing |
| A 2.03B | Third Floor Plan Lantern | A 5.34 | Building Partial Elevations |
| A 2.03C | Third Floor Plan East Wing | A 5.35 | Enlarged Elevations & Wall Sections - East Wing |
| | | A 5.36 | Enlarged Elevations & Sections - East Wing |

the overall shape of a building, architectural plans provide such fundamentally useful information as the dimensions of the spaces within a building, the intended uses of these spaces, and their occupancy capacities. Architectural plans also detail the locations of all the essential components of a building—stairwells, windows, doors, offices, restrooms, and so on—as well as the location of special-purpose rooms such as custodial closets, electrical rooms, and telecommunications rooms. Architectural plans form the basis for other plan sets, as in many cases the electrical, mechanical, and plumbing plans are simply layered on top of the basic architectural plan set.

A basic architectural plan set will include the following elements:

- Site plans: Entire building footprint and the surrounding area
- Floor plans: Each floor with walls, windows, columns, etc.
- Ceiling plans: Overhead features (clerestories, drop ceilings, soffits, etc.)
- Roof plans: Structural features of the roof and rooftop equipment
- Exterior and interior elevations: Vertical views of a building as it will appear when completed
- Sectional drawings: Views of a building as if it were sliced open to expose interior features
- Enlarged drawings: Portions of a building that require a close-up view
- Detail drawings: Complex features that must meet exacting specifications
- Exterior and interior finish plans: Floor, wall, and ceiling materials and finishes
- Egress plans: Building exits, exit paths, and places of refuge

## Site Plans

Site plans are detailed engineering drawings of planned improvements to the plot of land on which a building will be erected (see Figure 3.3). The site plan depicts the building footprint plus underground and adjacent structures. Underground structures may include water, power, and other utilities (e.g., sprinkler systems) as well as drainage facilities (e.g., sewer lines and runoff drainage). Surface structures may include roadways, parking lots, loading docks, sidewalks, exterior lighting, and landscaping. Site plans serve two important functions. First, they provide a bird's-eye view of the building footprint and its immediate surroundings; second, they provide, in conjunction with elevation drawings (described later in this chapter), a three-dimensional perspective of the completed building in its surrounding context. Most architectural software systems provide some capacity to render a three-dimensional illustration of a structure and its surroundings, but such

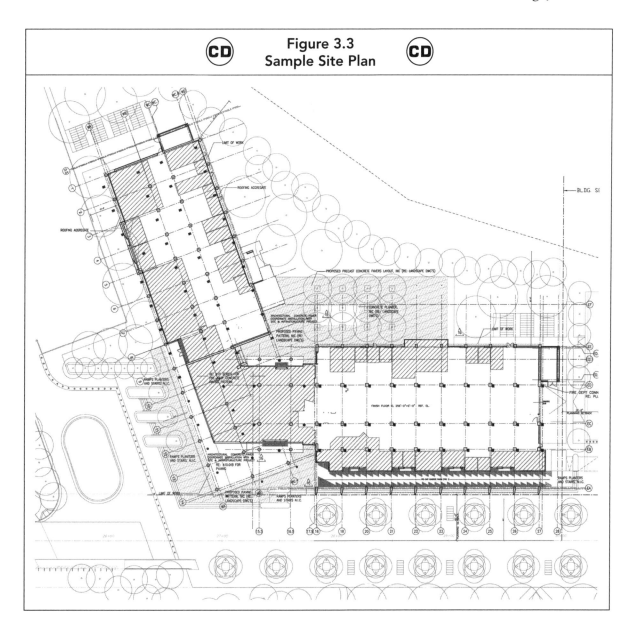

**Figure 3.3**
**Sample Site Plan**

three-dimensional renderings are ultimately derived from the site plan and elevation drawings. In some instances, three-dimensional representations will also be included in a plan set.

### Floor Plans

Aside from the site plan, floor plans are generally the simplest, least cluttered drawings in any plans set (see Figure 3.4). Floor plans can be thought of as maps of a building, and their purpose is to represent the basic exterior structure and interior subdivisions of a building. Floor plans provide dimensions of everything from the grandest reading room to the smallest storage closet; locations of such features as doors, windows, hallways, book stacks, and staircases; and a wealth of additional information that is important to those who use, or will use, a building. It is essential to examine floor plans with great care, as it is all but inevitable that doing so will uncover errors. And since most of the other plans

---

#### Errors on Building Plans

It would seem that on something as professionally planned and carefully controlled as a building project, serious errors should not happen. It would seem that no mistake could possibly slip past the trained eyes of architects, building inspectors, project managers, construction supervisors, foremen, and workers. But the fact is mistakes can and do go undetected. This may sound cynical, but if you go through a set of plans and do not find any errors, it means that you need to go back over them again because you undoubtedly missed some.

Plans should be reviewed not only prior to construction but also during construction in order to catch mistakes wrought by changes to the plans. On one project on which the authors worked, one of the executive architects asked if the library really needed a large storage closet in the first-floor elevator lobby. Without reviewing the plans, we immediately agreed that a closet was not needed, and so the architect removed it from the plans. That was fine until the elevator installers showed up a month or two later asking, "Where is the mechanical room for the elevator?" Oops. The executive architects managed to contrive a solution, but it was far from elegant and created a fair number of problems after the building was commissioned and occupied. It is possible that, had we looked at the plans one more time instead of shooting from the hip, one of us would have noticed the problem and prevented the mistake.

One possible reason that errors make their way onto plans and remain undetected is that construction professionals typically focus largely on micro and macro views of their projects, thereby allowing the items in between these extremes to be overlooked. The library's representatives on a building project, even if not trained construction professionals, can sometimes illuminate these in-between errors by asking questions when plans and the physical reality do not seem to match. It is common for errors on building plans to become apparent only as the pieces of the building puzzle are being assembled and someone says, "Hey gang, this doesn't make sense," at which point architects and builders confer and remediate the error. That "someone" could just as easily be the library's project liaison or an alert library staff member as an electrician, carpenter, or project manager.

When on-the-fly changes are made to building plans, it is critical that the as-built drawings (discussed in detail in Chapter 1) are updated to reflect the reality of the completed building. Helping to keep the as-built drawings on track is an area where a library project liaison who is paying attention and taking good notes can provide an extremely valuable service.

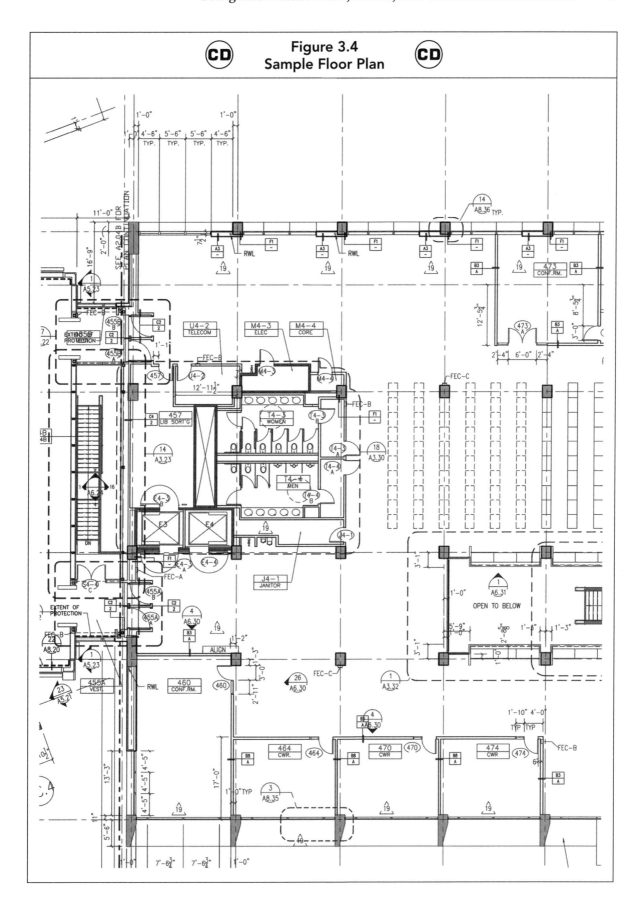

**Figure 3.4
Sample Floor Plan**

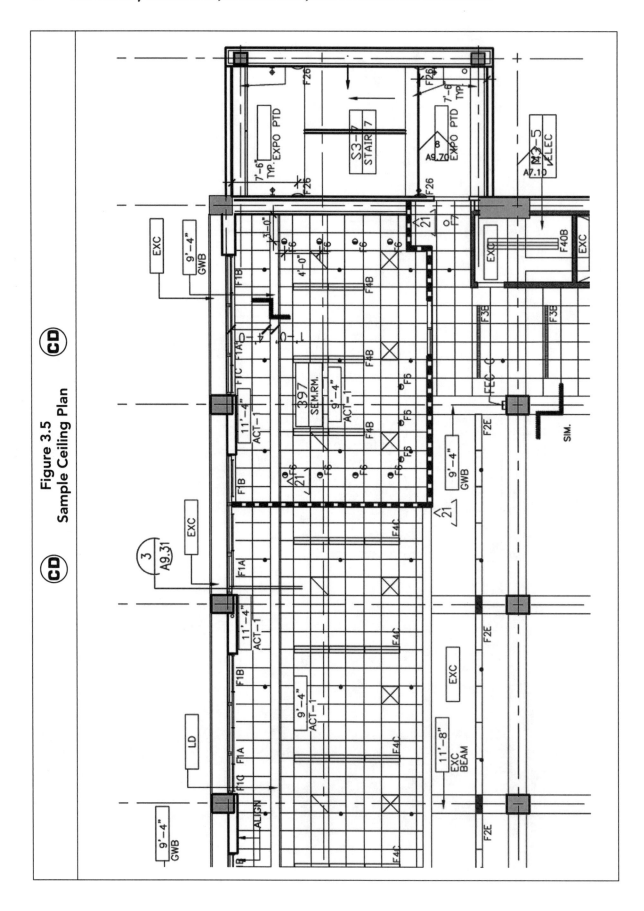

**Figure 3.5**
**Sample Ceiling Plan**

in a set are based on the floor plans, a small error on the floor plans can perpetuate itself into the other plans until it becomes a serious problem. Common mistakes to look for on floor plans include, but are certainly not limited to, the following:

- Doors that swing in the wrong direction or block other doors
- Missing windows or windows where no windows should be
- Incorrect placement of interior features (walls, fixtures, book stacks)
- Missing walls or walls where no walls should be
- Corridors or staircases that lead nowhere
- Void spaces that defy explanation
- Restroom stalls and fixtures that do not meet accessibility regulations

### Ceiling Plans

Although ceiling plans are somewhat difficult for a layperson to interpret, they are nonetheless important because they provide a great deal of information about how the ceiling in any given interior space will be constructed and look (see Figure 3.5, facing page). Modern buildings may incorporate many types of ceilings—including drop ceilings, clerestories, suspended ceilings (commonly referred to as t-bar and tile ceilings), soffits, open ceilings, and hard ceilings—and ceiling plans show not only which type of ceiling goes where, but also the location of such overhead structural features as beams and built-in lighting fixtures (such as recessed fluorescent panels, recessed incandescent can lights, and cove or indirect light sources). Although a building's electrical plans will detail lighting fixtures more completely, the ceiling plan is generally easier to interpret for the purpose of getting a sense of how the lighting will look and function once a building project is completed.

### Roof Plans

Also somewhat challenging to interpret, roof plans show the location of structures and equipment located on the roof (see Figure 3.6, p. 48). Roof structures include access and egress pathways (stairs, ladders), clerestories, skylights, and parapets. Equipment typically found on building rooftops includes HVAC equipment, ducting and piping, ducting and piping shafts, drains, prepared walkways, and other specialty items. Although it takes a practiced eye to envision it, roof plans can provide a picture of what a roofline will look like from the ground or from a higher floor of an adjacent building or wing. Roof plans can tip you off to the fact that what might be promised as a grand view from the fifth floor of the building's main wing could in fact be nothing more than a view of its four-story annex's rooftop parapet and shed-like HVAC room. Roof plans and their respective detail drawings provide information about what materials and construction techniques are to be used on various sections of the roof. In the past, flat-roofed buildings employed ineffective tar-and-gravel-based coverings; today, the preferred materials for flat-roof construction are continuous-membrane coverings or sealed-metal coverings. On green buildings, flat roofs may be covered with a layer of plant life. Buildings with sloped roofs may feature any of a variety of materials, including ceramic tiles, wood shingles, asphalt tiles, asphalt sheeting, or sheet-metal panels.

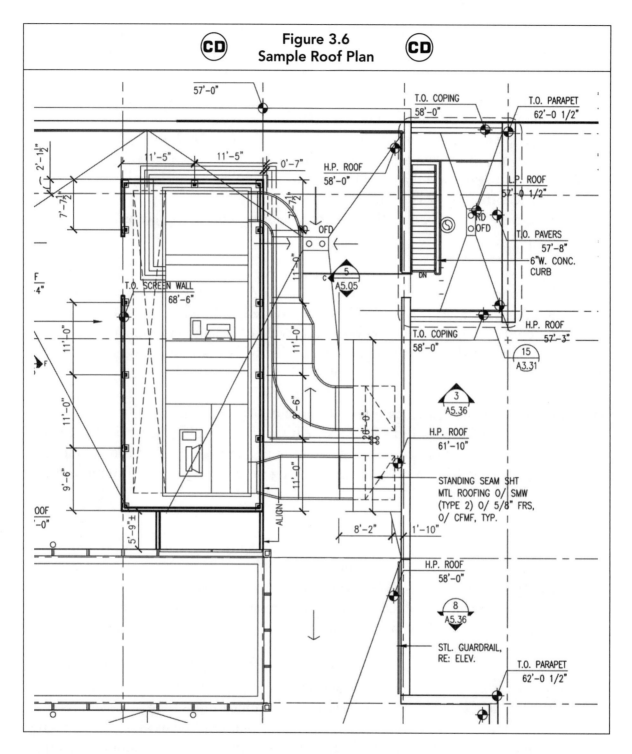

**Figure 3.6
Sample Roof Plan**

## Elevation Plans

Elevation plans (often called simply *elevations* by architects and builders) are drawings of a building in a two-dimensional vertical view. Normally elevations show only one side of a building, though the whole building from top to bottom is represented. Elevations can be exterior or interior views. As mentioned previously, when viewed in conjunction with the site plan, exterior elevation drawings can provide a good mental image of what the completed structure and its immediate surroundings will look like in 3-D reality. Or at least what the architect intends them to look like in 3-D reality. Exterior elevations will show building exterior features such as windows, exterior stairs and balconies, recesses and pop-outs, and door locations (see Figure 3.7, p. 50). Typically, elevations lack the measurements or details found on most other plan types. When viewed in conjunction with ceiling plans, interior elevations provide a clear idea of how various interior spaces will look and feel when completed and occupied (see Figure 3.8, p. 51).

### Sectional Drawings

Sectional drawings allow you to view an internal portion of a building as if it had been sliced open with a knife (see Figure 3.9, p. 52). This cutaway effect is somewhat similar to slicing open a layer cake that has lots of interesting fillings between the layers. Sectional drawings are frequently used to show interior features in context. For example, a sectional drawing could allow you to see the top-to-bottom layout of an entire staircase without walls or other obstructions to get in the way. Another typical use of sectional drawings is to show the relationship between adjacent features on each floor, as when the technique is used to illustrate shafts and columns that span the entire height of the building. Sectional drawings also show similar features that appear on each floor of a building, such as soffits and other ceiling features.

### Enlarged Drawings

Similar in purpose to sectional drawings, enlarged drawings are simply magnified (larger scale) portions of drawings contained in the site plan, floor plan, etc. They are intended to provide a greater amount of detail where small features or groups of features require illumination. This might include such features as a discrete suite of rooms or complex architectural forms like soffits, raised ceilings, or wall recesses.

### Detail Drawings

Detail drawings show builders precisely how complex or unusual features are to be assembled or constructed (see Figure 3.10, p. 54). In many cases, detail drawings depict engineered features that must be constructed and installed to exact specifications in order to perform as designed. Some of the most important detail drawings in any plan set are the representations of the building foundations and footings. Because foundations and footings are engineered based on the material characteristics of the soil and surface preparation, different footings and foundation compositions may be used under different portions of a single building. Detail drawings make these important differences clear to builders. Another excellent illustration of the use of detail drawings is in the construction of a steel structure staircase, a building component that, to withstand particular stresses and maintain rigidity, must be precisely welded or bolted together in accordance with the detail drawings. Windows are yet another building component that frequently requires extensive detail drawings to ensure that glass panels, mullions, seals, and other features function as designed.

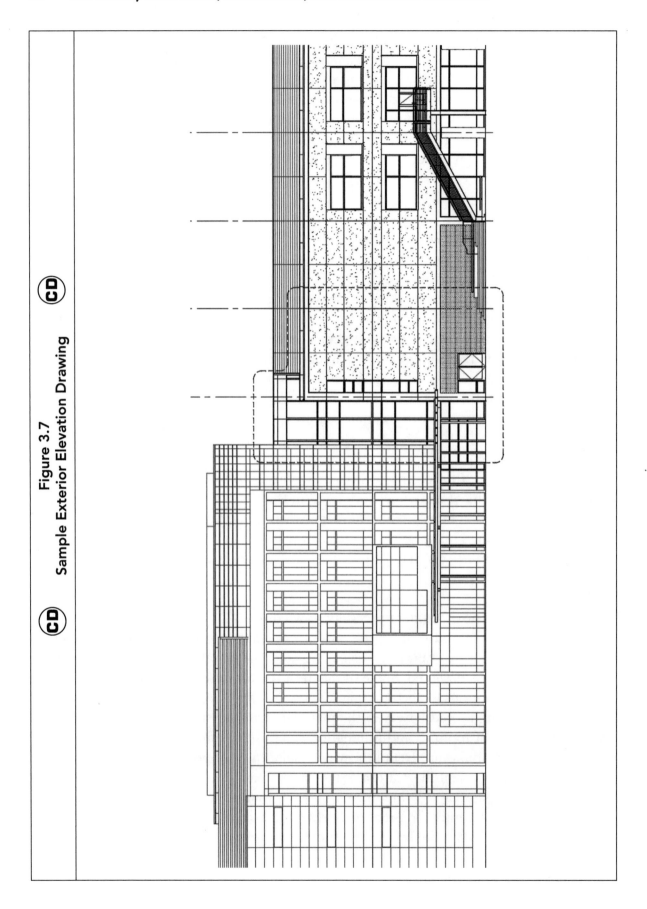

Figure 3.7
Sample Exterior Elevation Drawing

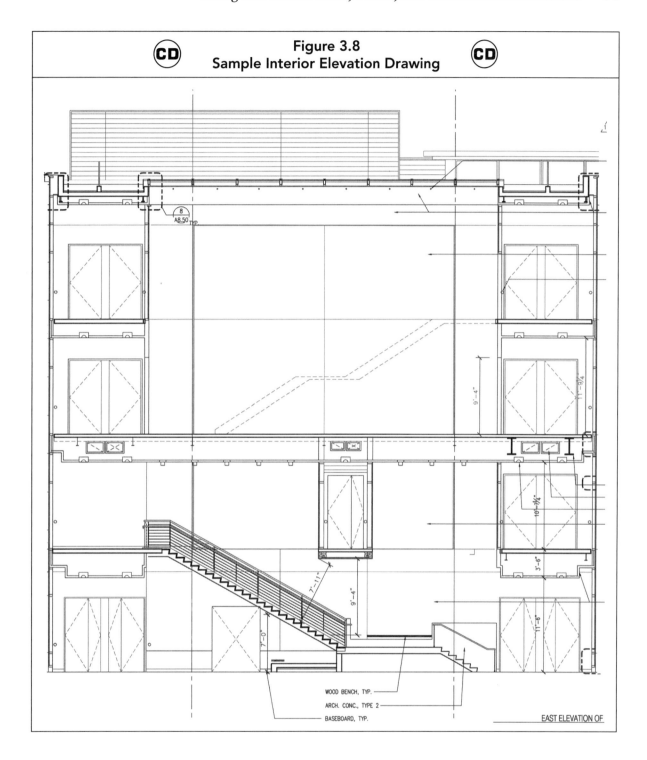

**Figure 3.8**
**Sample Interior Elevation Drawing**

## Exterior and Interior Finish Plans

As the name makes clear, exterior and interior finish plans detail the materials and finishes on both the inside and outside of a building. Finish plans will detail everything from surface texturing and wall coverings to carpeting and paint. Depending on the building project, it may be important that new finishing materials match existing materials in other parts of the building or match existing materials in nearby buildings. Carefully

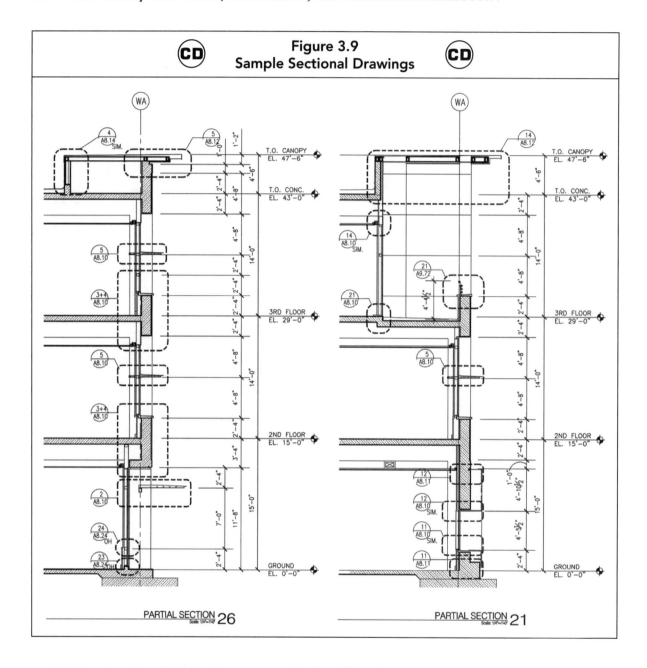

Figure 3.9
Sample Sectional Drawings

reviewing interior finish plans is worth the effort because, to a great extent, it is the finish plans that determine the impression the library building's interior will make on those who work in and use it (see Figure 3.11, p. 55).

While architects are knowledgeable about finishes, and while most architects consider themselves artists as much as artisans, the fact remains that not every architect has the best eye for interior design or is possessed of tastes that accommodate themselves to the culture of the library staff and users who must live with the finished product. For these reasons it is important to ask questions about materials and finishes and to clearly express preferences. For example, an architect who decides that a children's area should be finished with bare concrete and structural steel covered with black paint needs to be set straight by someone who actually understands what makes a library environment suitable for children. To create interior environments that are appropriate to their intended uses, it may be worthwhile to hire an independent interior designer who has library-specific design experience and is willing to spend the time to understand the needs and wants of library staff and users.

### Egress Plans

Because egress plans show occupation densities and emergency exit pathways, they have a big impact on the safety of building occupants (see Figure 3.12, p. 56). Amazingly enough, egress plans are sometimes created without consulting fire or safety professionals. If it appears that the local fire authorities were not properly consulted in developing egress plans, library officials should provide copies of those plans to their local fire or public-safety organization and request input. Also, just because egress plans comply with relevant codes does not guarantee that they actually make sense in an emergency evacuation situation. The local fire officials who would respond in the event of an emergency are in the best position to determine if on-paper egress plans will work in reality.

An important aspect of egress plans is the number of people who are expected to exit through a given pathway during an emergency. An egress plan that calls for emptying a room with a maximum occupancy of 200 through an exit that cannot possibly accommodate such a crowd is certainly unworkable. Another thing to consider when viewing egress plans is the concept of egress versus refuge. Large buildings will have not only exiting pathways but also areas of refuge where occupants may safely stay sheltered without actually leaving a building. Egress plans must be carefully examined to understand how these relationships will work out in a real emergency.

## Plans Not Included in the Architectural Plans Set

In addition to types of plans already listed, several other, more technical, types of plans comprise a significant part of a complete set of drawings for a building project (see Figure 3.13, p. 57). These include structural, mechanical, electrical, plumbing, technology, and security plans; as a group, they constitute the most complex drawings in any plan set. Construction professionals can interpret such complex plans because of their training and experience; it is not realistic to assume, though, that an amateur can become proficient enough to interpret complex plans without careful, guided study. Nonetheless, this section contains brief descriptions of each of these types of plans in order to provide a broad understanding of what these plans depict and how they fit into the plans set as a whole. Before any building project gets underway, the project manager and/or an independent professional from each field (e.g., an electrician, a plumber, a mechanical engineer) should review these detailed sections of the plan sets to ensure that they are correct and in compliance with local codes and regulations.

### Structural Plans

Structural plans show the foundations, framing, and loading plans for a building (see Figure 3.14, p. 58). Depending on the structural materials used, this plan set may

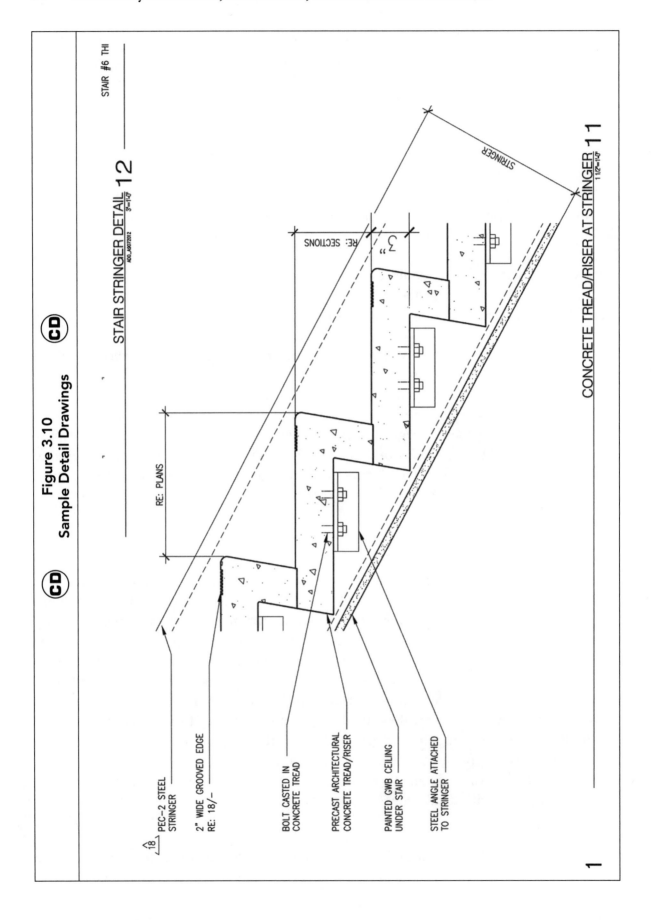

**Figure 3.10**
**Sample Detail Drawings**

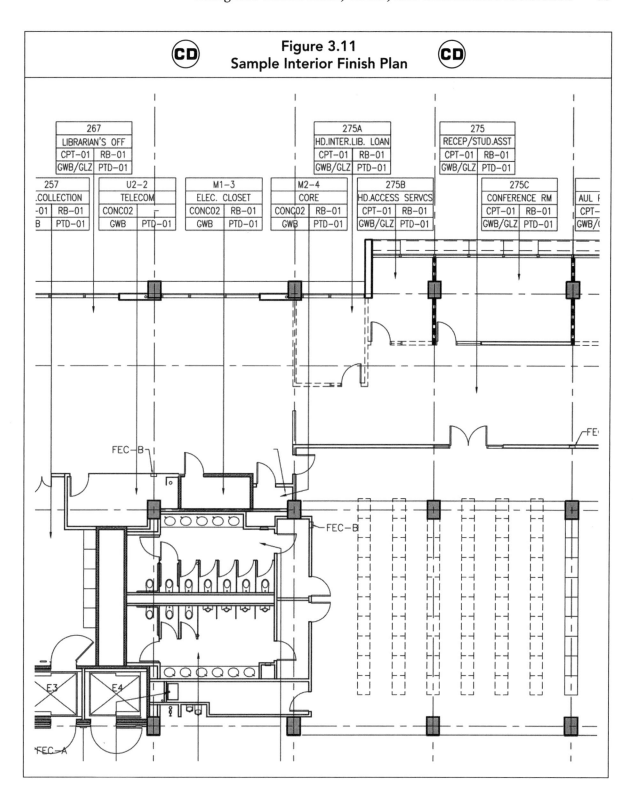

**Figure 3.11**
**Sample Interior Finish Plan**

include detailed plans for concrete, steel, metal decking, and roof framing. They will also show engineering data for gravity framing and loading data. If a library is to have a compact-shelving area that requires higher-than-normal floor-loading capacity, structural plans will include this detail.

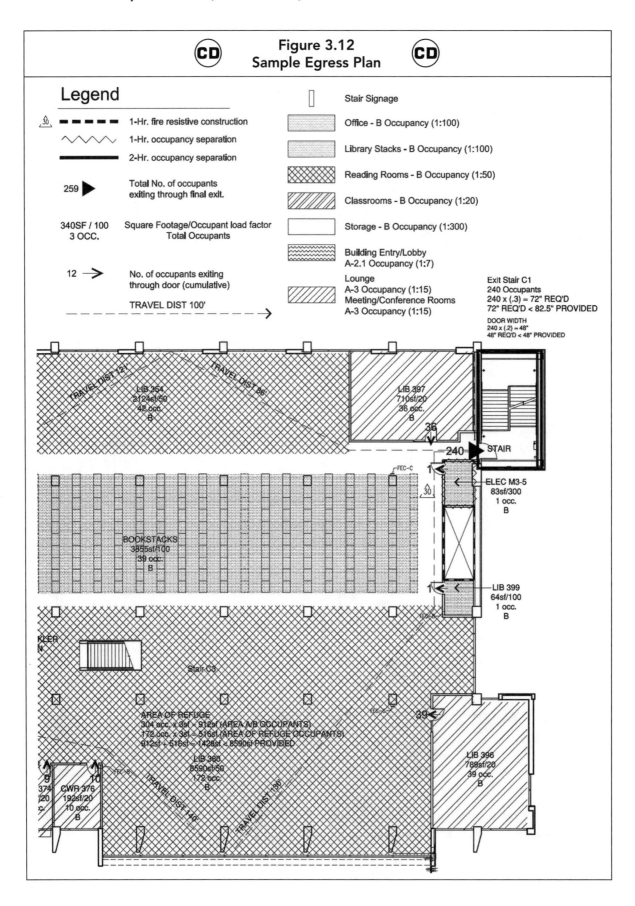

**Figure 3.12**
**Sample Egress Plan**

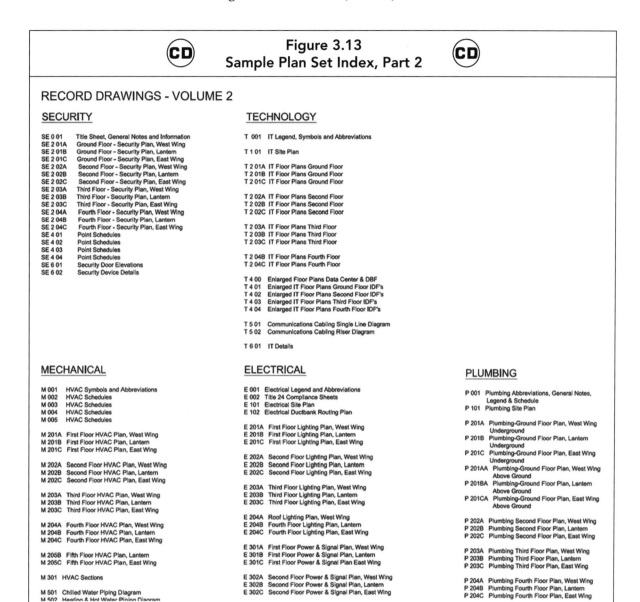

**Figure 3.13**
**Sample Plan Set Index, Part 2**

RECORD DRAWINGS - VOLUME 2

SECURITY

| | |
|---|---|
| SE 0 01 | Title Sheet, General Notes and Information |
| SE 2 01A | Ground Floor - Security Plan, West Wing |
| SE 2 01B | Ground Floor - Security Plan, Lantern |
| SE 2 01C | Ground Floor - Security Plan, East Wing |
| SE 2 02A | Second Floor - Security Plan, West Wing |
| SE 2 02B | Second Floor - Security Plan, Lantern |
| SE 2 02C | Second Floor - Security Plan, East Wing |
| SE 2 03A | Third Floor - Security Plan, West Wing |
| SE 2 03B | Third Floor - Security Plan, Lantern |
| SE 2 03C | Third Floor - Security Plan, East Wing |
| SE 2 04A | Fourth Floor - Security Plan, West Wing |
| SE 2 04B | Fourth Floor - Security Plan, Lantern |
| SE 2 04C | Fourth Floor - Security Plan, East Wing |
| SE 4 01 | Point Schedules |
| SE 4 02 | Point Schedules |
| SE 4 03 | Point Schedules |
| SE 4 04 | Point Schedules |
| SE 6 01 | Security Door Elevations |
| SE 6 02 | Security Device Details |

TECHNOLOGY

| | |
|---|---|
| T 001 | IT Legend, Symbols and Abbreviations |
| T 1 01 | IT Site Plan |
| T 2 01A | IT Floor Plans Ground Floor |
| T 2 01B | IT Floor Plans Ground Floor |
| T 2 01C | IT Floor Plans Ground Floor |
| T 2 02A | IT Floor Plans Second Floor |
| T 2 02B | IT Floor Plans Second Floor |
| T 2 02C | IT Floor Plans Second Floor |
| T 2 03A | IT Floor Plans Third Floor |
| T 2 03B | IT Floor Plans Third Floor |
| T 2 03C | IT Floor Plans Third Floor |
| T 2 04B | IT Floor Plans Fourth Floor |
| T 2 04C | IT Floor Plans Fourth Floor |
| T 4 00 | Enlarged Floor Plans Data Center & DBF |
| T 4 01 | Enlarged IT Floor Plans Ground Floor IDF's |
| T 4 02 | Enlarged IT Floor Plans Second Floor IDF's |
| T 4 03 | Enlarged IT Floor Plans Third Floor IDF's |
| T 4 04 | Enlarged IT Floor Plans Fourth Floor IDF's |
| T 5 01 | Communications Cabling Single Line Diagram |
| T 5 02 | Communications Cabling Riser Diagram |
| T 6 01 | IT Details |

MECHANICAL

| | |
|---|---|
| M 001 | HVAC Symbols and Abbreviations |
| M 002 | HVAC Schedules |
| M 003 | HVAC Schedules |
| M 004 | HVAC Schedules |
| M 005 | HVAC Schedules |
| M 201A | First Floor HVAC Plan, West Wing |
| M 201B | First Floor HVAC Plan, Lantern |
| M 201C | First Floor HVAC Plan, East Wing |
| M 202A | Second Floor HVAC Plan, West Wing |
| M 202B | Second Floor HVAC Plan, Lantern |
| M 202C | Second Floor HVAC Plan, East Wing |
| M 203A | Third Floor HVAC Plan, West Wing |
| M 203B | Third Floor HVAC Plan, Lantern |
| M 203C | Third Floor HVAC Plan, East Wing |
| M 204A | Fourth Floor HVAC Plan, West Wing |
| M 204B | Fourth Floor HVAC Plan, Lantern |
| M 204C | Fourth Floor HVAC Plan, East Wing |
| M 205B | Fifth Floor HVAC Plan, Lantern |
| M 205C | Fifth Floor HVAC Plan, East Wing |
| M 301 | HVAC Sections |
| M 501 | Chilled Water Piping Diagram |
| M 502 | Heating & Hot Water Piping Diagram |

ELECTRICAL

| | |
|---|---|
| E 001 | Electrical Legend and Abbreviations |
| E 002 | Title 24 Compliance Sheets |
| E 101 | Electrical Site Plan |
| E 102 | Electrical Ductbank Routing Plan |
| E 201A | First Floor Lighting Plan, West Wing |
| E 201B | First Floor Lighting Plan, Lantern |
| E 201C | First Floor Lighting Plan, East Wing |
| E 202A | Second Floor Lighting Plan, West Wing |
| E 202B | Second Floor Lighting Plan, Lantern |
| E 202C | Second Floor Lighting Plan, East Wing |
| E 203A | Third Floor Lighting Plan, West Wing |
| E 203B | Third Floor Lighting Plan, Lantern |
| E 203C | Third Floor Lighting Plan, East Wing |
| E 204A | Roof Lighting Plan, West Wing |
| E 204B | Fourth Floor Lighting Plan, Lantern |
| E 204C | Fourth Floor Lighting Plan, East Wing |
| E 301A | First Floor Power & Signal Plan, West Wing |
| E 301B | First Floor Power & Signal Plan, Lantern |
| E 301C | First Floor Power & Signal Plan East Wing |
| E 302A | Second Floor Power & Signal Plan, West Wing |
| E 302B | Second Floor Power & Signal Plan, Lantern |
| E 302C | Second Floor Power & Signal Plan, East Wing |

PLUMBING

| | |
|---|---|
| P 001 | Plumbing Abbreviations, General Notes, Legend & Schedule |
| P 101 | Plumbing Site Plan |
| P 201A | Plumbing-Ground Floor Plan, West Wing Underground |
| P 201B | Plumbing-Ground Floor Plan, Lantern Underground |
| P 201C | Plumbing-Ground Floor Plan, East Wing Underground |
| P 201AA | Plumbing-Ground Floor Plan, West Wing Above Ground |
| P 201BA | Plumbing-Ground Floor Plan, Lantern Above Ground |
| P 201CA | Plumbing-Ground Floor Plan, East Wing Above Ground |
| P 202A | Plumbing Second Floor Plan, West Wing |
| P 202B | Plumbing Second Floor Plan, Lantern |
| P 202C | Plumbing Second Floor Plan, East Wing |
| P 203A | Plumbing Third Floor Plan, West Wing |
| P 203B | Plumbing Third Floor Plan, Lantern |
| P 203C | Plumbing Third Floor Plan, East Wing |
| P 204A | Plumbing Fourth Floor Plan, West Wing |
| P 204B | Plumbing Fourth Floor Plan, Lantern |
| P 204C | Plumbing Fourth Floor Plan, East Wing |

## Mechanical Plans

The mechanical plans primarily include the HVAC drawings, schedules, details, and controls (see Figure 3.14). They may also include some plumbing information, depending on the particular type of HVAC installation.

## Electrical Plans

Because of their complexity, electrical plans are especially challenging for amateurs to interpret. A set of electrical plans will show every single receptacle, light fixture, and all the wiring back to the building's main power supply (see Figure 3.14). They will also detail any intermediary electrical rooms or panels. It is essential to ensure that every new or renovated building has adequate power capacity for all of the electrical equipment contained within it. If a building lacks power capacity and additional power is needed at a later date, installation will be much more expensive than if it was planned for during new construction or renovation.

### Plumbing Plans

Less complex than electrical plans, plumbing plans are still a challenge to interpret. A set of plumbing plans will include overall plans for the entire building with details of both specific systems and specific areas of a building (see Figure 3.14). Plumbing plans will detail fire-protection systems, HVAC supply systems, drainage systems, vent stacks, and potable water systems.

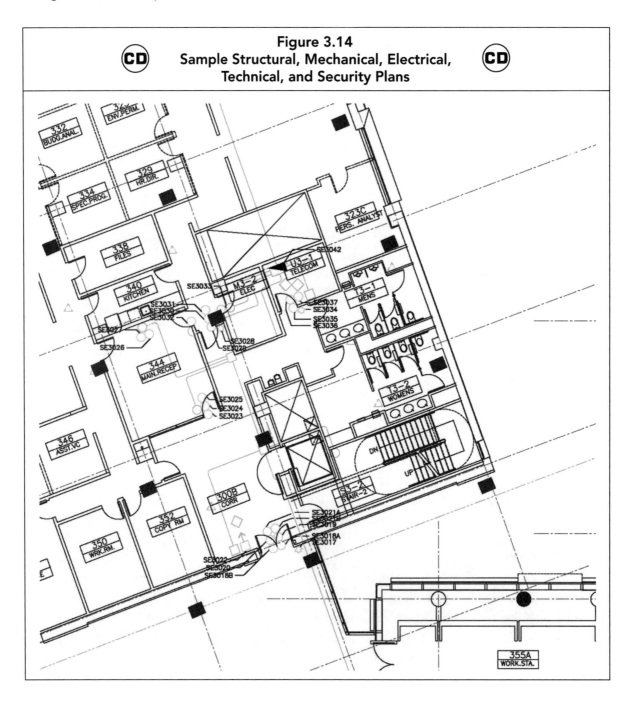

**Figure 3.14**
**Sample Structural, Mechanical, Electrical, Technical, and Security Plans**

### Technology Plans

Technology plans detail data cabling and routing (see Figure 3.14). It is fairly typical for data cabling to follow the same pathways as electrical wiring, though data usually has its own dedicated rooms or closets for patch panels and other equipment. Because technology infrastructure will change many times over a building's life span, it is best to provide separate data rooms or closets rather than installing data and electrical in shared rooms or closets. While combining the two may save some costs in the short run, over time it can create problems in terms of access to equipment and the future expansion of data or electrical systems. A qualified, competent information technology networking professional should review the technology plan to ensure that the plan is workable in the present-day reality and will allow for change and growth as technology evolves. For libraries, one important aspect of technology plans is that they include detailed layouts for technology-intensive rooms such as computer labs, conference rooms, and classrooms. Obviously, putting 25 computers in a classroom or lab space that is not designed to handle the data (or electrical) load is taking a quick march down the road to frustration and failure.

### Security Plans

Security plans provide information about doors, electronic access controls, alarms, security cameras, and, in some instances, emergency lighting and notification systems. As with the other specialty plans, security plans should be reviewed by a knowledgeable expert. This expert might be a representative from the local police department, an independent security-system consultant, or perhaps the same information-technology professional who examines a building's technology plans.

---

 Please see the accompanying CD for high-resolution images of sample building plans showing common architectural symbols and sample drawings/plans with annotations.

---

### Working with Scale Drawings

Building plans, like maps, are drawn to exact proportional scales. In architectural drawings using U.S. measurements, these scales are usually stated as fractions of an inch to the foot. For example, a common scale for residential architectural drawings is three-eighths-inch on the drawing equal to one foot on the real-world structure. This is generally written as 3/8" = 1'-0". In larger buildings, 1/8" = 1'-0" is the more common scale. While scales may be expressed in terms of a mathematical ratio (e.g., 1:48 is the same as 1/4" = 1'-0"), the ratio format is rarely, if ever, employed by architects. In countries that use the metric system, plans will display both ratios and the unit of measurement being used.

For anyone trying to interpret building plans, an architect's scale is an essential tool. The modern architect's scale consists of a triangular or trefoil ruler designed to accommodate 12 different scales (see Figure 3.15). Traditionally made of wood, modern architect's scales are

*(Continued)*

**Working with Scale Drawings** *(Continued)*

usually made of dimensionally stable hard plastic, though aluminum, brass, and other materials are sometimes used. Every architect's scale will have one flat surface dedicated to a single 12-inch, 1:1 scale rule divided down to either 1/32nd or 1/16th fractions of an inch, while all the other flat surfaces on the scale will display at least one relative scale each. At the end of each surface the relative scale will be represented by a fraction, a whole number, or a combination of the two (e.g., 1/8, 1/4, 3/4, 1-1/2, or 3). In all cases, these scales are to be interpreted as X" = 1'-0". The beauty of the architect's scale is that it allows you to instantly convert dimensions on a drawing to their real-world equivalents. For example, if you are working with building plans drawn to 1/8 scale, laying the 1/8 side of an architect's scale on the drawing will instantly tell you that the seminar room on the third floor is 20 feet wide or that the portico covering the main entrance extends 16 feet from the edge of the building.

A single trefoil-type architect's scale will contain all the scales commonly used by architects. Available from a variety of sources, including most office supply vendors, an architect's scale ranges in cost from a few dollars for a plastic model to ten dollars for one crafted from aluminum. The small cost is well worth it for anyone embarking on a building project.

**Figure 3.15**
**Photo of an Architect's Scale**

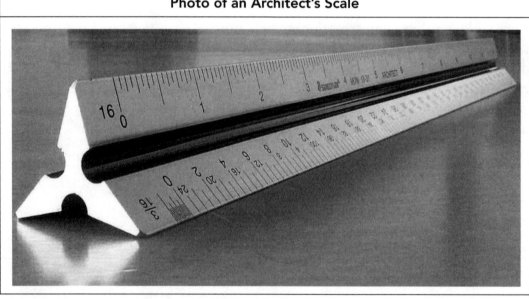

## Building Codes and Standards

Codes that set standards for building construction are not a new concept by any means. The Babylonian Code of Hammurabi, dating to 1790 BC, specified penalties as serious as death for a builder whose building collapsed and killed its occupants. Other examples of efforts to ensure the safety of buildings and their occupants exist throughout history, but it was not until the middle of the nineteenth century that, primarily in Western Europe and the United States, regulations and laws bearing close resemblance to what we think of today as building codes were developed. These first codes were the result of efforts to respond to numerous deadly fires in Europe and the United States, including some that burned significant portions of entire cities. Among the prime motivators of early efforts at developing safety codes were a number of disastrous nineteenth-century theater fires that resulted in appalling death tolls due to poor lighting, poor exiting provisions, and the use of highly flammable construction materials. Deadly factory fires were another motivator for safety reforms, the most notorious of these being New York City's Triangle Shirtwaist Factory fire, which took the lives of 146 workers. Insurance companies, weary of paying out large settlements as a result of fires and other potentially avoidable disasters, were another major force for the establishment of early building and fire codes.

Standardized building code development began in earnest in United States in the early 1900s with the establishment of the three major regional code authorities:

Building Officials Code Administrators International (BOCA)
- Region: East Coast, Midwest
- Major Publication: *BOCA National Building Code (BOCA/NBC)*
Southern Building Code Congress International (SBCCI)
- Region: Southeast
- Major Publication: *Standard Building Code (SBC)*
International Conference of Building Officials (ICBO)
- Region: West Coast, Midwest
- Major Publication: *Uniform Building Code (UBC)*

These three regional governing bodies continued in existence until the mid-1990s when they combined to form the International Code Council (ICC). The ICC, a nonprofit organization comprised of building and construction professionals, establishes and constantly updates codes via a process whereby any interested individual or group may submit a code-change proposal, which is then debated among ICC members and decided by vote. To date, the major publications of the ICC include the following:

- *International Building Code*
- *International Residential Code*
- *International Fire Code*
- *International Energy Conservation Code*
- *International Plumbing Code*
- *International Private Sewage Disposal Code*
- *International Mechanical Code*
- *International Fuel Gas Code*
- *International Wildland-Urban Interface Code*
- *International Existing Building Code*
- *International Property Maintenance Code*
- *International Zoning Code*

Note that several of the individual ICC codes listed reflect the organization of the separate sections that constitute a set of building plans (i.e., mechanical, fire, plumbing).

No coincidence, this organizational format reflects the close correlation between codes and plans.

Due to the complexity of building codes as well as regional preferences, many states and municipalities have not yet converted to the ICC codes and still use its predecessor, the International Council of Building Official's *Uniform Building Code* (*UBC*), or a combination of local codes with either the *UBC* or ICC codes, or even local codes with both the *UBC* and ICC codes. In fact, with the exception of federally legislated standards such as the Americans with Disabilities Act (discussed below), most states and municipalities in the United States alter national codes to accommodate local needs and conditions. For example, in California, codes require much stricter adherence to earthquake-resistant engineering in building design and construction than do codes in midwestern states. Similarly, in the Northeast and other cold-weather areas of the United States, codes generally require stronger roof design to withstand snow loading. Further examples of locally focused codes may be found in areas prone to flooding, hurricanes, etc. An excellent illustration of customized codes and construction requirements can be found on the website of the State of California Division of the State Architect, the agency which governs (among other things) all school construction in California. Other states and provinces have similar code-authority agencies, though the scope and powers of these agencies vary widely. See Table 3.1 for links to state and provincial building

| Table 3.1 Websites for U.S. State and Canadian Provincial Code Authorities | |
|---|---|
| **Authority** | **URL** |
| Alabama Building Commission | http://www.bc.state.al.us/ |
| Alaska Fire and Life Safety Regulations | http://www.dps.state.ak.us/Fire/regulations.aspx |
| Arizona Department of Fire, Building, and Life Safety | http://www.dfbls.az.gov/ |
| Arkansas Building Authority | http://www.arkansasbuildingauthority.com/ |
| California Division of the State Architect | http://www.dsa.dgs.ca.gov |
| Colorado Office of the State Architect | http://www.colorado.gov/cs/Satellite/DPA-EO/DEO/ 1247524014223 |
| Connecticut Office of the State Building Inspector | http://www.ct.gov/dps/cwp/view.asp?a=2148&q=305412 |
| Delaware Code | http://delcode.delaware.gov |
| District of Columbia Department of Consumer and Regulatory Affairs | http://dcra.dc.gov/DC/DCRA |
| Florida Building Codes | http://www2.iccsafe.org/states/florida_codes/ |
| Georgia Construction Codes | http://www.dca.state.ga.us/development/Construction Codes |

*(Continued)*

### Table 3.1
### Websites for U.S. State and Canadian Provincial Code Authorities *(Continued)*

| Authority | URL |
|---|---|
| Construction in Hawaii | http://hawaii.gov/dbedt/info/economic/data_reports/construction/ |
| Idaho Division of Building Safety | http://dbs.idaho.gov/ |
| Illinois Capital Development Board | http://www.cdb.state.il.us |
| Indiana Codes, Standards, and Other Rules | http://www.in.gov/dhs/2490.htm |
| Iowa Building Code Bureau | http://www.dps.state.ia.us/fm/building |
| Kansas Department of Administration, Facilities, Design and Construction | http://www.da.ks.gov/fp/Code/Code_ADAAG.htm |
| Kentucky Department of Housing, Buildings, and Construction | http://dhbc.ky.gov/ |
| Louisiana Office of State Fire Marshal | http://sfm.dps.louisiana.gov/ |
| Maine State Planning Office | http://www.maine.gov/spo/specialprojects/buildingcodes |
| Maryland Codes Administration | http://mdcodes.umbc.edu/ |
| Massachusetts Building Code | http://www.mass.gov/ |
| Michigan Codes and Standards | http://www.michigan.gov/ |
| Minnesota Construction Codes and Licensing | http://www.dli.mn.gov/Ccld.asp |
| Mississippi State Board of Architecture | http://www.archbd.state.ms.us/ |
| Missouri Office of Administration | http://oa.mo.gov/fmdc/dc |
| Montana Building Codes | http://BuildingCodes.mt.gov/ |
| Nebraska State Fire Marshal's Office | http://www.sfm.ne.gov/ |
| Nevada Fire Protection Engineering Bureau | http://fire.state.nv.us/Engineering.shtml |
| New Hampshire State Building Code Review Board | http://www.nh.gov/safety/boardsandcommissions/bldgcode/ |
| New Jersey Division of Codes and Standards | http://www.state.nj.us/dca/divisions/codes/index.html |
| New Mexico Regulation & Licensing Department, Construction Industries Division | http://www.rld.state.nm.us/cid |
| New York Division of Code Enforcement and Administration | http://www.dos.state.ny.us/code/ls-codes.html |
| North Carolina Office of State Fire Marshal, Engineering and Codes | http://www.ncdoi.com/OSFM/Engineering/engineering_home.asp |

*(Continued)*

**Table 3.1**
**Websites for U.S. State and Canadian Provincial Code Authorities** *(Continued)*

| Authority | URL |
|---|---|
| North Dakota State Building Code | http://www.communityservices.nd.gov/government/state-building-code/ |
| Ohio Board of Building Standards | http://com.ohio.gov/dico/BBS.aspx |
| Oklahoma State Fire Marshal Adopted Codes | http://www.firemar.state.ok.us/adoptedcodes.htm |
| Oregon Building Codes Division | http://www.bcd.oregon.gov/codeprograms.html |
| Pennsylvania Uniform Construction Code | http://www.portal.state.pa.us/portal/server.pt/community/uniform_construction_code/10524 |
| Rhode Island State Building & Fire Code Regulations | http://sos.ri.gov/library/buildingcodes/ |
| South Carolina Building Codes Council | http://www.llr.state.sc.us/POL/bcc/ |
| South Dakota State Fire Marshal | http://dps.sd.gov/emergency_services/state_fire_marshal/fire_laws.aspx |
| Tennessee Fire Prevention Division, Codes Enforcement Section | http://tn.gov/commerce/sfm/fpcesect.shtml |
| Texas Building Codes and Standards | http://seco.cpa.state.tx.us/sa_codes.html |
| Utah Uniform Building Codes | http://www.dopl.utah.gov/programs/ubc/ |
| Vermont Licenses and Permits | http://www.vermont.gov/portal/business/index.php?id=93 |
| Virginia State Building Codes and Regulations | http://www.dhcd.virginia.gov/StateBuildingCodesandRegulations |
| Washington State Building Code Council | https://fortress.wa.gov/ga/apps/sbcc/default.aspx |
| West Virginia Office of the State Fire Marshal, Plans & Review | http://www.firemarshal.wv.gov/ |
| Wisconsin Department of Commerce, Safety & Buildings List of Administrative Codes | http://www.commerce.state.wi.us/sb/SB-DivCodesListing.html |
| Wyoming State Fire Marshal, Codes and Standards | http://wyofire.state.wy.us/plan/codes&standards.html |
| **Canada** | |
| Canadian Commission on Building and Fire Codes | http://www.nationalcodes.ca/ |
| Canadian Codes Centre | http://www.nrc-cnrc.gc.ca/eng/services/irc/codes-centre.html |
| Alberta Building Codes & Standards | http://www.municipalaffairs.gov.ab.ca/cp_building_codes_standards.cfm |
| British Columbia Building Code | http://www.bccodes.ca/bccode_building.htm |

*(Continued)*

| Table 3.1 Websites for U.S. State and Canadian Provincial Code Authorities *(Continued)* ||
| --- | --- |
| **Authority** | **URL** |
| Manitoba Codes and Standards | http://www.firecomm.gov.mb.ca/codes.html |
| New Brunswick (Adopted National Code) | http://www.nationalcodes.ca/ |
| Newfoundland and Labrador (Adopted National Code) | http://www.nationalcodes.ca/ |
| Northwest Territories (Adopted National Code) | http://www.nationalcodes.ca/ |
| Nova Scotia Building Code Regulations | http://www.gov.ns.ca/just/regulations/regs/bcregs.htm |
| Nunavut (Adopted National Code) | http://www.nationalcodes.ca/ |
| Ontario Building Code | http://www.obc.mah.gov.on.ca/site4.aspx |
| Prince Edward Island Building Code | http://www.gov.pe.ca/cca/index.php3?number=16923&lang=E |
| Quebec Building Code - Safety Code | http://www.rbq.gouv.qc.ca/dirEnglish/BuildingCode/Safety Code.asp |
| Saskatchewan Building Standards | http://www.nationalcodes.ca/ |

code information for the United States and Canada. Also note that many counties and municipalities post local code information on their websites.

Adding to the confusing mixing and matching of building codes, several organizations besides the ICC continue to publish their own national codes. Most notably, the National Fire Protection Association (NFPA) publishes *National Fire Codes*, while the International Association of Plumbing and Mechanical Officials (IAPMO) publishes its *Uniform Plumbing Code*. Including in its membership representatives from virtually every firefighting organization in the United States as well as representatives from a number of foreign firefighting organizations, NFPA carries a great deal of weight within the firefighting community. Because the NFPA and ICC produce their own competing codes with somewhat different focuses and coverage, the two organizations have, as yet, failed to agree on a single national fire code. The story is similar in regard to IAPMO and ICC, with each organization continuing to produce its own specific code.

The Americans with Disabilities Act (ADA) is yet another factor shaping building codes and standards in the United States. Signed into law in 1990, the ADA regulates access standards for public facilities and provides standards for accessible design. Unlike the various building codes, the ADA is a federal law that applies uniformly across the United States. In addition to abiding by the ADA, several states have enacted their own, more stringent, accessibility standards, and some states have mandated that a percentage of any public funds used for building renovation must be dedicated to improving accessibility.

In a perfect world, codes and standards would not only be uniform but also insulated from the influence of special interests. Because this is not a perfect world, and because construction is big business involving such varied and powerful interests as architects, developers, lenders, insurance companies, builders, consumers, and public officials, the development and adoption of building codes is a highly political, far from impartial process. Builders, developers, lenders, and (to an extent) architects generally want fewer, less restrictive codes hampering their activities and driving up their costs. Insurance companies, most consumers, and many public officials want stronger codes to ensure that public and private structures are well built and safe. On top of all this, the whole permitting and codes-enforcement system can be something of a cash cow for local governments, a circumstance which further hinders the impartiality of building codes, as some cities and counties manipulate (some would say abuse) the system to create income streams.

Regardless of which authority issued the building code, and regardless of the code's impartiality (or lack thereof), the general rule is that buildings must be built to meet the code that is in effect when the project is approved, an action which may occur several years before construction actually begins. For existing buildings, it is possible that renovations based on changes in building codes may be mandated at any time, especially when those code changes directly involve life safety. The more common scenario is for an existing building to be brought up to current building codes only when it undergoes a major renovation, remodeling, or expansion. The cost of bringing an older existing building up to current code can be so expensive as to be a deal breaker for a proposed renovation, remodeling, or expansion. In some cases, existing buildings are demolished because building new is less expensive than bringing the existing building up to code.

## Construction Professions

Just as it is beneficial for an architect involved in designing a library to know something about the specific jobs performed by library staff, it is beneficial for library staff involved in a library building project to know something about the specific jobs done by those working on the project. This section focuses on those construction professions that are most likely to be present on library building projects; as such, this is not a comprehensive list of all construction professions.

There is considerable specialization within the construction professions. To some extent this specialization is based on training and knowledge; a brick mason cannot be expected to do a crane operator's job, and vice versa. More significantly, construction specialization may also be enforced by union rules and licensing regulations. Union rules may declare a particular type of work to be the exclusive domain of members of the appropriate union. Licensing regulations legally prohibit unlicensed workers from doing certain types of work, notably (but not exclusively) electrical work, plumbing, and elevator installation and maintenance. The influence of union rules will vary from location to location, while licensing regulations tend to be more universal. The benefits of specialization are better-built and safer buildings; the downsides are higher cost and, in some cases, slower progress. The painter or carpenter standing right there might very well have the skill and knowledge to hook up that light fixture, but it is simply against the rules for him or her to do a job that requires a licensed union electrician. By the same token, no member of the library staff, no matter how handy, should take matters into his or her own hands by performing any work that must be left to construction professionals.

## Managerial and Administrative Construction Professionals

A **general contractor** is the individual or firm holding primary responsibility for managing a building project and providing all of the material, labor, equipment, and services necessary for completing the project. As the signatory to the contract for the prime construction of a project, the general contractor assumes the risks that come with bidding on a project while, at the same time, standing to reap the rewards of successfully fulfilling the contract. For very small projects the general contractor is often a single individual who participates in the hands-on work of construction. On larger projects the general contractor will be a firm with many employees. As the chief on-site representative of a large general-contracting firm, the **construction superintendent** is the person directly responsible for field supervision of the project and completion of the work.

One of the main functions of a general contractor is to hire, oversee, coordinate, and pay the **subcontractors** (aka *subs*) who are responsible for completing various parts of the project. For example, the general contractor for a large building project would likely select an electrical subcontractor to perform the electrical work rather than directly engaging electricians to do the work. It is also possible for subcontractors on large projects to hire their own subcontractors to complete some parts of the work.

Just as the general contractor is represented on site by the construction superintendent, the owner of a building is represented on site by a **building project manager** (aka *construction project manager*) whose main job is to look after the owner's interest. Though working closely with the construction superintendent and other members of the general contractor's team, the building project manager is the owner's employee, not the general contractor's. On large projects the building project manager is assisted by a team of other project managers and inspectors whose job it is to make sure all work is carried out in accordance with the formal construction documents.

**Executive architects** are also involved in the construction process in that they are called upon to clarify questions from the field regarding the working documents, make changes to the working documents as problems are encountered, and render the as-built drawings that document the actual work done.

## Hands-On Construction Professionals

**Carpenters** work with wood, as well as such other materials as plastic, fiberglass, or drywall, and are employed, at one point or another, on almost all building projects. While carpenters may be generalists, there are specialties within the field. The following specialist carpenters are likely to be encountered on a library building project:

- **Framers** are carpenters who work on the structure of wood-framed buildings. On typical residential or light commercial building, framers first erect the 2x4 studs and the rafters that comprise a building's frame and then attach plywood siding and subfloors to the frame. On a large steel-and-concrete building, framers erect interior stud walls and perform other tasks related to creating rooms within the larger structure.

- **Trim carpenters** specialize in doors, molding, window trim, baseboards, and other decorative woodwork. Trim carpenters may also install cabinets.
- **Finish carpenters** (aka *joiners*) do the type of detail-oriented carpentry associated with cabinets, fine furniture, and other wooden objects that carry with them exacting requirements for artistry.

**Cement masons** (a category that includes concrete finishers and terrazzo workers) place, finish, and repair concrete. Cement masons build and align the forms into which concrete is placed; control the placement and leveling of placed concrete; float concrete to bring a fine paste of cement to the surface; round the edges of concrete to prevent chipping; and put grooves in the concrete to allow for expansion. Near the end of the process, concrete masons finish the concrete by either smoothing it for a decorative effect or giving it a rough, nonslip texture. Concrete masons may also embed decorative pebbles in concrete, tint it, or stamp it with decorative patterns.

There are many devices for placing concrete, ranging from simple wheelbarrows to concrete pumps, truck-mounted cement mixers (aka *concrete wagons*), and concrete skips suspended from cranes.

**Drywall installers and tapers** install drywall (so called because it can be used only in spaces that are protected from high levels of moisture) on interior walls and ceilings. Also known by the names *gypsum board, wallboard,* and *plasterboard,* drywall is functional in that it provides soundproofing and a small measure of fire resistance, but it is also decorative in that it finishes off an interior space and can be painted any color. While drywall installers (aka *hangers*) fasten drywall to studs or other framework and tapers prepare drywall for painting by removing imperfections, it is possible for a single person to do both jobs. A skilled drywall team works with such precision that the joints between the drywall boards and the screws holding the boards in place are rendered invisible after the drywall has been taped, floated with drywall joint compound, and painted. For areas where some moisture may be present, such as restrooms, drywall crews will install water-resistant greenboard or cement board, the latter being the more water-resistant of the two materials.

**Electricians** are skilled tradespersons licensed to install, inspect, and repair wiring in buildings, ships, and stationary machinery. Electricians may also install network cabling.

**Elevator installers and repairers** are licensed to install, repair, maintain, and inspect elevators, escalators, and similar devices. **Elevator adjusters**, the most skilled elevator installers and repairers, have the job of fine-tuning elevators to make sure they travel at the right speed and stop smoothly and exactly at each floor. On modern computer-controlled elevators, any changes to the program controlling an elevator require the service of an elevator adjuster.

**Flooring installers** may install and repair carpet (broadloom or carpet tiles), wood, sheet goods (linoleum and vinyl), tile, and other floor finishings that serve both decorative and functional purposes. In some cases, these materials may be installed on walls and ceilings as well as on floors. Installing each type of flooring requires its own set of skills and knowledge, so many installers specialize in only one material.

**Glaziers** install, cut, replace, and remove glass in all its forms, including windows (exterior and interior), glass partitions, and decorative glass. They also work with such glass substitutes as plastics, granite, or marble. On large buildings, glaziers build the metal frameworks that support large glass panels or curtain walls and install the glass into those frameworks.

**Hazardous materials removal workers** are most likely to be present during renovations of older buildings, and the materials they are most likely to remove are asbestos and lead (including lead-based paint). Though the removal of hazardous materials can add significant, and sometimes unanticipated, costs to a renovation project, such safety-mandated expenses are all but unavoidable.

**Heating, ventilation, and air-conditioning (HVAC) technicians** install, repair, fine-tune, and clean HVAC systems. The installation of the motors, compressors, pumps, fans, ducts, pipes, thermostats, and switches that control a building's indoor climate normally takes place after a structure has been erected and clad but before interior finishing (drywall, ceilings, floor coverings) is installed. HVAC has become an increasingly important and complicated component in new and newly renovated buildings because proper HVAC is key both to reducing a building's energy consumption and to maintaining a healthy, comfortable indoor environment.

**Heavy-equipment operators,** as the name implies, operate such devices as bulldozers, backhoes, excavators, pile drivers, graders, forklifts, compactors, cranes, dump trucks, and the like. As might be expected, the type of heavy equipment on any given library project depends both on the scope of the project and where on its timeline the project is. In the early stages of the construction of a new multistory, steel-and-concrete library building you would expect to see bulldozers and graders doing site preparation, followed perhaps by pile drivers pounding a building's piers into place. Large cranes, on the other hand, would not appear on site until the structural steel starts to go up. Operating heavy equipment requires significant training, skill, and practice. For example, the precision required for lifting structural steel into place is so demanding that operating a large crane is said to be more difficult than piloting an airplane. Because heavy equipment is so dangerous, keeping people safe while it is in operation is a significant worksite safety issue.

**Hod carriers** (aka *hoddies*) carry bricks, blocks, stones, mortar, and other construction materials as part of a team working on a masonry project. Hod carriers may be unskilled laborers or they may be apprentices in the first stages of learning to become masons.

**Insulation workers** specialize in installing heat or frost insulation to reduce a building's energy consumption. They also insulate such equipment as boilers and steam pipes to reduce heat loss and prevent injuries. Properly installed insulation materials can also reduce noise, a matter of special interest for libraries.

**Ironworkers** (aka *erectors*) are involved in just about any job that requires building with iron, steel, aluminum, or other metal. In fact, the job title *ironworker* is a holdover from times past, as today's ironworkers are far more likely to work with steel than iron. On a large concrete-and-steel library building, ironworkers will begin by assembling the cranes and derricks necessary to hoist a building's structural steel members (beams, girders, and columns) into place. The ironworkers will then perform the job of connecting the structural steel members that comprise a building's frame. Two major specialties within the ironworker field include:

- **Reinforcing iron and rebar workers** (aka *rod busters*) cut, bend, set, and wire into place the reinforcing bars (commonly known as *rebar*) that are used to strengthen concrete. Reinforcing ironworkers also work with the steel mesh and tensioning cable systems that are sometimes used to strengthen concrete.
- **Ornamental ironworkers** install curtain walls (non-load-bearing walls and window frames), metal stairs, handrails, and other nonstructural metal components found in most buildings.

**Laborers** are unskilled workers who do some of the most physically demanding work on any building project. Their work may include digging, lifting, carrying, and other menial tasks. Typically the lowest paid employees on any worksite, laborers may or may not be unionized, depending on local laws and customs. In spite of laborers' low pay and low status, their work is vital to even the most high-tech, automated worksite, as it would be impossible to complete a building project without laborers performing the tasks that machines simply cannot do.

**Masons** (aka *brick masons, block masons, stonemasons*) specialize in building processes that involve shaping and assembling individual units (bricks, concrete blocks, glass blocks, stones) and joining them together, with or without mortar, to form structures.

**Painters** apply paint, stains, varnish, or other finishes to a building's exterior, interior, or both. In general, interior painting is largely decorative while exterior painting serves both decorative and protective purposes. Besides selecting and applying the appropriate paint (or other finish) for any given job, painters are responsible for preparing surfaces to be painted. For interior work, such preparations may involve patching and taping drywall, removing old wallpaper, sanding rough surfaces, caulking seams and cracks, filling nail holes, and so on.

**Pipe layers, plumbers, pipe fitters, and sprinkler fitters** are related fields, though there is enough difference that individuals tend to specialize in just one field.

- **Pipe layers** dig and grade trenches for sewers, drains, water mains, and gas lines. Pipe layers install and join pipes that may be made of a variety of materials, including cast iron, plastic, clay, and concrete.
- **Plumbers** install and repair the pipes, tubing, fixtures, and appliances necessary to move clean water into a building and move waste out. Plumbers also install and repair gas lines. Because plumbing is crucial to public health and safety, plumbing work is heavily regulated and finished plumbing work must adhere to a complex set of codes.
- **Pipe fitters** install low- and high-pressure pipes for heating and cooling systems of the sort used in large library buildings. They also install the automatic controls that regulate the flow of water and/or air through those pipes.
- **Sprinkler fitters** install and repair automatic fire-sprinkler systems.

**Plasterers** practice one of the most ancient of building techniques, the application of plaster (aka *mud*) to create very durable, paintable coverings on walls and ceilings. As with drywall, plaster serves both practical (sound- and fireproofing) and decorative purposes. While the number and complexity of techniques for plastering make the profession more of an art than a trade, most techniques include the application of an initial *brown coat* which is then covered with a smooth, paintable *finish coat* (aka *white coat*).

**Roofers** install and repair all types of roofs, typically working with roofing materials composed of tar, asphalt, gravel, wood, rubber, thermoplastic, metal, or some combination thereof. Properly installed roofs not only protect buildings and their contents from water damage but are a key component in reducing any building's total energy consumption.

**Stucco masons** apply stucco to the exteriors (and, sometimes, interiors) of houses and light commercial buildings. Similar to plaster, traditional stucco is composed of lime, sand, and water, though the modern version often incorporates strengthening polymers into the mix. In the past, stucco, like plaster, was spread over wooden laths to give it additional strength; since the middle of the twentieth century, metal-wire mesh or netting has replaced wood laths. Stucco exteriors are especially popular in the states of California, Arizona, New Mexico, and Florida.

A **teamster** is, in modern usage, a truck driver. The work of teamsters who drive very large trucks is somewhat akin to that of heavy equipment operators. While a teamster (lower case) may well be a Teamster (a member of the International Brotherhood of Teamsters, an influential labor union), not every teamster is a Teamster, and vice versa.

## Conclusion

If completing a library building project were a football game, the set of plans would be the coach's book of plays, building codes would be the rules of the game, and construction professionals would be the players. We library professionals who get involved in building projects are something like team owners. It is not our job to suit up and run out on the field. It is not our job to call the plays or interpret the rules. But because we have so much at stake in the outcome, it is important that we are familiar with the playbook, understand the rules, and know the players so that we can, in our own way, contribute to the success of our team.

# II

# Library-Specific Construction and Renovation

# 4

# Spaces within the Library: A Survey

The purpose of this chapter is to survey and generally describe the attributes of various spaces commonly found in libraries. Though the final dimensions and details of library spaces will be drawn up by architects who (it is hoped) fully understand the functions of the library spaces they are designing, this chapter provides a useful preprogramming review for those with experience planning library building projects. This chapter will be even more useful to library staff who are involved in their first building project and also to nonlibrarians who have been invited to participate in the programming process.

## Public Areas

### Library Entrances and Exits

It is wonderful for a library to feature a drop-dead entrance point where the mere act of stepping into the building transports visitors into a magical world of books and knowledge. Wonderful is wonderful, but there are a number of practical considerations that come in to play when planning a library entrance. One of the most important of these considerations, security, is covered in detail in Chapter 7, "Library Security and Safety in Building Design and Construction." Emergency-only exits, which are distinct from ordinary entrance/exit points, are also covered in Chapter 7.

It is best to avoid an entrance/exit scenario in which people step directly from the outside into a library quiet area. The unavoidable noise of those entering and exiting is certain to disturb anyone trying to read or study. Placing such aids as building directories, floor maps, and appropriate directional signage just inside a library entrance will help visitors get their bearings. There should be a clear line of sight between the library entrance and a staffed service point—the nearer to the entrance the better.

For the entrance/exit doors themselves, there are two main options: manual or automatic doors. Manual doors are usually less expensive and require less maintenance than automatic doors, though this is not always the case when dealing with high-quality manual balance doors that can be operated even by persons with disabilities. The use of less expensive, harder-to-operate manual doors most often requires the installation of at least one power-assisted door activated by a push button marked with a handicapped symbol.

Automatic doors eliminate the need for a special power-assisted door and are a boon not only for people with disabilities but also for anyone carrying a load of books, pushing a stroller, wrangling three or four children, or otherwise not in a good position to manage a manual door. Automatic doors that slide open and closed have major advantages over automatic (and manual) swinging doors. First off, sliding doors do not swing open to whack the faces or, during sandal season, break the toes of unwary library users. Second, sliding doors will continue to operate effectively in winds strong enough to rip most swinging doors right off their hinges.

In especially windy areas, revolving doors, though expensive, are worth considering for their ability to function well in the face of strong winds. (Next time you attend an American Library Association meeting in Chicago, notice how many buildings in the Windy City feature revolving doors.) Unless it is large enough to accommodate a wheelchair, a revolving door may require the installation of a separate door for wheelchair access. A typical combination is a revolving door plus an adjacent single-width automatic sliding door for wheelchair access.

In any area subject to strong winds, heavy precipitation, extreme temperatures, or blowing sand, dust, or leaves, a portal-style entrance/exit may be the answer. With a portal arrangement those entering the building go through a set of doors that takes them into an alcove; from the alcove, one must pass through a second set of doors to enter the building proper. Going in reverse, anyone leaving the building first enters the alcove before exiting to the outside. A portal-style arrangement will help keep wind, rain, snow, dirt, cold, and heat out of the building while also giving those in the alcove an area in which to raise or lower umbrellas, button or unbutton coats, shake off snow or rainwater, and otherwise prepare to enter or exit the building. Portal or not, library entrance/exit areas should offer conveniently located trash cans and also provide walk-off grates and mats to reduce the amount of trash and dirt entering the building.

### Library Stack Areas

Library stack areas are typically defined by standard library book stacks manufactured of metal and finished with end panels made of wood, metal, or composite materials. End panels should include accommodations for range signage.

Stacks may be single or double faced. Shelf depth for single-faced stacks ranges from 8 to 12 inches; for double-faced stacks, 16 to 24 inches. The industry-standard width for book stack shelves is 36 inches, with deviations from this standard considered custom widths.

A single set of shelves running from the floor to the top of the book stack is referred to as a *unit*. Standard units range in height from 42 inches (which might be used in a children's area) to 90 inches (common in research libraries), with many in-between heights readily available and custom heights always an option. At a height of 90 inches, a unit will accommodate seven shelves spaced for standard (nonoversized) books. A double-faced unit fitted with 14 (seven per side) 36-inch-wide shelves provides 42 linear feet of shelf space, which, at an average of eight volumes per linear foot, translates to a capacity of 336 books per double-faced unit *if filled to maximum capacity*. However, working capacity for library stacks is never 100 percent. While the actual working capacity will vary from library to library, and will even vary within a single library depending on how a particular set of stacks is being used, loading the book stacks to at most 70 percent of maximum capacity is a realistic (if admittedly ballpark) figure for a hypothetical average library. Working from this 70 percent estimate, the working capacity for a double-faced unit comes out to 235 books.

The footprint for each unit of shelving must include space for the shelving itself plus extra space to allow aisles between rows of stacks. Single-faced shelving requires 10 to 14 square feet per unit, while double-faced shelving requires 18 to 22 square feet per unit (Siems and Demmers, 2003: 3).

---

### Sample Planning Exercise

1. A library planning an expansion wants to add stack capacity to accommodate 7,000 books.
2. Assuming no oversized books and assuming the stacks are filled to 70 percent of capacity: 7,000 books √ 235 books per double-faced unit = 29.7 double-faced units, a number which is easily rounded off to 30 double-faced units.
3. 30 double-faced units x 20 square feet per unit = approximately 600 square feet to accommodate 7,000 books.

---

An important consideration in the Sample Planning Exercise is compliance with the Americans with Disabilities Act (ADA) of 1990. Interpretations of this law vary from state to state, and you should check with your state disabilities office for appropriate guidelines. The general rule of thumb is that a wheelchair requires about 48 inches for maneuverability. The state of California guidelines provide a fairly simple formula for book stacks that meets federal ADA guidelines:

- Book stack aisles should be minimum of 36 inches wide.
- Each row of stacks should not exceed 21 feet in length (a maximum of seven sections at standard width of 36 inches each).
- Cross aisles should be minimum of 36 inches wide.
- End aisles should be minimum of 44 inches wide.

Obviously, single-sided wall-mounted stacks do not require a break every 21 feet. If it is possible to make all aisles 44 inches wide, it is best to do so. Aisles of that width also have the benefit of allowing two average-sized people to pass without becoming intimately acquainted with each other.

Book stacks should be laid out perpendicular to overhead lights in order to allow as much light as possible to get down between the stacks. If laid out parallel to overhead lights, it is possible for a book stack to almost entirely block out the light from above. Book stacks should not be exposed to direct sunlight or high levels of reflected ultraviolet (UV) rays as either one can damage books over time. Protection from UV rays can be achieved by locating stacks in windowless areas or by using window products that filter UV rays. UV filtering is becoming an increasingly common practice as contemporary green-building practices call for more, not fewer, windows in order to save energy and contribute to a more comfortable environment for work and study.

Because of their weight when loaded with books, standard book stacks must be erected on floors capable of supporting loads of at least 150 pounds per square foot. Standard floors for an office space, for example, are designed to support about half that load and will eventually fail under the weight of loaded book stacks. When dealing with older buildings where detailed specifications may not exist, only qualified structural engineers are capable of determining whether a floor is capable of supporting book stacks.

In areas of seismic activity, state and/or local building codes call for high standards of reinforcement for library book stacks. When planning library stack spaces in such areas, be sure to consult local codes.

When remodeling an area containing book stacks that have been in place prior to 1990, be aware that the Americans with Disabilities Act requires wider spacing between the stacks than was standard when the stacks were originally installed. This means that remodeling a pre-1990 stack space will likely require the removal of some stacks and, therefore, result in a decrease in the number of books that can be housed in that space.

### Compact Shelving Areas

The virtue of compact shelving is its ability to store more material in less space than conventional book stacks or industrial storage racks. Compact shelving (which is also known as *high-density shelving* or *movable-aisle shelving*) saves space because a single relocatable side aisle provides access to multiple rows of shelving. Mounted on a rail system, compact shelving can be either motorized or manually operated. In a small installation, compact shelving will require half of the floor space of equivalent-capacity static shelving; in larger installations, compact shelving requires one-third of the floor space of equivalent-capacity static shelving (Siems and Demmers, 2003: 22). All compact shelving comes with safety devices that halt movement should the shelving come in contact with a person, book truck, kick stool, or other object.

Compact shelving can be used in public spaces, where it typically stores books, micro-formats, DVDs, and other materials that members of the public can either check out or use on their own in the library; in public-access settings, the shelf depth of compact shelving is typically equivalent to the shelf depth of standard static book stacks (8 to 12 inches single faced; 16 to 24 inches double faced). In nonpublic spaces, such as special collections, reserve-reading rooms, and archives, compact shelving may store anything from books to manuscripts to realia; the depth of shelves on this type of compact shelving varies widely but is typically much greater than for standard book stacks.

Compact shelving does have some drawbacks. As long as one compact-shelving aisle is open, materials in other rows are completely inaccessible, making compact shelving impractical for storing heavily used collections. Compact shelving is more expensive to purchase and install than static library book stacks and, because of its weight when fully loaded, requires even stronger floors than do static book stacks. In most existing buildings compact shelving can be installed only on the bottom floor of a building, directly on top of the foundation slab. In any case, only a qualified structural engineer can determine whether a particular floor is capable of supporting compact shelving.

## Reading Areas

Library reading areas may be adjacent to, intermingled with, or far removed from the book stacks. The classic furnishings for a library reading area are wooden library tables outfitted with fixed tabletop lamps and matching wooden chairs. Other furniture options for reading areas include individual carrels, soft seating (armchairs and couches), and casual fun furniture for children's and young adults' reading areas.

When determining how many library tables can fit into a given floor plan, remember to allow not only for the square footage of the tables themselves, but also space for chairs to be pulled out as well as space for aisles around tables. Allow about 60 inches between square tables, 54 inches between round tables. The rule of thumb for aisles is that an aisle wide enough for two people to walk comfortably abreast (about 48 inches) is wide enough for a wheelchair to maneuver and will meet the requirements of the Americans with Disabilities Act. The spacing of soft seating and fun furniture is more flexible than for traditional tables and chairs, but there still must be space for people to move around with ease and for wheelchairs to maneuver. Whatever the type of furniture, it is better to underfurnish a space than to cram in the maximum amount of furniture possible, as doing the latter makes a room feel crowded and uninviting.

With the wide adoption of mobile computing devices (laptops, etc.) access to power and data connections (wired or wireless) from each seat in a reading area has become standard and should be factored into any reading-room plan.

## Periodical Rooms

The typical periodical room features slope-fronted periodical display shelving that allows for the display of the most recent issue of a periodical and also provides space to store a dozen (give or take) copies of back issues. Back issues are typically stored beneath the display shelf, which may itself be hinged to provide easy access to back issues.

Periodical rooms usually provide some seating for those who wish to read in the room and also provide an ample number of photocopiers, though the rise of online journals has, in many academic and research libraries, reduced the demand for copying of print-format periodical articles. Periodical rooms may also provide newspaper racks for current newspapers as well as microformat readers for accessing older periodicals and other materials available in microformats.

The designation of "current periodical (reading) room" is routinely used by those libraries that separate current periodicals from older bound issues, typically binding and then storing the latter in their main book stacks. The designation of "periodical room" is used by libraries that keep current and bound issues in the same location, with such spaces typically having a mixture of periodical display shelving and traditional book stacks for bound volumes.

The ambiance of periodicals rooms can range from the rather clinical atmosphere found in many research libraries to the clubby feeling favored by public libraries.

### Copier/Printer Areas

It is possible for libraries to scatter copiers or printers (or, increasingly, devices that are both copiers and printers in one) all around a library, to cluster them in designated copier/printer rooms, or do a bit of both. Wherever they go, copier/printers present certain challenges:

- Because the use of copier/printers generates considerable noise, placing them far from reading areas or inside designated, ideally soundproofed, rooms helps to preserve quiet.
- Clustering copier/printers in designated rooms instead of scattering them around a building also has the advantage of making the machines easier to service and resupply.
- On the other hand, clustering copier/printers in designated rooms can make them difficult for library users to find and often removes them far from actual points of need.
- When machines are clustered, copier/printers areas may require supplemental cooling and ventilation.
- Copier/printers have specific electrical requirements and so cannot simply be plugged in to the nearest outlet. Standard electrical circuits will fail under the power demands of copier/printers.
- Modern copier/printers that incorporate scanning technology require network connections so users can e-mail documents they have scanned.
- Heavily used copier/printer spaces benefit from being situated near shelving to hold copied items prior to reshelving.
- Volume copying and printing produces lots of waste paper, so any space in which copier/printers are clustered requires supplemental trash and recycling capacity.
- One or more lockable spaces to store such copier/printer supplies as toner and paper is a necessity for any busy printer/copier operation. The closer such storage spaces are to the copier/printers, the better.

### Classrooms

Library classrooms are used for many purposes and therefore come in many shapes and sizes. That said, there are some universals to consider when planning any library classroom space.

Although equipping a library classroom with auditorium-style rows of seating allows the largest number of students to fit into a given space, there are instructional benefits in furnishing library classrooms with loose chairs and tables that can be easily reconfigured for different instructional styles, including active learning, group work, seminars, or traditional lecture-style classes. Table 4.1 (adapted from a guide created at

**Table 4.1**
**Estimated Square Feet Needed per Student**
**by Room Type and Furnishings**

| Square Feet per Student* | Room Type | Furnishings |
|---|---|---|
| 29–35 | Seminar | Movable tables and chairs |
| 28–32 | Conference | One large table and chairs |
| 24–28 | Classroom | Tablet armchairs |
| 30–39 | Classroom | Movable tables and chairs |
| 24–27 | Classroom | Fixed table and movable chairs |
| 20–22 | Auditorium | Auditorium seats with tablet arms |
| 28–30 | Auditorium | Fixed tables with movable chairs |

*These estimates include space for an instructor.

*Source*: Adapted from Emory University College Classroom Working Group, 2010: 17.

Emory University) gives good rule-of-thumb estimates for the amount of square footage to provide per student in various types of instruction and meeting spaces.

It has become increasingly common to provide a computer at each library classroom seat so students can practice information skills as they are being taught. Desktop computers are the least expensive option for classrooms, though these can get in the way when the classroom is being used for non-computer-dependent activities (a book talk, a knitting class, etc.). Laptop computers can be more expensive than desktops and also require a secure space (such as a lockable cart or closet) in which they can be stored and charged, but their use makes for a more flexible classroom space.

When a classroom is outfitted with multiple computers, the electrical circuits must be sufficient for running or, in the case of laptops, charging however many computers are assigned to that classroom. In addition, the classroom's network infrastructure, whether wired, wireless, or both, must be robust enough to allow all the computers in the room to access the network simultaneously without delays. Floor boxes are the most flexible way to distribute power and wired data connections around a classroom and keep dangling power and data cords to a minimum as tables and chairs are rearranged.

The capability for computer projection is a must for today's library classroom. The best arrangement is for overhead, wall-mounted, or rear projection so that the projector is safely out of the way and has an unobstructed shot at the surface on which it projects. The options for projection surfaces included ceiling-mounted screens (motorized or manual), drywall painted with special projector-screen paint, or interactive whiteboards. For smaller classrooms and meeting rooms, a large display monitor (either LCD or plasma, almost certainly flat screen) may be used in place of projection. Auditoriums and large classrooms may require multiple projectors or some combination of projectors and monitors to provide adequate visibility throughout the space.

Computer projection works best when the lighting can be closely controlled. A library classroom should be equipped with lights which can be dimmed or which are zoned so that some can be turned off when projecting. Blinds (manual or motorized) capable of darkening the room for projection are a necessity.

Though too reflective to serve as projection surfaces, garden-variety whiteboards remain a useful feature in any library classroom. Traditional chalkboards should not be used because they produce dust that is harmful to electronic equipment and, potentially, human beings.

Each classroom should have a lectern or instructor's desk. This can be as simple as a traditional wooden lectern designed to hold an instructor's notes or as complex as the high-tech media-control consoles that incorporate electronics for managing projection, lights, and sound.

Larger classrooms benefit from built-in sound systems to amplify both the instructor's voice as well as any audio played during an instruction session. See Chapter 5, "Library Interiors," for information on classroom furniture.

### Auditoriums

In many ways nothing more than larger versions of classrooms, auditoriums usually feature fixed seating laid out in rows, often in the form of theater-style seats mounted on a sloped floor. For a lecture-hall-style auditorium, seats may include folding tablet arms to aid note taking. It is possible to equip an auditorium with fixed tables and movable chairs, though this arrangement is less common. Table 4.1 contains per-student square-footage estimates for auditoriums.

The computer-projection and lighting needs of auditoriums are similar to those of a classroom, though the scale is larger. The grandest auditoriums often have a booth located above and behind the audience from which technicians can control projection, lighting, and sound. In lecture-hall-style auditoriums, a high-tech console at the front of the room makes it possible for a single instructor to control projection, lighting, and sound during a lecture. With few exceptions, auditoriums require robust, often quite sophisticated, sound systems that may incorporate echo-dampening features into the design of the space.

### Public-Access Computers

Public-access computers capable of doing more than accessing the local library catalog began showing up in libraries in the 1990s and are still widespread as the first decade of the twenty-first century rolls to an end. Operating under such labels as *computer labs*, *computer clusters*, or *learning commons*, it is common for such operations to boast more than 100 public-access computers.

The space needs of computer clusters are similar to those of a classroom space with fixed tables and movable chairs: roughly 25 to 27 square feet per computer workstation (see Table 4.1). Computer clusters typically require space for one or more printers (plus trash and recycling bins) and possibly a service desk.

While computer workstation furniture can take many forms, it is best to avoid any furniture too specifically designed to accommodate one particular type of computer hardware; once that type of hardware is no longer in use, reusing such furniture for other purposes is difficult if not impossible. The only type of seating appropriate for computer use is a sturdy, fully adjustable swivel chair on casters. Another important contributor to comfortable computing is glare-free overhead lighting.

Every computer cluster requires sufficient electrical circuits to power the computers and printers housed within it. Computer clusters also require a network infrastructure (most likely wired) sufficient to meet the needs of multiple simultaneous users.

When a number of computers are housed within a closed space, the heat they generate will require supplemental cooling.

Good sight lines are important in computer clusters as they allow staff to see when users need assistance; they also discourage theft, vandalism, and other inappropriate behavior.

### Stand-Up Computers

Libraries provide stand-up computer areas for the convenience of library users who need to make only quick use of a computer. Indeed, the purpose of placing computers in stand-up arrangements is to discourage users from settling down for a long session of e-mail or web browsing. Stand-up computers are often clustered in small groups located near service points so that users can easily ask for assistance and library staff can keep an eye on the equipment; alternatively, stand-up computers may be scattered around a library so users can access them at points of need.

A successful stand-up computer operation requires the usual ready access to power and network connections along with sturdy, stable, and adjustable stand-up furniture that provides good cable management in order to eliminate the danger of dangling cords. The best stand-up computer furniture provides one or more fastener plates or holes through which a security cable can be fed and locked in order to safeguard computer hardware. In any cluster of stand-up computers, one or more machines must be set to wheelchair-accessible height. Along the same lines, stand-up computers must be spaced far enough apart to allow a wheelchair to maneuver.

### Miscellaneous Service Points

Library service points can be single purpose—reference only, audiovisual materials only—or a single point may provide multiple services, such as with a combined reference, interlibrary loan (ILL), and circulation desk. Although the continued use of the word *desk* to describe library service points harkens back to the most traditional model of library service, as libraries rethink service in the age of online information, the resulting service points often end up transformed into solutions far removed from the iconic solid wooden fortress separating the gatekeeper librarian from information-seeking supplicants. In extreme instances, libraries are completely doing away with desks as service points become mobile or virtual in an effort to bring services to users rather than asking users to go to these services.

During the planning of any library building project, the decisions a library makes about its future service points—including their number, locations, physical formats, and intended functions—will shape library services for years to come. Such decisions should not be made lightly, nor should they be made in a design vacuum that does not take into account the library's future. Most important, this is one element of library design where the architects need to listen more than they need to lead.

In general, service desks must be located where they can be seen by library users and where those staffing the desk can observe what is going on around them. Accommodations for technology are undeniably important for today's service points, but it is worth repeating that the furniture will always outlive the technology du jour; for this reason, designing in flexibility to accommodate the unknowable technology of the near future is key.

Certain library service points, such as reserve reading collections or ILL operations, are closely tied to materials that come in physical formats. Obviously, these types of service points must have space to organize and store the physical materials that they provide to library users.

### Map Rooms

The needs of the classic map room are simple: large, unobstructed tables; flat cases to store maps; good lighting; and large-format copying machines. As more maps become available in digital form, plotter printers are becoming map-room necessities. Map libraries that wish to deliver map contents in digital format will benefit from large-format scanners.

Map cases are available in several sizes and types. Metal map cases are always preferable to wood or other organic material for preservation purposes. Hamilton brand map cases were the standard in many libraries for most of the twentieth century. While the Hamilton company no longer exists, their size 3J map case and similar units are still manufactured by other companies. The 3J case consists of a five-drawer unit with drawers that are 55-1/4 inches wide by 44-5/8 inches deep and 2-5/8 inches high. This drawer size will accommodate most standard-sized maps. Most map case units are stackable, but caution should be used when stacking more than three high.

Generally, two types of footings are available for map cases: four-footed (at the corners) and a full perimeter base. The four-footed base is more solid and allows for cleaning under the cases but concentrates the floor loading at those four points. The full perimeter base distributes weight better but does not allow for access to the floor beneath the cases. Generally, the same rules apply to map cases as with compact shelving. An important safety note: map cases should never be moved while stacked. They should always be disassembled and moved as five-drawer units.

Most companies that manufacture map cases provide some method for seismic anchoring. Ideally, map cases should be anchored to the floor, the base should be bolted or clamped to the cases, and each unit should be secured to the next with clamps. If you live in an earthquake-prone area, the last thing you want is a stack of map cases skittering across your reading room.

Ample space should be planned around map cases. If you have cases facing each other, ideally the aisle should allow adequate walking space between the cases even when drawers from each opposing map case are pulled fully open at the same time.

## Special Collections/Archives

The public areas of special collections/archives tend to take the form of very traditional reading rooms furnished with wooden library tables and chairs. As a preventive measure against theft or misuse of materials, the tables and chairs in special collections/archive reading rooms are arranged so that a single library staff member can observe each person in the room from a strategically placed service desk. Because copying in special collections/archives is tightly controlled, public copiers are not normally placed in the reading room. The entryways to special collections/archives are often outfitted with public lockers because briefcases and backpacks, along with a variety of other items, are not allowed inside.

Mounting displays is an important part of the mission of most special collections/ archives, so display cases are often located at their entrances or inside their public areas. Because special collections/archives are often used to show off library treasures to VIPs, such areas (or a special conference/meeting room within such areas) may be outfitted with particularly elegant furnishings. If artwork is displayed in a special collection/ archive, appropriate spot lighting should be included in the design of the space.

## Microformat Area

Depending on the size of the microformat collection and amount of use it gets, microformats may be located within another area (or areas) of the library, such as reference, government documents, or current periodicals, or they may be treated as a discrete collection. Wherever they are located, microformats require storage cabinets appropriate for the particular format or formats (microfilm, microfiche, or microcard) as well as machines for viewing and copying microformats. Copying microformats to paper is traditional, but machines that copy microformats to digital formats are becoming increasingly popular because of their convenience and greenness (no paper or toner required). Microformat areas require electrical circuits capable of supporting microformat machines and, where digital copying is an option, network connections so that users can e-mail their digital copies.

## Audio/Visual Rooms

In its most traditional form, the library audio/visual (A/V) room contains everything in a library's collection that is neither print nor microformat, such as vinyl recordings (78, 45, and 33-1/3 RPM), audiotapes (reel-to-reel, eight-track, cassette), compact-disc recordings, films (often in 16 mm format), filmstrips, videotapes, and DVDs/Blu-ray discs. In addition, the A/V room contains spaces and equipment for listening to/viewing the materials in its collection. Some A/V rooms include soundproofed rooms for listening/ viewing; most provide headphones for private, nondisruptive listening.

The coupling of web services such as Pandora, iTunes, Netflix, Hulu.com, and YouTube with small personal computing devices (tiny laptops, netbook devices, web-enabled cell phones) has seemingly transformed the whole world into a giant A/V room. Where this transformation will leave the traditional library A/V room remains to be seen, but so long as libraries maintain media collections, a space within the library to access those collections will be necessary.

### Government Documents Room

Government document collections can include international, federal, state, or local documents. Traditionally, government documents collections have been heavily oriented to print and microformats. However, starting in the 1990s many governments (notably, but by no means exclusively, the U.S. federal government) began cutting back the printing of documents in favor of digital formats in order to reduce costs and provide for wider dissemination of government information. This means that the average government documents room needs to be outfitted with book stacks, microformat cases, microformat reader/copiers, library tables, chairs, and some number of networked public-access computers to facilitate access to online government information. A service desk may also be part of the mix depending on the level at which the library supports access to its documents collection.

### Meeting and Study Rooms

If public, school, academic, and special libraries have any one thing in common, it may be that there are never enough meeting or study rooms. Although there is no clear distinction, a rule of thumb is that any room that accommodates six or fewer people is a study room; six to twelve, a meeting (or conference) room. Any room that accommodates more than twelve is typically considered a seminar room or classroom. See Chapter 5, "Library Interiors," for more details on furniture for study and meeting rooms.

Adequate soundproofing for study and meeting rooms prevents them from becoming a nuisance to adjacent quiet-study areas. See this chapter's Acoustics sidebar for more details on this subject.

As technology has become an essential component of the way people learn and collaborate, it has also become an essential component of study and meeting rooms. Today's study and meeting rooms require sufficient power and networking (wired and/or wireless) to support multiple computers. The presence of whiteboards (regular or interactive) and display technology increase the usefulness of study and meeting rooms. For study rooms, display technology might consist of a large flat-screen display monitor to which a library user can connect a laptop computer; for meeting rooms, display technology may include projection devices similar to those found in classrooms.

Due to the increasing popularity of teleconferencing and web conferencing, the inclusion of a wired telephone jack will extend the capabilities of meeting rooms, though some way to prevent library users from making unauthorized long-distance or harassing calls from such jacks is necessary in most library settings.

Very large formal conference rooms may incorporate features not found in ordinary meeting and conference rooms; these features may include cloakrooms, storage closets (for such items as stacking chairs, easels, and lecterns), and even small kitchens for food service.

**Acoustics**

Large public buildings tend to be noisy places simply by virtue of their size and the number of people they accommodate. Particularly in libraries, noise is a problem. If you are ever alone in a large building, you will realize how much noise is present just from the building systems—blowers, elevators, fluorescent lights, water moving through pipes. When people and all their individual noise-producing devices are added to the mix, it is a wonder that we are able to function in such an environment. For these reasons, architects and designers go to some effort to mitigate noise, particularly in public buildings such as libraries. Unfortunately, the success of these efforts varies wildly. The fact is that there is a bewildering array of factors that can influence noise in a particular building or space. These include:

- Size and shape of the space (wall height and ceiling shape)
- Materials used in construction of floors, walls, and ceiling
- Windows (quantity, type, or lack thereof)
- Flooring material (carpeting or linoleum)
- Furniture
- Wall decorations (artwork, monitors, signs, etc.)

Spaces or rooms that need to be quiet or isolated from other spaces should have interior walls and ceiling insulated with acoustical insulation. Sheetrock is usually preferable to bare or painted concrete. Carpeting is generally the quietest floor covering. Acoustical wall coverings are a further improvement, but simply adding artwork can help a great deal.

## Children's Rooms

If the design of any room in any library calls for wild creativity, it is a children's room. How materials are organized and displayed; themes that can be played out through colors, decoration, and furnishings; the types of activities the room supports—all can be approached with great imagination and a sense of fun.

Even when being creative and having fun, there are still down-to-earth realities to consider:

- Locating the children's room close to a library's main entrance makes it easier for small children (and parents with strollers) to reach their destination while eliminating the need for children to parade past grumpy, quiet-seeking adults.
- On the other hand, locating a children's room close to the main entrance opens the possibility of a child getting out of the library unnoticed by parents or staff. Like many design issues, there are two conflicting schools of thought on the best approach.
- Proximity to water fountains (at least one of which at child height), restrooms, diaper-changing facilities, and nursing stations is a big plus for a children's room. A near-perfect solution is to locate a gender-neutral family restroom near the children's room so that a parent can take a child of either gender to the restroom while enjoying full privacy.

- The furnishings and fixtures found in children's rooms must be as durable and safe as they are whimsical and attractive.
- Although children's rooms should be designed to accommodate children, many children use these rooms in the company of parents who do not readily fit into child-sized furniture; locating at least some adult-sized furniture in the children's room will help keep a trip to the library from becoming a parental dread. Along the same lines, soft seating in which both child and parent can enjoy a cozy read together will win a lot of fans.
- Good sight lines are especially important in children's rooms, as both parents and library staff need to keep an eye on the kids.

The activities supported by children's rooms vary from one library to the next, ranging from computer use to crafts to puppet shows to homework assistance. If there is, however, one universal children's room activity, that activity would be story time. Story time

---

### Getting Creative with the Children's Room

Many libraries can boast of a creatively designed children's room. The following summary of what was done at Florida's Jacksonville Public Library is just one recent example of what can be done with a children's room (Gubbin and Lamis, 2009).

The Jacksonville Public Library offers two distinct rooms for youngsters: the Children's Library and the Teen Library.

#### The Children's Library

- The unifying theme of the Children's Library is the natural environment of the Jacksonville, Florida, region.
- As children enter the Children's Library, they pass through a sculpture that represents high swamp grasses and hear an audio track of natural sounds.
- Inside the room, the swamp theme is continued with a blue-and-green color palette, porthole-shaped interior windows, and custom furniture pieces resembling alligators, manatees, lotus blossoms, turtles, snails, leaves, and mushrooms.
- The Children's Library storytelling space is a theater with the feel of an outdoor space. After children enter the theater through a screened porch—a structure which is traditional in the South—a perched robotic owl welcomes them and introduces programs.
- Computer technology is integrated into the Children's Room to complement traditional print materials without overwhelming them.

#### Teens' Library

- The ambiance of the Jacksonville Public Library's Teens' Library is described as "cool clubhouse."
- The Teens' Library is adjacent to the library's Popular Materials section, a favorite area and collection for teens that is itself designed to feel like a coffeehouse and bookstore.
- The Teens' Library features bright colors, communal seating, and video screens scattered throughout the space.
- Hyperbolic speakers contain the sounds from video displays to specific zones in front of each display.
- The Teens' Library offers café-style seating, banks of computers, salvaged retro-cool 1960s' furniture, and areas for quiet study.

spaces in children's rooms may be as modest as a casual nook in which a dozen or so children can gather to hear a story read out loud; as grand as a stand-alone space that is, in effect, a theater within the library; or something in between.

While smaller libraries tend to have just a single children's room, it is possible to have separate children's rooms targeted at different age ranges. For example, creating a distinct library space for teenagers, often featuring media devices and computers in addition to traditional books, is an emerging trend in public libraries. However the under-eighteen population is divided up, rooms catering to specific age ranges offer collections, themes, furnishings, and technology appropriate to the needs, interests, and abilities of their intended audiences.

All but the smallest children's rooms incorporate a service point of one sort or another.

### Restrooms

Though hardly a glamour spot, restrooms are possibly the most asked for, and most heavily used, rooms in any library building. The number and sizes of restrooms will be determined by building architects based on the size and predicted occupancy of the building. While there is no perfect location for restrooms, they are best located where they are unobtrusive yet easy to find. The ideal restroom is resistant to graffiti and vandalism as well as easy to clean and maintain without looking as if the fixtures were ordered straight from a prison-supply catalog.

As mentioned, features such as diaper-changing stations, nursing facilities, and family restrooms are desirable in libraries that cater to children.

### Cafés

As historical library taboos against food and drink break down, cafés are turning up in more and more libraries. Library cafés may come in the form of prefabricated kits or built from the floor up, though even the latter process routinely incorporates such prefabricated components as countertops and cabinets. Whatever its form, a library café requires electrical circuits sufficient to power any heat-generating devices (typically coffeemakers) and refrigeration units; a water supply and drains; and networking to support credit-card transactions.

With rare exceptions, library cafés must comply with local food-safety regulations. Before doing any design work on a library café, it is vital to thoroughly understand local regulations and make sure that the design of the café is in compliance.

Café furniture must be comfortable, attractive, resistant to spills, and easy to clean.

## Nonpublic Spaces

Under the financial pressures that squeeze major building projects, it is frighteningly easy to shortchange nonpublic spaces in favor of public spaces. After all, is it not the height of selfishness to fight for the library staff lounge or librarian offices when the public's need for space is so great? In fact, no. For however selfish it may seem, failing to provide staff with the space to do their jobs well will end up shortchanging both library staff and library users. To be effective, any organization that serves the public needs some spaces where the public does not normally go. A restaurant must have a kitchen. A sports stadium must have locker rooms. A bank must have vaults. And libraries, too, must have their nonpublic spaces.

### Break Room/Lounge

Library staff need a place to eat, relax, chat, and throw the occasional party without the public there to observe. The typical break room requires tables and chairs suitable for eating, a refrigerator, a sink (with optional garbage disposal), cupboards for dishware, a microwave, and a coffeemaker. Soft seating, including a sofa or two, makes a nice addition, as does some extra storage space for things like the office holiday decorations or the volleyball net annually hauled out for the staff picnic.

### Office Spaces

In modern office settings, the size of office spaces are standardized and any competent architect knows how to fit them into a floor plan. The trick for library planners is to ensure there are enough office spaces to accommodate current library staff plus enough to allow for anticipated growth. The two main types of office spaces are private offices and cubicles. Some organizations have clearly defined rules regarding which categories of employees get private offices and which get cubicles. In less structured organizations, the general rule is that managers who need privacy in order to deal with confidential business or employment matters must have private offices; for everyone else, a private office versus cubicle is a judgment call. The two main advantages of cubicles are that they cost less than private offices and make it possible to seat more staff in a given space; the big disadvantage is that cubicles lack privacy.

While there are many options for furnishing computer-age office spaces, the standard requirements include:

- a fully adjustable swivel chair on casters;
- a desk or table compatible with computer use;
- a set of desk drawers;
- one or more file cabinets;
- one or more guest chairs;
- shelves for storage; and
- power and network connections.

The standard furnishings for cubicles are similar, though cubicles may dispense with guest chairs and file cabinets.

### Backroom Workspaces

A number of library units require backroom workspaces in which to carry out specialized tasks and to house special equipment. Archives, for example, require nonpublic spaces in which to organize and store archival materials, work surfaces on which to process archival collections, and space for archival supplies and equipment. Other examples of library units with special backroom needs include special collections, technical services, digital assets, acquisitions, binding, and information technology.

The point here is not to compile a laundry list of every library unit that might need backroom workspaces. Each library has its own list of operational units, and the staff of any given library knows what their operational units are. What is important is that the backroom needs of each operational unit are put on the table during the programming phase of a library building project so that those needs are taken into consideration in the overall programming process. In the excitement of creating fabulous public spaces, it is easy for designers to forget about the seemingly mundane but vital space needs of the largely invisible engines that make a library run. The aesthetics of a well-designed, fully functional mail room or reshelving area are not going to make anyone's jaw drop, but good luck running the average library without these types of backroom workspaces.

### Storage Spaces

If meeting and study rooms are the one kind of space the public side of a library never has enough of, then storage spaces are the backroom equivalent. Libraries have all sorts of stuff to store—ranging from nesting chairs to printer/copier paper to disaster-recovery supplies to you name it—and never enough space to store it all. In addition to being sufficient to meet a library's needs, storage spaces should be lockable, strategically located, and designed with flexibility in mind so they can be easily repurposed as storage needs change.

### Server Rooms

A library server room is perhaps the most highly specialized backroom space that any library will ever contain. Designing a successful server room requires input from not only library IT staff who understand current and anticipated local needs but also professional IT design consultants. The standard components of a server room include:

- a dedicated HVAC system to cool the server room to the proper temperature for server hardware;
- a dedicated, non-water-based fire-suppression system;
- extraordinary electrical and network capacity to meet the needs of multiple servers;
- cable management via overhead trays and/or raised-floor system; and
- server racks.

## Conclusion

Just about every library will have one or more spaces that do not exactly fit into any of the categories listed in this chapter, and it is certainly incumbent on any library that is programming a building project to bring such spaces into the programming mix. However, this survey of library spaces should serve as a good starting point for considering how the pieces that make up the puzzle of a nascent building project might go together to form a complete and functional library building.

## References

Emory University College Classroom Working Group. 2010. *Emory College Classroom Design Guide*. Atlanta, GA: Emory University. http://college.emory.edu/home/assets/documents/facilities/classroomGuidelines.pdf.

Gubbin, Barbara A.B., and Alex Lamis. 2009. "Jacksonville Public Library Children's and Teens Libraries." IFLA.org. Milan, Italy, World Library and Information Congress: 75th International Federation of Library Associations Conference and Council, August 23–27. http://www.ifla.org/files/hq/papers/ifla75/103-gubbin-en.pdf.

Siems, Earl, and Linda Demmers. 2003. *Library Stacks and Shelving*. Libris Design Project. U.S. Institute of Museum and Library Services, California State Library. LibrisDesign.org. http://www.librisdesign.org/docs/ShelvingforLibraries.pdf.

# 5

# Library Interiors

For any new library building or major expansion project, the initial buzz will always focus on the exterior of the building. When architects' concept drawings are unveiled, everyone wants to see the exterior views first. What will the finished building look like from outside? Will it be impressive? Will it fit in well with its surroundings? Of course, once a library building opens, most visitors spend far more time inside the building actually using the library than they do standing in the parking lot admiring the asymmetrical boldness of the building's postmodernist roofline. The truth is, a pleasing and usable library interior can overcome even the most humdrum exterior. The exterior of a typical Barnes & Noble superstore is nothing special, but step through the doors and the store's pleasing interior causes you to forget that you are, in fact, between a chain restaurant and a discount hair salon in some cookie-cutter strip mall.

Aesthetics aside, good interior design can actually support a library's programs. Take an obvious example: A library user walks into a library space where the walls are painted bright colors, the carpet pattern features characters from Mother Goose, and the furniture and book stacks are half sized. Because of these interior-design cues there is no need for a sign announcing that this is the children's room or explaining the purpose of this space. Similarly, good interior design can tell library visitors that they are in a space intended for quiet reading, holding meetings, enjoying a snack, or getting assistance from library staff. From an operational point of view, library interiors are far more important than library exteriors, and so the many choices that shape a library's interior must be guided by the greatest possible knowledge of both interior-design principles and the library's programs.

It is also important to note that interior design is a crucial element of smaller projects, not just new buildings and major renovations. Remodeling a library entrance or special-collections room, renovating a library space water-damaged by a burst pipe, converting what was formerly staff space into public space (or vice versa)—all are examples of smaller projects on which interior design choices, including flooring, paint, furniture, and window coverings, and so on—matter a lot. What kind of message should the remodeled/renovated/converted space send? Should it feature an entirely new, distinctive look? Should it blend in seamlessly with the rest of the library building? How can the space's new interior design support the purpose of the space by helping library users understand what it is for and how to navigate it without signage or human assistance? While the questions are representative, the point is universal: even small projects generate big decisions about interior design.

## Furniture, Fixtures, and Equipment

Furniture, fixtures, and equipment (FF&E) is an accounting term for describing all the movable property required to run a business (or a library). If a library staff member can have a solid grasp of only one element of a major building project, that element should be FF&E. One reason for this is that FF&E has great impact on the look and function of a completed building's interior, the part of the building that is really of most concern to library staff. A second reason is that it is far more likely that library staff will have input on FF&E choices than on major architectural features. Members of the library staff rarely get to choose the building's exterior cladding, but they might be allowed to pick out the chairs.

---

### A Working Definition of FF&E

Imagine a building. Turn it upside down and shake vigorously. Everything that falls from the floor to the ceiling is FF&E.

---

Of course there are some subtleties surrounding what does or does not come under the rubric of FF&E. For example, a carpet that is glued to the floor is not FF&E, while a loose area rug is. Permanent library book stacks are not FF&E, while the bookcases in library offices are. Distinguishing between what is or is not FF&E is more than an exercise in accounting semantics. Most large construction projects come with two distinct budgets: one for construction (foundations, walls, mechanical systems, roofs, and all of the other stuff that does not go flying when the building is turned upside down) and one for FF&E. While the rules laid down by funding authorities will vary, such rules typically stipulate that money cannot be moved from the construction budget to the FF&E budget, and vice versa. There is a good reason for this mandated separation. If, under the tremendous pressures of just getting a construction project finished, it were possible to raid the FF&E budget for the $200,000 needed to cover the unexpected cost incurred after historic artifacts are uncovered during excavation or for the $300,000 needed to cover a sudden uptick in the price of steel, virtually every building larger than a single-family home would open its doors with no furniture, fixtures, or equipment on the premises. Which is not to say that, rules notwithstanding, budget-shifting gamesmanship does not take place. For example, suppose the construction budget needs a boost because of a sudden worldwide concrete shortage. As a result, plans are altered so that staff offices that were originally to be built of studs and drywall (construction budget) are replaced with modular offices (FF&E budget). The money not spent on studs and drywall can now go to offset the cost of concrete, but the money spent on modular offices is no longer available for FF&E items like library tables and carrels.

Because architects, contractors, and project managers tend to be so intensely (and rightly) focused on the construction side of any project, it is incumbent on those who will ultimately occupy the building to protect the FF&E budget from excessive plundering. While it is easy enough for an architect or contractor to walk away from a completed but woefully under-furnished library building, it is not at all easy for library staff to make a functional library of an empty shell. Along similar lines, it is not unheard of for a library building to be built or expanded with no budget provision whatsoever for furniture. In such a scenario it may turn out that money for furniture will somehow materialize in a timely fashion. Or perhaps that furniture can be acquired piecemeal over time. The former is a huge gamble. The latter is completely undesirable. Any opportunity to undertake a new building or expansion project that does not include a budget for furniture is not nearly the opportunity it might seem at first blush.

---

**Absolutist Alert**

Anytime a group of people are brought together to work on a building interiors project, some of those involved will make absolutist statements like:

*"Never put arms on rolling chairs because they will just get beat up when they bang into the edge of the table."*
True, but if you have to sit in a rolling chair for more than about 30 minutes, a chair with proper adjustable arms is far more comfortable than one without.

*"Always use hard-surface flooring in a library. Carpet is too much trouble to clean."*
True, but carpet dampens noise and insulates cold subfloors. Also, high-quality, commercial-grade carpet in a color chosen to hide dirt is not especially hard to keep clean.

*"Never put sofas or loveseats in an academic library. Students will just sleep in them."*
True, but students have to sleep somewhere, and at least it gets them into the library.

Absolutist ideas about library interiors can be dead-on. However, they can also be passé notions based on a rather narrow band of previous experience. The point is that all absolutist statements (including those made by the authors of this book) should be challenged, not meekly accepted.

---

## Expert Advice

Having the services of a professional interior designer written into a project's budget can be a huge plus. An interior designer's knowledge of color, style, and available products can save time and money while producing an immensely pleasing and functional result. Interior designers may be employees of a project's main architectural firm or they may be independent contractors. The value of the former is that they are likely to be fundamentally in tune with the overall design intent of the building's architect, while the value of the latter is that they are not (in other words, an independent interior designer may be able to stand back and make decisions based more on the needs and desires of the building's tenant than on those of the building's architect). Interior designers employed by large furniture vendors are another source of expert advice. While it is important to remember that such designers come with an inherent conflict of interest—their job, in the end, is to get you to buy as much of their company's product as possible—their knowledge of product lines and professionally trained design sensibilities can be great assets. Besides, their services incur no direct cost to the library. (Their services are, of course, calculated into the price charged for the furniture, so they are not really free.) The danger of working with any interior design expert is the risk that a tunnel-vision designer may hijack the project, imposing an interior look and feel that is highly idiosyncratic, impossibly trendy, or completely out of touch with library programs.

It is quite possible that a library's parent organization will have an interior-design expert on staff who will work with library staff. While such experts can be an excellent source of advice on both design and on the product lines available for the project at hand, it is still important that such experts work with library staff and not act in an authoritarian manner.

On the other side of the coin, it is quite possible to end up involved in a building project for which no expert interior design advice is available. The usual practice in such a situation is to turn the interior design process over to a worthy amateur chosen from the staff of the library or its parent institution. The end result of such an approach is entirely dependent on the knowledge, talent, tastes, and openness to outside input of the chosen individual. The fact that the rare-books cataloger's lovely home could grace the cover of *House Beautiful* is nice, but pastel floral prints are not necessarily the best choice for the young-adult room. The assistant director of the county's facilities department may have done a bang-up job with the new jail, but a chair's ability to withstand vomit should not be the chief criteria for picking library furniture.

### Group Process and Interior Design

Regardless of whatever amount and quality of interior design advice is on hand, good group process increases the chances for success. Bringing multiple voices into the mix prevents the final result from turning into a single individual's design statement and increases the chance that absolutist ideas will be challenged. It is crucial, though, to keep in mind that good group process means more than simply forming an interiors committee. Good group process is not a committee:

- that sits quietly while a domineering leader tells the members what they should think;
- that is not representative of a wide spectrum of stakeholders;
- whose large size makes it unwieldy (a committee of five to seven active, engaged participants is a good size for most projects);
- that operates with a dearth of information and/or constructive guidance;
- that feels it must reach total unanimity on all decisions; and
- whose decisions are really nothing more than suggestions subject to fickle veto by some higher authority (architect, library director, donor, etc.).

What makes for good group process? Besides reversing the negatives just listed, good group process is fostered by:

- a committee chair who actually believes in group process and has some experience facilitating it;
- committee members who are well supplied with information and constructive guidance, possibly in the form of:
  - full information on the budget, timeline, and programmatic realities of the project;
  - selected crash-course readings on interior design, library usability, and other topics directly related to the project (furniture and interior design catalogs, print or electronic, may be part of the selected readings); and
  - field trips to other libraries, interior design or furniture showrooms, furniture factories, and so on.

### *Purchasing Considerations*

Before embarking on any interior design project, it is crucial to be familiar with all purchasing rules that may impact the process. Purchasing rules will vary from funding authority to funding authority, and even from project to project, but examples of limitations to watch out for include:

- requirements that all, or some percentage of, furnishings be purchased from one or more precontracted vendors (including, in some cases, prison industries);
- price caps on certain classes of items (e.g., no more than $n$ dollars may be spent on a sofa);
- deadlines by which FF&E funds must be encumbered and/or items received;
- requirements to submit Requests for Proposals (RFPs) for purchases over a specified dollar amount; and
- written justifications for purchases over a specified dollar amount.

One purchasing trap to watch out for is hidden costs above the publicized base purchase price. These costs may include sales taxes, shipping, short-term storage, and final installation and assembly. Be aware that you cannot directly compare list prices that, for example, do not include shipping and installation with those that do. Short-term storage can be an unpleasant budget surprise. When a tractor trailer load of fine wood furniture pulls up in May to a building that, due to construction delays, will not have a roof or windows until July, you cannot tell the driver to come back later. Nor can you put the furniture out on the lawn (or at least where the lawn is supposed to be laid down in a couple of months). All you can do is find local warehouse space and, quite likely, pay dearly for both the space and the added cost of eventually transporting the furniture from the warehouse to the library.

Unless all of the furniture for a project is purchased under preapproved contracts, it is likely that an RFP will be issued to solicit bids from furniture manufacturers or vendors. See the Appendix for a detailed look at the art of writing a furniture RFP.

## *Date Stamping*

Before considering what features may be desirable in library furniture, it is important to be aware of the problem of date stamping. Date stamping occurs when library furniture, which may be in use for decades, is dominated by styles and color combinations strongly associated with a specific time period. A classic example of date stamping can be seen in the avocado green, harvest gold, and orange color palette that was pervasive in the late 1960s and early 1970s. While 40-year-old library furniture featuring these colors may have a limited retro appeal, most people see it as ugly and passé. On the other hand, 100-year-old library chairs and tables built in the more restrained Mission style still look handsome or, at the very worst, neutral, when seen with twenty-first-century eyes. It is always tricky to identify what constitutes a passing fad and what will stand the test of time, and almost every style and color palette will endure a period of disfavor, but the best way to avoid date stamping is to take design cues from styles and colors that have stood up over the years.

One situation where date stamping is not an issue occurs when a library purchases a relatively small amount of furniture with the idea that it will be replaced after a fairly short period of service, say, five to ten years. An example of this might be furniture for a library café.

## *Choosing Furniture*

When choosing furniture for a library, there are four principal considerations:

- Aesthetics
- Functionality
- Comfort (ergonomics)
- Durability and maintenance

### Aesthetics

The first fact to accept about library furniture is that some percentage of the population is going to hate the look of whatever furniture ends up in the library. Once you have accepted this fact and let go of the notion that you are going to please everyone, the trick becomes keeping the number of haters to a minimum. The best way to do this is by choosing furniture that coordinates well with both the look and the programmatic function of the space it will occupy.

The attractiveness of any piece of furniture is determined by its style, materials, and colors in combination with how the piece interacts with the interior space which it occupies. There are many furniture styles in the world, some of which are not much seen outside of antique stores, some of which are not much seen outside of photo spreads in hipster design magazines. With rare exceptions, library furniture should fall somewhere between these extremes. There is no magic formula for picking the perfect furniture style, but picking a style that clashes with the space it will occupy is a nearly surefire way to go wrong:

- High-Gothic chairs in a dark stain are probably not the best choice for a steel-and-concrete Brutalist-style building.

- Danish modern is a little iffy in a venerable reading room that features stained-glass windows and cherubs flitting across a Rococo ceiling.
- Victorian-style claw-foot chairs in the children's room might induce nightmares among the clientele.

All of which is a negative way of restating the idea (worth repeating) that furniture should coordinate with the look and the function of the space it occupies. Extreme furniture can work well in an extreme space. For example, sofas featuring partially exposed frames of rough-hewn knotty-pine and cushions covered in forest-green fabric could look right at home in a vernacular library building designed to evoke the cedar lodge houses of northwestern costal tribes. On the other hand, conventional furniture tends to work well in more conventional spaces. Traditional prairie-style chairs and tables might be just right in a traditional, conservatively designed reading room dominated by straight lines and right angles.

Adding new furniture as part of a project to remodel some portion (possibly as little as one room) of an existing building brings special challenges. One approach is to seek out new furniture that so exactly matches existing furniture as to be interchangeable with it. This is not always possible, especially when the existing furniture has been around long enough to show signs of wear that new furniture pieces lack. If the manufacturer of the existing furniture is no longer in business or has changed lines, obtaining exact copies may be impossible. (When you acquire new furniture, it is good practice to contractually require the manufacturer to provide detailed shop drawings. With shop drawings, it is possible for someone other than the original manufacturer to, at some future time, closely replicate existing furniture even if the original manufacturer is no longer in business.) A different approach is to select furniture that is clearly different from the existing furniture yet still complements it; that is, to mix rather than to match. For example, if the existing library furniture is mission style, you might furnish the remodeled space with mission-style furniture but use a lighter or darker wood species to clearly distinguish it from the older furniture. Or you might choose for the new furniture a contrasting style—say, for example, modernist versus prairie style—but incorporate wood species, colors, or other design elements that reference the existing furniture.

Especially in larger buildings, it is desirable to acquire more than one style of furniture in order to set the tone for different spaces within the library as well as to add some variety. Group meeting and study rooms might be equipped with office-style furniture (rolling swivel chairs, modular tables on casters) to provide a high-tech look while facilitating a collaborative style of working. A leisure reading room might feature casual furniture that invites users to get comfortable and relax. A classic special-collections room might feature very formal, even somber furniture to set a serious, studious tone. And rooms for children and young adults should have furniture that appeals to, and meets the needs of, the intended users of those spaces. Furniture choices can also set the tone for library service areas. A classic reference desk in which there is a rigid barrier between the supplicant library user and the enthroned library staff sends one message, while a more open design in which the furniture invites users to come in and collaborate says something completely different.

With rare exceptions, the materials of which furniture is built include wood, metal, plastic, upholstery (fabric or leather), or some combination of the above. The style or, in some cases, function of a particular piece of furniture often determines the materials that make up the piece. Modernist furniture is very likely to combine metal, often chromed metal, with plastic or molded plywood. Classic library study tables and chairs are chiefly wood, though tabletops may consist of a composite surface (such as Marmoleum), while study chairs may feature seats that are padded and upholstered. While it is common to think of furniture materials more in terms of their impact on durability (a topic that is taken up in the next section) than in terms of their impact on overall attractiveness, materials matter in both arenas. For example, a stacking chair with a molded-plywood seat and back is going to look much different from a chair of the same style with a plastic seat and back (see Figures 5.1 and 5.2). Neither chair is right or wrong, but choosing one material over the other is a design decision.

It is worth noting that some furniture materials may be controversial. Furniture made from certain exotic, endangered, or nonsustainably harvested wood species can draw objections from environmentalists. Leather upholstery has the potential to draw complaints from animal-rights advocates as well as from followers of certain religions. Controversial wood species can easily be avoided, as there are plenty of noncontroversial choices on the market; indeed, many furniture manufacturers proudly advertise the fact that they

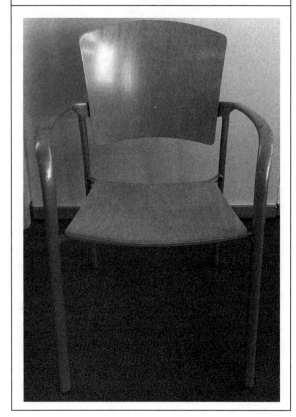

**Figure 5.1**
**Molded Plywood Chair**

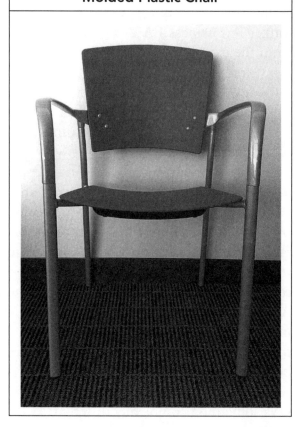

**Figure 5.2**
**Molded Plastic Chair**

use only sustainably harvested wood. Modern high-quality leather substitutes are so difficult to distinguish from the real thing that informing library users that such furniture does not actually use leather becomes an issue. An added bonus of high-quality leather substitutes is that they wear better than the real thing.

Color, the third component of furniture attractiveness, is one of the most difficult elements to get right. Of all the places where a bit of trained, genuinely expert help is useful, choosing colors is at the top of the list. A key determinant of furniture color is the color palette of the building's interior. A neutral interior color scheme not only leaves room for interesting furniture color choices, it practically demands color to break up the monotony of white(ish) walls and drab floor coverings. Note that color contrast can come from wood as well as from upholstery. For example, cherry wood furniture produces a surprising amount of color contrast in an otherwise color-neutral room. On the other hand, boldly colored floor coverings and/or bright wall colors may be best complemented by a somewhat neutral furniture palate.

Within a single space, a level of consistency among furniture colors helps to define the space. Consistency does not mean that every piece of furniture must be exactly the same color, merely that the colors be complementary. One way to achieve consistency without uniformity is to include some pieces covered in a multicolored upholstery material and accent them with pieces covered in solid colors taken from the color palette of the multicolored material. Mixing and matching pieces upholstered in fabric with pieces upholstered in (real or imitation) leather or suede is another strategy for producing variety without clashing. As with furniture styles, varying furniture colors from one space to the next helps define spaces and the activities that take place within them. For example, in a library in which all the wood furniture is light maple, putting furniture made of a dark wood species in one special space makes a dramatic statement that the user has entered a part of the library that is different from the rest of the building.

### Functionality

It is a mistake to confuse *functional* with *utilitarian*. Although a folding metal chair is utilitarian, someone forced to spend a four-hour stretch sitting in one is not going to describe it as *functional*. "Crippling," perhaps, but not "functional." In a broader and better sense, *functional* means a lot more than *utilitarian*. To be functional, a piece of furniture must help someone to do something better than they could without that piece of furniture. Office workers sit in adjustable swivel chairs on casters because such chairs are highly functional for a person who must sit for long periods of time while using a computer, answering a phone, meeting with people who enter the office space, retrieving files, and so on. Brightly colored, small-scale, whimsical pieces of furniture are highly functional for a children's reading room because they meet the needs—and expectations—of the users of that room. Library carrels that provide a modicum of privacy while allowing enough space for books, papers, laptops, and other research tools are highly functional for individual studiers. Note that, as in the example of the furniture in a library children's room, the appearance of the furniture can be an integral part of its function rather than an optional frill. Just because a piece of furniture is plain or ugly does not mean that it is functional; just because a piece of furniture is attractive does not mean that it is merely decorative and therefore incapable of also being functional.

Ergonomics is an important aspect of functionality and the subject of more than a few book-length treatments. Before attacking a pile of books on ergonomics, however, consider that any reputable manufacturer of commercial furniture has studied ergonomics far more than anyone outside the furniture business ever will. More than likely, that manufacturer has been producing ergonomically correct furniture for many years. Does this mean that you should blindly trust manufacturers? No. But instead of spending a lot of time studying ergonomics, request some full-sized samples of a manufacturer's products and spend a lot of time sitting on them. (As a rule, do not request full-size samples of furniture until after an initial winnowing process has taken place and there is a short list of finalists. Unless the manufacturer grants permission for destructive testing, full-size samples should be returned to the manufacturer in the same condition in which they were received.) Better yet, get a lot of people of different shapes and sizes to spend a lot of time sitting on the samples. The more time and people, the better. Replace your normal desk chair with a sample library study chair for a day. If it feels good after an eight-hour day at an office desk, it is probably going to feel good to anyone using it at a library study table.

Acquiring furniture that meets the requirements of the Americans with Disabilities Act (ADA) is, in a sense, merely a means of ensuring that library furniture is functional for the broadest possible spectrum of users. One approach to meeting ADA requirements is to specify that some percentage of the library's furniture meets ADA standards. The problems with a percentage approach include the fact that users who need to use ADA-compliant furniture must locate it among all the noncompliant furniture, that it may be necessary to label such special furniture as ADA compliant, and that the existence of special furniture can be stigmatizing to persons with disabilities. A better approach for meeting ADA requirements is to specify that every piece of library furniture be ADA compliant. Acquiring 100 percent ADA-compliant furniture eliminates all of the problems listed above, yet it is not difficult to do nor is it costly. Because the Americans with Disabilities Act has been on the books since 1990, furniture manufacturers are now well accustomed to producing compliant furniture. Whatever ADA solution you choose in the end, avoid any ADA furniture that includes cranks, levers, lifts, or other mechanical parts. Besides often being difficult for persons with disabilities to use, device-laden furniture is subject to failure over time.

How well furniture accommodates technology is another element of its total functionality. In older libraries you can occasionally spot tables sporting circular indentations designed to accommodate inkwells, a technology that once flourished but has all but vanished. The latter-day version of the inkwell holder is post-1990 library furniture fitted with shelves, holes, pop-ups, troughs, and waterfalls intended to accommodate the desktop computer technology of an era that had yet to discover flat-screen monitors, USB connections, pervasive wireless, Bluetooth, small-form-factor computers, and so on. It will not be long until people look at this cohort of furniture and ask, "What were they thinking?" Accommodating technology may continue to be important for many years, but best practice demands that technology be accommodated in a manner that can be undone when the technology in question is no longer being used. For example, instead of putting a hole in a tabletop and inserting a metal-and-plastic power/data pop-up, consider a device that can be screwed into the bottom of the tabletop and, at some later date, removed with no visible damage (see Figure 5.3). (Many of the most intricate pop-up power/data devices are nearly impossible for anyone with arthritis or small hands [such as children] to open. Also, some devices are so unintuitive that many users who do possess the manual dexterity to use the devices cannot figure out how to do so without instructions.) Furniture will almost always outlive technology, so follow the practice of a good conservator and do not do anything to the furniture that cannot easily be undone by those who come after you.

### Durability and Maintenance

Once a library building project is complete and any new furniture has been moved in, it is a rare occurrence for more furniture money to come into the coffers any time soon. This means that library furniture must be durable enough to last for many years; in some cases, for many decades. There are a number of points to consider when choosing furniture that will last:

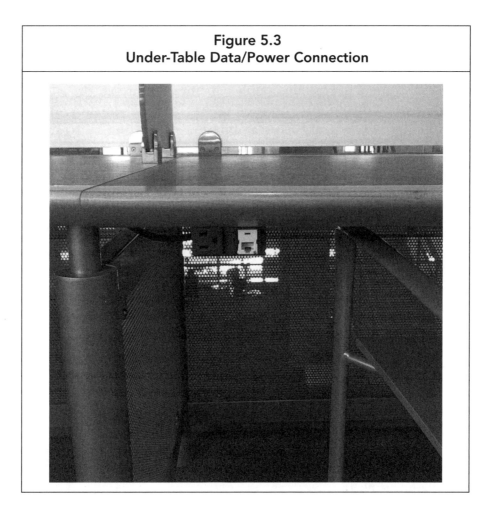

**Figure 5.3**
**Under-Table Data/Power Connection**

- Furniture built for the home market will not last long in a public space. All library furniture must be commercial grade.
- Cheap furniture does not last. In fact, in the long run, cheap furniture is not cheap. A $400 wooden library chair that lasts for 50 years cost $8 per year of use. A $150 wooden library chair that lasts for 15 years costs $10 per year of use, and this factors in neither the significant cost of disposing of worn-out furniture nor the cost of staff time involved in acquiring multiple replacements for the $150 chair during the 50-year life span of the $400 chair.
- A manufacturer's track record can reveal much about the durability of the furniture it produces. Check with other library or institutional users of furniture lines you are considering to learn how well the furniture has held up. If possible, visit sites that have been using the furniture for several years to see for yourself how well it has stood the test of time.
- Ask the manufacturer to provide full-sized furniture samples that you do not need to return and then conduct some destructive testing. Have the burliest person you can find sit in a sample chair and tilt back as far as possible. Dump a cup of coffee on the seat. Take a permanent marker, write on the fabric, and then see how well it cleans up. The Facilities Department at the University of California, San Diego Library takes destructive testing even further, hurling chairs from a loading dock and attacking them with knives and hammers (Kennedy, 2004). If a piece of furniture quickly falls apart during in-house tests, it is not going to last out in the open where the public will put it to the test every day.
- Require manufacturers to provide double-rub abrasion ratings for any upholstery products they use. One double rub is equal to the abrasion caused by a person sitting on the upholstery and then standing up. The rating number reflects the number of double rubs the upholstery can withstand before it begins to show noticeable wear. The double-rub rating for general contract upholstery is 15,000, while the double-rub rating for heavy-duty upholstery is 30,000. An alternative durability rating employs the concept of cycle abrasion. A fabric's cycle-abrasion rating is the number of times the fabric can be rubbed in a figure-eight motion against an abrasive material before showing noticeable wear. The cycle-abrasion rating for general contract upholstery is 20,000, while the cycle-abrasion rating for heavy-duty upholstery is 40,000.
- Upholstery materials come with codes that indicate how the material should be cleaned:
    (**W**): Water-based cleaners only.
    (**S**): Dry-cleaning solvent only.
    (**WS**): Water or dry-cleaning solvent.
    (**X**): Vacuum or brush only. No liquid cleaners.
  Obviously, upholstery that can only be vacuumed or brushed is not going to do well in an environment in which liquid spills and pen marks are likely. For any upholstery, it is a good idea to obtain samples, make them dirty, and then see how well the fabric cleans up.

### *General Types of Library Furniture*

While atypical or even unique furniture pieces are a possibility in any library, most library furniture falls into one of several familiar categories.

### Library Study Tables and Chairs

This is classic, bread-and-butter library furniture. Largely constructed of wood, library study tables and chairs may include metal elements, nonwood tabletop surfaces, and padded seats. Properly built and maintained, this type of furniture should last for 50 years and possibly much longer. It is not difficult to find furniture of this type that has been in use for 100 years and is still going strong. For a library study table, consider providing 48 inches of width and 30 inches of depth for each seat at the table. While this amount of space may seem overly generous, it provides enough room for books, a backpack, a notebook computer, and other user necessities.

### Carrels

Carrels are yet another classic type of library furniture. The traditional high-topped library carrel provides lots of user privacy but also blocks views and makes possible a number of undesirable behaviors. The trend in libraries is toward low-rise carrels, while carrels that include lockable compartments for the convenience of preferred library users (traditionally faculty and graduate students) are increasingly seen as anachronisms. If carrels provide less than 48 inches of width per seat, users tend to sit only at every other carrel, so providing a seemingly generous amount of space is actually a better use of resources than skimping.

### Technology Furniture

Today all library furniture, including study tables and carrels, is technology furniture and should be capable of accommodating power and data needs. But, as mentioned, furniture always outlasts technology and so permanent alterations to furniture in the name of accommodating technology should be avoided. Just think of all the library computer-lab furniture still in service that was built to accommodate a 15-inch CRT monitor and the standard beige box tower or desktop case, both of which since have given way to less space-hogging hardware. While such computer-lab furniture is still usable, it is hardly ideal for the technology in use today or, most likely, for the technology that will be in use 10 or 20 years from today. Above all, avoid buying a piece of furniture purpose-built to accommodate a specific piece of technological hardware. When that hardware is no longer needed, what remains is either a misfit piece of furniture or fodder for the local landfill.

### Stand-Up Computer Carrels

Stand-up computer carrels are a special type of technology furniture commonly seen in libraries. Such furniture must be sturdy, stable, adjustable, and able to provide good cable management to eliminate the danger of dangling cords. The best stand-up computer furniture provides one or more loop holes to which a security cable can be attached in order to safeguard computer hardware. In any cluster of stand-up computers, one or more machines should be set to a wheelchair-accessible height, and stand-up computer carrels must be spaced far enough apart to allow a wheelchair to maneuver.

### Classroom Furniture

Classroom chairs should be designed to remain comfortable for the duration of the longest class session held in the room. A well-designed unpadded chair is good for about an hour; padded chairs are more suitable for longer sessions; also, chairs fitted with armrests are more comfortable for long periods of sitting than are chairs without armrests. Chairs fitted with casters, though more expensive than static chairs, are well suited both to computer work and to the easy rearrangement of seating layouts. Stacking chairs, even if lacking casters, are easy to move and may be stored out of the way when not in use. Arranging stacking chairs in rows without tables will provide the largest number of seats in any given space, though the only instructional style for which such an arrangement is functional is a traditional lecture during which the students remain largely passive.

Chairs with tablet arms can, at least in theory, eliminate the need for tables, but tablet arms are not big enough or sturdy enough to compete with tables. Using a computer—even a small laptop—on the average tablet-arm chair is a trick best left to circus performers.

Static classroom tables are the standard for classrooms equipped with desktop computers, as routinely rearranging tables loaded down with computer boxes, monitors, keyboards, and mice is impractical. Under other scenarios, such as laptop-equipped classrooms, tables on casters allow for easy rearranging of the furniture layout, with desk-sized one-person tables providing the greatest flexibility for forming rows, horseshoes, and group clusters of various shapes and sizes. Folding-top tables can be readily stored away without taking up a lot of room, adding to a classroom's flexibility, but it is important that folding tables come with extremely robust fittings so they do not turn into wobbling nightmares after six months of use.

### Study, Meeting, and Conference Room Furniture

Meeting and study rooms are traditionally equipped with one or more tables of appropriate dimensions, plus chairs of appropriate number, for the size of the room. While static chairs are traditional, chairs equipped with casters better lend themselves to the way meeting and study rooms are used in the twenty-first century, which is to say such spaces tend to be used more for active collaborative work than as refuges for solitary reading and study.

Formal conference rooms tend to be furnished with a higher grade of furniture than is used for less formal spaces and may include credenzas and other storage-type furniture. Very large conference rooms may also include a complement of stacking chairs to accommodate larger-than-normal crowds for special events, open public meetings, and the like.

### Soft Seating

Soft seating—sofas, loveseats, armchairs, floor pillows, beanbags, ottomans, and so on—adds warmth and comfort to a library. Well-chosen fabrics and styles can bring color into the library and help set the tone for the spaces they occupy. Besides aesthetic

> ### Chair Rails
>
> Any public space in which there are both chairs on casters and drywall requires some kind of chair rail system to protect the walls from the inevitable gouges and scratches caused by rolling chairs. Adhesive chair-rail strips made of tough composite materials are available in just about any color and provide the most protection for the lowest cost.

considerations, other things to look for in soft seating are comfort, durable frames, and durable, easily maintainable upholstery.

### Occasional Tables

Occasional tables are commonly used in conjunction with soft seating as they provide handy places for library users to set books, backpacks, and the like. Younger users will happily sit on the floor and use an occasional table as a desk. Occasional tables in libraries need to be sturdy because users will move them, use them as footrests, and sit on them.

### Benches

A judiciously placed bench, perhaps near a checkout desk or just inside the library entrance, is a real convenience for anyone who needs a place to plop for a minute. When architects call for built-in benches, such benches are part of the construction budget rather than the FF&E budget. Movable benches acquired as part of a furniture purchase (FF&E budget) need to be sturdy and heavy enough so that they are not easily moved. Although nothing says "Welcome to prison" quite so much as the practice of bolting library furniture in place, benches are a possible exception to this rule.

### Furniture for Children

Not merely small in scale, library furniture for children should appeal to children through its forms, colors, and potential for fun. As bright and fun as it may be, children's furniture must be durable, easy to maintain, comfortable, safe, and, in many cases, able to accommodate technology. In addition to a children's room, many public libraries now offer special spaces for teens. While the furniture for teen spaces may be superficially similar to furniture for adults, its colors and styles and functions should fit the needs of a group that, for example, may prefer a floor pillow to a sofa, a beanbag to an armchair.

### Furniture for Staff

This category includes furniture for office spaces and service points. All the rules for aesthetics, functionality, comfort, durability, and maintenance apply just as much to staff furniture as they do to furniture for library users. There is a delicate balance between trying to acquire furniture that fits the way people work without acquiring furniture that is so specific to the way a particular person works at a particular time that the furniture is no longer functional when people or times change.

### Café Furniture

A library café, once cutting edge, is now rather commonplace. Obviously, café furniture needs to be resistant to spills and easy to clean and maintain. Tall tables and stools are classy looking, but they are an obstacle for children and people with disabilities. Some café furniture is intentionally designed to be a little uncomfortable so that customers do not linger too long; employing move-along furniture is arguably acceptable if done judiciously, but as a general rule using discomfort to manage human behavior is something to avoid.

### Stacking Chairs

Stacking chairs are used in spaces that are temporarily configured to seat large numbers of people, often in an audience configuration. Stacking chairs must be stackable (of course); strong enough to withstand the rigors of regularly being moved, deployed, restacked, and moved again; light enough to be easily handled; and comfortable enough for at least two hours of continuous sitting. If stacking chairs happen to be attractive, that is a bonus. Stacking chairs that come with their own dollies will save labor. Closets in which to store the chairs when not in use are a real convenience. If you know you will be using stacking chairs and the building is still in the planning stages, let the architects know that they should include space for storing stacking chairs.

### Lamps

Lamps add a touch of elegance to a room and are a great aid to library users when ambient light is insufficient. Fixed-in-place tabletop lamps are standard because they are not prone to the accidents that will inevitably befall freestanding floor or table lamps. Also, fixed-in-place lamps are hard to steal. Incorporating power and data connections into the bases of fixed-in-place lamps is an elegant and unobtrusive way to meet power and data needs without excessively carving up the furniture.

### Display Cases

Freestanding display cases may be purchased with FF&E funds, while built-in cases are typically paid for out of the construction budget. One advantage of freestanding cases is that they can be moved, though not necessarily with ease. Criteria for evaluating display cases include:

- The cases must be secure enough to protect items on display from theft or vandalism.
- The glass should filter ultraviolet light in order to prevent damage to printed materials left on display for longer than a week or two.
- The cases must be big enough to display the size or amount of items the library is likely to display yet small enough to fit in the spaces available.
- The cases must be designed to provide easy access to anyone mounting or taking down a display.
- If the cases include internal lighting systems, that lighting must be adequate and designed so as to not damage items on display.

- As with any furniture, the cases should be attractive and of a design appropriate to the spaces they will occupy.

Somewhat related to display cases are art display systems. These typically involve a rail that is permanently secured to a wall and from which adjustable rods are suspended. Curators can quickly and securely fasten framed artworks to the rods without doing any damage to the wall. Art display systems of this type are a worthwhile investment for any library that intends to display framed artworks.

### Construction-Budget Items

As mentioned above, library staff typically do not get much say on items—especially big-ticket items—that are part of the construction budget. However, there are a few construction items that are so important to a library building's interior—yet such a small part of the overall construction budget—that it is worth making the voice of the library heard when it is time to make decisions about these items.

#### Paint

Architects may provide clear and exact specifications for what colors of paint will be applied, and where, in a library interior; in such a circumstance, the architect's plan is likely to prevail unless there are objections from some other quarter. Any such objections must be raised before the paint has been purchased and mixed if there is any hope of altering the preordained color scheme. On the other hand, architects may take a more collaborative approach to interior colors and choose to bring the building's tenant in on the color selection process. If you are fortunate enough to work with such open-minded architects, don't pass up the opportunity. Whether paint colors are chosen from the top down or the bottom up, be aware that if the construction budget gets tight, the color plan may devolve to picking a single shade of white and painting the entire interior in that color—the least expensive, least interesting paint option.

#### Floor Coverings

Modern library buildings typically employ one or more of a limited number of floor covering types:

- **Concrete:** Typically stained or polished when used in a library interior, concrete requires little maintenance and lasts close to forever. Concrete can be cold and does nothing to dampen noise.
- **Ceramic tile:** The good and bad characteristics of ceramic tile are similar to those of concrete. Though not as long wearing as concrete and more expensive, ceramic tile offers greater color options.
- **Wood:** Though wood has high aesthetic value, it is expensive and requires conscientious maintenance. Most often, wood is used in spot applications.
- **Laminate:** Laminate flooring can mimic the look of wood at a lower cost than the real thing. The surface of laminate is more durable than wood but, unlike wood, it cannot be refinished.

- **Carpet:** Carpet dampens noise, insulates cold subfloors, is less expensive than wood, and is available in any color combination imaginable. Carpet is less long-lasting than some other flooring materials, is susceptible to staining, and requires regular cleaning, though high-quality carpet in a good stain-hiding color requires less maintenance than its reputation might suggest.

  The two types of carpet typically used in library settings are broadloom and carpet tiles. Broadloom carpet comes in large rolls and is installed wall to wall over the top of a carpet pad. Carpet tiles come in individual squares that incorporate padding. Properly installed, high-quality carpet tiles cannot be distinguished from broadloom. If a carpet tile becomes damaged or badly stained, it can be pulled up and replaced with a new tile, though fading and wear of surrounding tiles may prevent a perfect match. Beware of cheap carpet tiles that can quickly wear out or fail to adhere.

  Area rugs are not carpet and usually come out of the FF&E, rather than the construction, budget. Area rugs can provide nice accents to special areas within a library, but they must be installed so that they do not create a trip hazard.
- **Resilient flooring:** Typically glued to a subfloor, resilient flooring can be made of sheet vinyl, linoleum, cork, and other man-made or natural materials. High-quality resilient flooring can be a good choice for high-traffic areas, especially back-room spaces where there is a lot of foot and book-truck traffic.

Decisions about floor coverings are typically made early in the design process. Once the type of flooring has been chosen, color choices still remain. Having library staff involved in flooring (and paint) color choices is especially helpful if those same staff will be making choices about furniture colors which, of course, must be coordinated with paint and floor covering colors.

### Lighting

Other than the already discussed table or freestanding lamps, lighting is part of the construction budget and should be specified by the architect. The three most important things about library lighting are that it not be too little, not be too much, and that the lights over the book stacks should run perpendicular to the stacks, not parallel.

### Book Stacks

Though library book stacks are standardized as to shelf width and stack height, and though a relatively small number of specialist companies sell and install library stacks, decisions about book stacks should never be left to architects or builders. Library staff must be involved in deciding how many book stacks are needed, where they should go, what color they should be, and what type of end panels they should have.

## Conclusion

Because the interior of a library building is where all of the activities that we associate with actually using a library take place, creating an attractive and functional library interior must be a top priority in any library building project. Because interiors will be repurposed many times over the course of a building's existence, designing with an eye on the future is key. It is necessary to consider not only how the library is used today but also how it might be used in five, ten, or more years in the future. Aesthetics will be, of course, an important consideration when making choices about interior designs, colors, and furnishings. While both expert advice and constructive group input can be a great help in making aesthetic decisions, remember that no design concept, color, fabric, or furniture form is going to please everyone. Be prepared to hear some criticisms at the end of the project, and reassure yourself that, if you have done your best to consider the broadest array of options and follow inclusive decision-making processes, the criticisms will represent the feelings of only a tiny minority, not the population at large.

## Reference

Kennedy, Mike. 2004. A Study in Comfort. *American School & University*, September 1. ASUmag.com. http://asumag.com/mag/university_study_comfort/index.html.

# 6

# Library Wayfinding

Although the word *wayfinding* has multiple meanings, the one that really matters to librarians comes from the field of architecture and is concerned with how human beings orient themselves and choose paths within a built environment. To state an obvious but significant truth, successfully finding one's way through a library's physical environment is essential to successfully accessing the information resources available from that library. Though the basic tools for enhancing wayfinding seem simple enough—building design and signage—putting those tools together effectively is a challenging task that is far easier to get wrong than right. Getting wayfinding wrong creates significant, long-lasting problems because a hard-to-navigate building reduces library users' success and satisfaction while increasing the workload for library staff who must repeatedly answer directional questions.

## Conventionality Fosters Usability

In *Wayfinding: Designing and Implementing Graphic Navigational Systems*, Craig Berger notes that until the twentieth century public buildings were constructed along conventional, and therefore familiar, lines. Churches, ranging from the tiniest village chapel to the grandest urban cathedral, were laid out according to a standard design convention (Berger, 2005: 20). Train stations—unlike their modern equivalent, airports—were also laid out to a standard pattern (Berger, 2005: 71). This adherence to convention meant that a nineteenth-century traveler familiar with, say, the Union Pacific Depot in Boise, Idaho, would have had little trouble negotiating the Grand Central Depot (later Station) in New York City, even though the latter dwarfed the former. To some extent, this conventionality at one time extended to public library buildings. It may be an exaggeration to say, "Seen one Carnegie Library, seen 'em all," but it is not a huge exaggeration. Prior to World War II, academic libraries, too, were built to a conventional standard, one well described in 1940 by academician and library philosopher Harvie Branscomb: "The architecture of most college libraries, for example, with the books kept in a darkened central stack, surrounded by a few carrels or desks, and with one or more reading rooms out front, is an imitation of research libraries. This plan represents an effort to make available a great collection of books to a relatively few research workers" (Branscomb, 1940: 10–11).

Since World War II, the design of public buildings, including libraries, has trended away from adherence to conventional designs. We apply adjectives like *unique, surprising, innovative,* and *different* to the buildings we love; adjectives like *predictable, conventional,* and *generic* to the buildings we scorn. Conventionality still rules, however, when it comes to the architecture of contemporary consumer culture, as evidenced by the cookie-cutter designs that dominate the world of multiplex movie theaters, supermarkets, hotels, retail stores, and restaurants. For the grandest example of conventionality in consumer-culture architecture, consider the design of any large North American shopping mall:

- Completely surrounded by parking areas
- Limited number of well-delineated entrances and exits
- Large anchor stores at each end
- Central food court
- Directional kiosks with color-coded maps and store indexes near each entrance
- Movement between floors chiefly by escalator

While malls and other consumer-oriented establishments may be taken to task for their bland sameness, their navigability and usability are remarkable. Drop a busload of North American shoppers at a mall they have never before seen in their lives, and they will find their way around with little or no need to ask for assistance. Drop those same shoppers at an outpost of any casual-dining chain, and they will know exactly how to navigate the premises and partake of the services provided regardless of whether that restaurant is trimmed up to look like Granny's attic or a Tuscan villa.

Such ease and familiarity is not the case with most libraries, especially those built since 1945. When people walk into an unfamiliar library, they might reasonably assume that there will *probably* be a reference or help desk somewhere within sight of the main

---

### Navigability: Websites and Libraries

Contrast the idiosyncratic state of library spaces with the example of highly navigable websites, all of which take every possible advantage of web users' familiarity with established web conventions. For example, navigable websites employ a single color (typically, but not necessarily, blue) to differentiate a text link from ordinary text because this is a convention that even novice web users understand. Similarly, highly navigable websites never disable the web browser's back arrow because it is such a widely understood convention. When websites deviate from convention, whether out of carelessness or some desire to stand out, it sows confusion and reduces usability. Web-usability guru Jakob Nielsen describes idiosyncratic websites as being "like an anthill built by ants on LSD, . . . [they] don't fit into the big picture and are too difficult to use because they deviate from expected norms" (Nielsen, 2004). The situation for library buildings is actually worse because there are so few expected norms to begin with, much less from which to deviate.

entrance and a circulation desk somewhere near the exit, but for everything else that goes into a library—from map collections to restrooms to microformat machines—there are no standard conventions for placement. Government documents might just as easily be in the basement or on the top floor as located in some entirely different building on the other side of campus. One library may have DVDs front and center because of their popularity, while another may have them stashed away in a media room in some back corner of the building. Because there are no standard conventions, the navigation of each library building is a skill that must be learned individually, either by asking a human being for help or by making use of whatever wayfinding cues the library provides.

## Enhancing Wayfinding in the Library

It is too late to undo 60-some years of uncoordinated library architecture in order to impose conventions that would make any given library space as familiar—and, therefore, as usable—as the average shopping mall or supermarket. What libraries can do, though, is employ the tools of wayfinding to make library buildings as intuitive to navigate as they can possibly be. Designing a new building is, of course, the ideal opportunity to consider wayfinding issues and devise clever, even elegant, solutions for allowing library users to successfully navigate spaces and collections. For existing buildings, remodeling and renovation projects provide great opportunities to remediate wayfinding problems that tend to become increasingly worse as a building grows more crowded and as existing spaces are repurposed for uses and collections nobody could have imagined back when the building was first on the drawing board.

### *Avoiding Obstacles to Wayfinding*

One of the basic rules of medicine is, "First, do no harm." When a building project serves up the opportunity to improve wayfinding, the best way to do no harm is by consciously avoiding the mistakes that make libraries hard to navigate in the first place:

- **Overcrowding:** Too much of anything—books, furniture, equipment—makes a space feel cluttered and hard to navigate. While it may be possible to squeeze a few more ranges of stacks or library study tables into that beckoning rectangle on the draft floor plan, it may not be worth the wayfinding pain that comes with overcrowding.
- **Broken runs of call numbers:** Often a result of overcrowding, a random break in a run of call numbers is bound to sow wayfinding confusion among library users. Coming to the end of the 691 call numbers and discovering you must follow some lengthy, serpentine route to find the spot where the 692 call numbers start is not conducive to user success.
- **Special locations:** Special locations certainly have their uses, with a public library children's area being the most obvious example. However, it is easy for a library to overdo special locations to the point where they hinder wayfinding. Every time something is pulled out of the general collection and placed in a special

location—local-history room, media collection, graduate reading room, librarian's office—an obstacle has been placed between the user and the information. Worse, the often-cryptic catalog abbreviations used to indicate a special location only add to wayfinding problems. It is ironic that a library will go to great lengths to develop a website where nothing is more than two clicks away from the homepage while, at the same time, burying books in special locations that are the real-world equivalent of five clicks away. A building project provides a good opportunity to reevaluate a library's special locations and to seriously question the need for each. That special location containing all of the library's books about railroading (catalog abbreviation *RRRR*) may be a joy for a handful of die-hard railroading buffs, but for the majority of library users is it more hindrance than joy?

- **Physically hidden locations**: Somewhat related to special locations, physically hidden locations include all of those rooms and alcoves that are simply hard to find unless you know where they are. The fact that these locations may be poorly marked or located far down forbidding passageways only adds to the wayfinding problems they pose for library users.

- **Convoluted routes**:

  *To get to the Library Annex, go to the fourth floor of the Main Library and cross through the Annex corridor. Use Annex stairs or elevators to move from floor to floor within the Annex. Return to the Annex fourth floor to reenter the Main Library.*

  *To access the Library Media Center, exit the Main Library Building and reenter through the North Entrance near the Auxiliary Parking Lot.*

  Wayfinding nightmares such as these should never be allowed to happen in the first place; if they already exist, they most certainly should not be allowed to survive a major remodeling, renovation, or expansion.

- **Multiple service points**: Nobody likes being bumped around from one service point to the next—think of the department of motor vehicles cliché of standing in line for an hour only to be told to go stand in another equally long line. Ideally, a library user should be able to go to a single, prominent, impossible-to-miss service point for everything from checking out a book to getting a reference question answered to asking for directions.

- **Poor signage**: Signage is such an important component of wayfinding and so complex a subject that it is dealt with at length in its own section in this chapter. Suffice it to say that poor signage is a major detriment to wayfinding in far too many library buildings.

### Design as a Wayfinding Tool

Good building design is a powerful, sometimes overlooked, wayfinding tool. In a building designed with wayfinding in mind, users can get where they need to go without the need for extensive signage or human guidance; in a building poorly designed for wayfinding, seemingly no amount of signage and guidance can ameliorate inherent challenges to wayfinding. To a large extent, building design that supports wayfinding is the responsibility of the building-project design team; as experts, the design architects and their supporting team should thoroughly understand wayfinding issues and how to address them through good design practices. However, it is the responsibility of library stakeholders to communicate to the design team that wayfinding is a top priority for the library.

Good sight lines are fundamental to a building that lends itself to wayfinding. If library users can walk through a library entrance and immediately see the library's main staffed service point and, ideally, several of the library's most popular collections and services, more than half of the wayfinding battle has been won. Essential building infrastructure such as stairs, elevators, book returns, water fountains, and restrooms (or at least clear signage pointing the way to the restrooms) needs to be easily findable, not hidden away.

A building's design can further enhance wayfinding when such elements as color, graphics, and furnishings are integrated so that each library space's function becomes self-evident. A big part of wayfinding, after all, is simply realizing you have found the place you are looking for once you have come upon it. For example, a children's room that looks like a children's room—small-scale furniture, bright colors, animal-shaped kites hanging from the ceiling—tells library users the purpose of the space even from a distance and even if those users do not happen to see the sign identifying the space as the children's room. Along the same lines, a media area designed to resemble a retail video store—retail-style displays instead of traditional library stacks, walls decorated with movie posters, an overhead monitor constantly showing movie trailers—is much easier to spot and identify than the same space designed to look just like the periodicals room which looks just like the microformat room which looks just like the special-collections room, etc. Of course, there is the argument that borrowing design cues from retail spaces sends the wrong message; after all, "This is a library, not Starbucks!" And of course it is true that the retail design aesthetic (if the word *aesthetic* can be used in such a context) can be taken too far, and also true that such a look is not appropriate for every library or library space. But to repeat the idea that this chapter began with, in a consumer culture the architectural conventions with which people are most familiar are those of the retail world, and, like those conventions or not, adherence to them increases a space's navigability and usability.

Color can be an effective element of wayfinding design, especially when thoughtfully integrated into carpeting and wall colors. There are, however, some limitations to the use of color. The total number of wayfinding colors must be small, and the colors must be distinctive. Expecting library users to distinguish between pink and rose, or lavender and light purple, is not going to enhance wayfinding, especially for that part of the population which suffers from some degree of color blindness. (In the United States, this amounts to about 7 percent of males and 0.4 percent of females.)

Distinctive or prominent architectural features in a library can aid wayfinding. For example, if a library boasts a fountain or sculpture or other major work of art that is all but impossible to miss, the feature can be used as a wayfinding landmark on maps, in written or oral directions, or in signage.

### Maps in the Library

Maps can, of course, be great tools for wayfinding, though they come with their own problems. Printed maps that library users can carry around with them are an ongoing expense for the library and inevitably create a litter/recycling problem. Wall-mounted maps avoid the problems of printed maps and can offer the added bonus of "You Are Here" markers, but once users step away from a wall-mounted map they must maintain a mental picture of the map to get where they need to go, something that is not always easy to do when dealing with a complex route. Also, those who are not skilled at orienting a flat map to three-dimensional reality get little benefit from maps, regardless of their format. An emerging high-tech solution is the digital map kiosk, a device that displays on-screen digital maps and allows users to print out paper maps with customized directions to the location they are seeking. On-demand maps could prove to be a litter/recycling problem, but the theory is that they would be less of a problem than preprinted maps that visitors can grab by the handful. Finally, it is imperative that all maps be kept up-to-date; old maps make great historical documents, but they are not much use for wayfinding.

### Library Signage

*The food is just awful. And plenty of it.*

After building design, signage is the most important tool for wayfinding. If there is one truism about library signage, it is that most of it is not very good. Understanding the mistakes that lead to bad signage is the first step on the road to creating good signage.

#### Signage Principles Are Not Understood

Visit any successful business that depends on good signage—large discount or grocery stores are prime examples—and take the time to notice the quality of the signage. It will be attractive, unconfusing, consistent, well situated, highly legible, and not so abundant as to cause confusion. This does not happen by accident. Wherever you see successful signage, you know that someone has put considerable thought into creating it. In fact, there is a large body of scholarly and trade literature dealing with signage, an area of research and practice that draws heavily from the fields of psychology, marketing, and architecture. In too many libraries, on the other hand, signage appears to have been put up without even a basic understanding of the fundamentals of good signage. Even a small amount of research can go a long way toward improving a bad signage environment.

#### Signage Is Not Valued

It is hard to imagine a library that would allow major changes to its top-level webpages without approval from upper-level managers, if not from the library director personally. Similarly, a library newsletter is unlikely to be distributed without first having been approved by someone near or at the top of the library's management structure. In contrast, decisions about signage are too often made at a low level by library staff who do not necessarily think in terms of what a sign might be communicating and how that communication fits into the library's larger communication goals. Libraries need to recognize that signage is a powerful communication medium with as much or more impact than more high profile, and often more valued, electronic and print media.

**Signage Decisions Are Tactical, Not Strategic**

There is some problem in the library. Or, at least, somebody has complained about something:

- People are talking on cell phones.
- Nobody can figure out how to use the VendaCard machine.
- The reference desk constantly gets questions about where the media room is located.

If there is a problem, and especially if there is a complaint, it is natural to feel the need to react. To make a tactical move. To put up a sign. Or even better: a whole bunch of signs. But what feels natural is not always right. One pitfall of putting up a sign as a reaction to a problem (real or perceived) is that it is often done without much thought as to whether the new sign will actually solve the problem.

*"We've plastered this place with no-cell-phone signs, but people just keep yakking away in spite of them. I guess we need more signs."*

Even in those cases when a sign solves (partly or completely) a particular problem, those who posted the sign often fail to ask whether a sign is the *best* way to solve the problem. Putting up a sign that says, "Warning: Minefield" might partially solve the problem of accidental deaths and injuries, but a better solution is to clear the field of mines. (And the best solution is, of course, to have never planted the mines in the first place.)

More than being a reaction to a perceived problem, putting up a sign can be an over-reaction. A plastic-framed sign sitting on a service desk reads:

*Staff* only *permitted behind the desk.*

The question of whether such an off-putting sign is an overreaction often goes unasked. How frequently do nonstaff actually wander behind the desk? Does the frequency of trespassing justify a sign? Does the sign actually prevent trespassing or is it routinely ignored? When nonstaff go behind the desk, are the problems this creates serious enough to justify a sign? Was the behavior of relatively few library users, possibly as few as one, the reason for a sign that growls at everyone? Is the sign still needed? What would happen if it disappeared?

The need (real or perceived) to put up a sign is often itself a sign that something is wrong with the system. Instead of a sign detailing a set of complicated instructions on how to use the 20-year-old VendaCard machine, the real solution is to replace the outdated machine with a new one that does not require a user-instruction manual. Instead of a series of paper signs pointing the way to the media room, maybe the media room needs to be moved from the back corner of the seventh-floor annex to a more prominent location? Or maybe the media room has outlived its usefulness and its holdings should be shelved in the main stacks along with the books? Maybe the most heavily used media items need to be served up online so users do not have to find their way to the media room in the first place? Whatever the answer to the problem, the point is that a sign is not necessarily the best solution. And, most of all:

*Never use signage to address a problem that signage cannot solve.*

## Signage Is Used Defensively

Something in the library is flawed. A machine is malfunctioning. Some library system is badly designed. A library protocol fails to meet the reality of users' needs. Up goes a defensive sign. The sign then allows a staff member to ask an upset patron, "The VendaCard machine ate your five-dollar bill? Didn't you see the sign saying that it only takes ones?" Being able to point to a sign may make library staff feel vindicated, but it has zero palliative effect on library users.

## Signage Yells at Users

Want to create a hostile library environment? Follow these simple steps:

- Put up as many signs as you can containing words such as *no, must, forbidden, only, prohibited,* and *do not.* And do not neglect the good, old circle-slash symbol.
- Use *plenty* of italics, underlining, and **bold-faced** text. Better yet, use ***underline*** ***all three at once***.
- Do ***not*** scrimp on the exclamation points*!!!!*
- If you splurge on color, be sure to use ***plenty of red!!!!***

## Signage Is Badly Designed or of Low Quality

What are the core components of badly designed and low-quality signage?

- The sign, or the lettering on it, is the wrong size.
  - A sign intended to be seen from a distance is too small to be read.
  - A sign intended to be seen up close is larger than it needs to be.
- The sign is too wordy to take in at a glance.
- The font is not highly legible.
- There is not enough negative space around the lettering.
- There is poor contrast between the color of the lettering and the color of background.
- The meaning of the wording or symbols used on the sign is unclear.
- The sign is made from cheap materials. (Paper signs are evil.)
- The sign is poorly mounted.
  - It is crooked.
  - It is hung on a surface that is not flat.
  - It is attached with Scotch tape, masking tape, thumbtacks, etc.
- The sign is placed where it is difficult to see or is not placed at the point of need.
- The sign is so old that it has become shopworn or the information on it has gone out-of-date.

A big part of the problem with poor-quality signage stems from the fact that signage is seen as a cheap solution to a problem. And if you are looking for a cheap solution, the logic goes, then why not put up the cheapest possible sign? Why not? Because good signage is not cheap and bad signage is not effective. In fact, acquiring and installing a well-made sign could add up to more than the cost of actually fixing the root problem the sign is intended to remedy. If the budget does not allow for the acquisition of a well-designed, well-made, and attractive sign, it is better to put up no sign at all.

### There Is Too Much Signage

Library signage tends to build up over time, like barnacles fouling the hulls of ships. Unlike ships, however, libraries rarely heave to and scrape off the built-up accumulation. Overusing signage results in visual noise, the equivalent of a roomful of people all talking so loudly that a listener cannot distinguish one conversation from another. Faced with too many signs, people stop paying attention to any signs at all.

## The Architectural Signage System

The backbone of signage in any building should be built on a unified architectural signage system that enhances wayfinding and identifies spaces within a facility. Types of signs in an architectural signage system can be broken down into the following broad categories:

- Building identification
- Directional
- Regulatory
- Informational

Architects will have nearly exclusive responsibility for, and control over, the first two categories of signs, while building tenants, such as library staff, should (but do not always) have considerable control over directional and informational signs.

### Building Identification

Building-identification signage typically consists of exterior signs that must adhere to institutional signage standards. For example, almost all colleges and universities have campus signage plans that detail requirements for all building-identification signage: size, placement, materials, fonts, type sizes, colors, backgrounds, lighting, and logos. On older campuses it is not unusual to see exterior building-identification signage that meets contemporary campus standards for identifying buildings while simultaneously displaying historic, carved-in-stone building-identification signage; in some cases, the new and historic signage identify the same building differently. Local governments, school districts, and corporations may also implement standards to unify the signage identifying their various buildings. Finally, building-identification signage within historic districts or in cities with strict signage ordinances may also be required to meet specific aesthetic or size standards.

### Regulatory Signage

Regulatory signage includes all signs mandated by legislation or building codes for reasons of public safety or equal access. Examples of regulatory signage include signs identifying room numbers, exits, wheelchair access, firefighting and other emergency equipment, hazards (such as laboratories that contain biohazards or lasers), room capacity, elevators, and stairways. Building-evacuation maps are yet another example of regulatory signage. The size, placement, and special characteristics (Braille lettering, illumination) of regulatory signage must meet all of the requirements called for in the applicable codes. Regulatory signage may call for the use of symbols as well as text, and any symbols used must conform to the appropriate standards. In the United States, regulatory signage must comply with the Americans with Disabilities Act.

For any major building project, regulatory signage should be part of the unified architectural signage system and paid for out of the construction or remodeling budget. With some room for variation, regulatory signs within a single building should share a consistent appearance in terms of fonts, materials, and colors, though there can be color variation when it is used as an element of a wayfinding system in which distinct sign colors help distinguish different functional areas within a building.

### Directional Signage

In a perfect building, there would be no need for directional signage. Nobody has yet designed that perfect building, so directional signage is a necessary part of wayfinding. Three considerations stand out when it comes to directional signage:

- Use minimal directional signage.
- Use bump points to help with directional signage placement.
- Consider the best placement of directional signs.

#### MINIMALIST DIRECTIONAL SIGNAGE

If you have ever driven on a major freeway in an unfamiliar city and come upon an overpass that is plastered from one side to the other with those familiar white-on-green directional signs, you understand what it is like to be overloaded with directional signage. It is not always better to have more directional signs than fewer, and it can actually be worse. In an entirely new space, resist the temptation to overload it with directional signs; in an existing space, seriously consider taking down all of the existing directional signage and starting over with the mind-set of making wayfinding work with the fewest possible signs.

#### BUMP POINTS

Bump points are those places in any building where people routinely stop or slow down as they decide which way to go next. Because determining bump points is impossible until the public can be observed actually using the building, one good strategy is to open a new or remodeled space with low-cost temporary directional signage and wait until you have determined the bump points before installing permanent directional signage (including building maps) at those bump points. There are, however, two caveats for temporary signage.

1. You must set the date by which the temporary signage will be replaced with permanent signage. Temporary signage must not be allowed to remain in place until it starts to look ratty.

2. The quality of the temporary signage must be reasonably good. Printed signs on foam-core backing make for acceptable temporary signage; anything on sheets of paper or handwritten is unacceptable.

Going beyond signage, a major bump point is a great place to deploy human assistance in the form of a help desk.

PLACING SIGNS

While it is helpful to discover through observation that the space on the second floor where the east and west wings meet is a bump point, there remains the question of where directional signage should go so that people actually see it at the moment of need. Should it go on the north wall of the west wing? The south wall of the east wing? Should there be a double-sided sign suspended from the ceiling? Should directional signs be placed right at the bump point, or should they be placed where they can be seen on approach to that point? There is no manual to answer these kinds of question, but careful observation of how people behave at the bump point combined with thoughtful consideration of every option (i.e., do not slap a sign in the first place you think of and call it good) go a long way toward finding the best solution. Again, temporary signage may help determine the best placement option for permanent signage.

While there is a tendency to think of signs as always being mounted flat against a wall, this is not the only option. As suggested above, signs can be suspended from a ceiling. They can also be mounted on stands or mounted perpendicular to, rather than flat against, a wall.

## Informational Signage

Informational signage tells building users where they are or what they can (or cannot) do. Some informational signage, such as room identification signage, is also regulatory signage. Informational signage can also be directional. Say that a copier room is located in the middle of a long hallway. A perpendicularly mounted, double-sided sign reading COPIER ROOM is informational in that it identifies the space, but it is directional in that it can be seen from either end of the hall and thus guide library users to the copier room. Most of the signage mistakes mentioned (too much signage, signage that yells, tactical versus strategic signage) involve informational signage, so it is crucial to think carefully before deciding whether an informational sign is needed.

A special type of informational signage is donor-recognition signage. Whether it takes the form of generic engraved brass nameplates on a walnut plaque or elaborate tributes that move into the realm of high art, donor-recognition signage is rarely integral to library wayfinding. The most important considerations for donor-recognition signage is that it be attractive and appropriate for the space in which it is set and that it not in any way hinder wayfinding or library operations.

## *Signage Materials*

### Plastic Signs

While signs made of wood, stone, metal, or glass are employed for wayfinding purposes, signs incorporating such materials tend to be more decorative than utilitarian.

The same is true of signs that make use of neon, LED, and other specialty light sources. In contemporary buildings, signs made from plastic do most of the wayfinding work. Plastic signs are popular because they are inexpensive, lightweight, and come in a variety of attractive colors. Because plastic is a good material for engraved Braille letters, it is almost inevitably used for regulatory signs identifying rooms and spaces within a building.

One common method of lettering plastic signs uses a computer-guided blade to carve through the top layer of a plastic blank composed to two plastic sheets of contrasting colors. Once the carving is complete, the top layer of plastic forms the background of the sign while the exposed under layer forms the letters. There are also various reverse engraving processes for lettering plastic signs. A second common method of lettering plastic signs is by using laser-cut vinyl letters. Vinyl lettering is attractive and inexpensive. It is possible to remove vinyl lettering in order to reletter a plastic sign, though there may be problems with fading and residue if the relettered sign has been in use for a long time.

---

### Signage Formatting 101

**Fonts**

San-serif fonts dominate signage; that said, it is worth remembering that there are choices within the san-serif universe. Helvetica, believe it or not, is not the only san-serif font.

Lettering on signs that must be read from a distance, such as overhead signs, must be at least three inches high. On the subject of overhead signs, one urban legend about the Americans with Disabilities Act has it that even overhead signs must include Braille lettering. This is a total myth. Only those signs that can be reached by a normal-sized person, such as regulatory room-identification signs, are required to have Braille lettering.

**Negative Space**

The legibility of a sign is enhanced by negative space; simply put, lettering that fills the entire sign is less readable than lettering set within wider margins (see Figures 6.1 and 6.2).

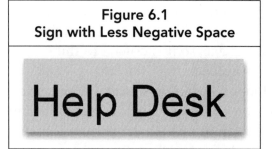

**Figure 6.1**
**Sign with Less Negative Space**

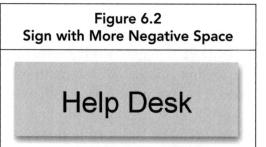

**Figure 6.2**
**Sign with More Negative Space**

**Contrast**

High contrast between the color of lettering and the color of the sign background on which the lettering appears adds to the legibility of the sign. The highest contrast is between black and white, though for large signs the contrast between true black and pure white is too stark; combinations such as black letters on a light gray background are more common. Low contrast combinations such as yellow and orange are almost unreadable and must be avoided.

*(Continued)*

---

**Signage Formatting 101** *(Continued)*

One point to consider when choosing colors is that dark text on light background tends to appear larger than a light version of that same text on a dark background (see Figures 6.3 and 6.4).

| **Figure 6.3**<br>**Sign Using Arial 22 Point Dark**<br>**on Light Background** | **Figure 6.4**<br>**Sign Using Arial 22 Point Light**<br>**on Dark Background** |
| :---: | :---: |
| 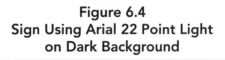 | 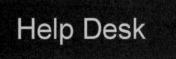 |

**Centering**

Centering text is good for one or two lines of text. More than two lines of centered text becomes hard to read.

---

### Framed Signs

Various commercially produced frame systems provide an attractive way to display low-cost, easily updatable signs. And such frames are the only way to make paper signs acceptable. The caveat is that if a library is going to use frames to display paper signs that are created in house, then those paper signs must be well designed and the library must have a high-quality, large-format color printer to produce them. An 8.5-by-11-inch sign floating in a frame designed to hold a 17-by-22-inch sign looks amateurish at best.

---

**Information Resources for Library Signage and Wayfinding**

There are a number of websites with good information about signage, including the library-specific page "Library Signs and Displays" (LibrarySupportStaff.com, 2010). Ellen Bosman (2010) provides a good starting point for signage research with her webpage "Creating a User Friendly Library with Signage: Selected Bibliography." A notable recent book on the topic of wayfinding is Craig Berger's (2005) *Wayfinding: Designing and Implementing Graphic Navigational Systems.*

---

## Digital Signage

Digital signage is a form of "narrowcasting" which displays multimedia or video content. Typically though not necessarily part of a network, a digital sign consists of a computer (sometimes referred to as a "media player" or simply "player") attached to a projector or display screen (LED, LCD, or plasma). Retail businesses pioneered digital signage, but noncommercial organizations, including some libraries, employ it as well. Digital signage offers a number of advantages over traditional signage:

- Is easily updatable
- Allows precise timing of messages
- Delivers multiple messages (at times simultaneously) on a single display
- Delivers audio and video content
- Offers interactive features
- Is potentially more attention grabbing than static signage

The chief disadvantage of digital signage as compared to static signage is the high initial cost for hardware, software, and installation. In addition, the staffing costs for creating new signage content and managing signage streams must figure into the digital signage cost equation. Even at its high price, digital signage can be just as ineffective as static signage if the designers of the digital content make the same mistakes made by designers of bad static signage. A digital sign that is hostile, confusing, or difficult to read due to bad graphic design is no better than its static equivalent. The technology may be different, but the principles that underlie effective static signage also hold for digital signage.

Although the rapidly advancing technology of digital signage is as dynamic as the signs themselves, the following sections cover digital signage basics that should hold true for the foreseeable future.

### *The Basics: Digital Signage Hardware*

The hardware for a typical digital signage installation consists of a display screen or projector that presents content (still images, video, sound), plus a media player (essentially an on-board computer) that controls the display and playback of content. When choosing displays, it is best to choose displays specifically designed for digital signage as opposed to purchasing (much cheaper) generic screens, such as consumer flat-panel televisions. The latter will not hold up as long as purpose-built digital signage displays and do not support the resolution and refresh rates necessary for high-quality images. Another important advantage to purpose-built displays is that most have their media players built into the display or incorporated in such a way that each media player is, in effect, an integral part of the display. With non-purpose-built displays, such as flat-panel televisions or large-screen computer monitors, comes the problem of securing the media player where it is out of the way and safe from tampering, theft, and vandalism. Solutions might involve putting the media player behind a wall, in the ceiling, or in a lockbox, with the end result likely proving expensive, ugly, or both.

The size of the display used depends on its purpose and setting. A display placed where viewers' eyes will be within a few feet of the screen need not be stadium sized. For example, a digital display that is mounted near eye level on a stand next to a service desk is often about the same size as an average desktop computer monitor. Yet a display mounted near the ceiling of a vaulted grand entrance needs to be big enough to be seen and read from floor level, so it will likely be much larger. The trick is to use the smallest display that will still do the job effectively, as every additional inch of screen size increases the cost of the display. For large displays, projectors are a more cost-effective option than LCD, LED, or plasma screens.

Every digital signage display needs access to power as well as to the data that it displays in the form of content. Obviously, there must be a source of electrical power within a few feet of wherever a digital sign is installed. As for supplying data, there are three means of doing this:

- Stand-alone digital signage
- Wired networked digital signage
- Wireless networked digital signage

### Stand-Alone Digital Signage

Stand-alone digital signs are self-contained units on which data is loaded via "sneaker net." That is, someone walks up to a display with some kind of storage device (such as a USB drive or a DVD), loads the storage device into a slot in the media player, and transfers the data. Stand-alone displays are a good option when there are no network drops located near that *perfect* location for a digital sign or when plans do not call for installing a large number of digital signs. Even if the future holds out the possibility of many digital signs in a library, starting with a single stand-alone sign is not a bad way to get comfortable with digital signage technology.

### Wired Networked Digital Signage

Wired networked digital displays connect to data drops via standard Ethernet cables and receive data from a remote server located somewhere on the network. This is the best option for digital signage systems consisting of more than a few displays and where network drops already exist (or can be readily installed) at the locations where displays should go. Employing a server allows human content managers to remotely control any number of displays from their desktops. Even modestly priced digital signage servers are capable of controlling upward of 200 networked displays.

### Wireless Networked Digital Signage

Wireless networked digital displays receive data via wireless nodes. With a wireless network the placement of displays does not depend on the proximity of data drops. There is, however, a limit on the maximum distance between a digital signage display and the node that serves it. In typical library settings this limit works out to one node per floor. The chief disadvantages of wireless networks are that they are somewhat slower and generally not as robust as wired networks. As with its wired cousin, the data for wireless digital signage is provided via a server.

### The Basics: Digital Signage Software

Regardless of hardware, a digital signage system is no better than the software behind it. While local needs will always vary from one library to the next, and not all of the following capabilities are absolute requirements for every installation, digital signage software should:

- display multiple still images with a high degree of control over order, frequency, length of display, and expiration date;
- operate across standard network infrastructure (CAT 6 cable);
- support a wide variety of standard file formats;
- provide a decentralized end-user interface which allows multiple frontline staff to act as content managers with the ability to create, post, and manage content;
- display video with the option to turn audio on or off at any display;
- display live webpages;
- support (at least potentially) touch-screen functionality; and
- support (at least potentially) two-way, real-time voice-and-video interaction between a library user in front of a digital display and a library staff member at a service point.

### Interactive Signage

Procuring digital signage software that supports two-way, real-time voice-and-video interaction speaks to the largely unexplored possibility of interactive digital signage in libraries. While touch-screen technology is the most familiar mechanism for interacting with digital displays, digital displays exist that allow users to interact through their cell phones. A digital display could allow users to choose from a menu of how-to videos addressing common questions or, as mentioned, allow users to print out customized maps and directions. Perhaps most promising for libraries are displays offering two-way audio/video communication in real time. A display so enabled makes it possible for a user in a remote part of a library to see and talk to library staff located on another floor or even in a different building. In return, public service staff can see and talk to the user and provide further assistance by displaying relevant webpages, maps, or other digital information. Imagine a single library staff member sitting in front of a web cam providing public service during off-peak hours to several branch libraries via interactive digital signage. The potential cost savings could be considerable and more than pay for the cost of implementing the digital signage system in the first place.

### Locating and Presenting Digital Signage

What makes a good location for a digital sign? As mentioned, the first necessity is ready access to power and (at least for networked signs) data. Certainly a busy space where the information displayed can reach a large number of people is an ideal location for digital signage. A remote location where users may have questions but not easily find any staff nearby to assist them is also a good area for placement. On the other hand, digital signage does not belong where it will unduly disturb library users. Typically, this includes those parts of a library intended for use as quiet study spaces. While it is obvious that displays which present audio can disturb users, even silent digital signs can be disturbing in some settings. One solution to the problem of presenting audio in an otherwise quiet space is directional speakers which allow their output to be heard only when a listener is within a limited "spotlight" of sound (Fischetti, 2007: 96–97).

Once a location is chosen, the most common way to present digital signage is to mount a display on a wall. Suspending a digital sign from a ceiling is another common technique. Digital signage can be used with either floor stands or desktop mounts. Although desktop- and floor-stand-mounted signs will always require power and data regardless of where they go, they are relatively mobile, making it possible to place them almost anywhere there is a need for signage. Because such signs tend to be located in close proximity to the people viewing them, their screens do not need to be as large as signs mounted near a ceiling or high on a wall. Kiosks can be an effective way to present interactive digital signage. In the past, the term *kiosk* implied a computer screen mounted in a substantial piece of furniture; today, kiosks come in trimmer, less imposing designs.

Short-throw projectors capable of displaying a large image without the need to be placed more than a few feet distant from the surface on to which they project are becoming an increasingly important part of the digital-signage hardware arsenal. Because they can easily be mounted in the ceiling, short-throw projectors are less susceptible to theft or vandalism than wall-mounted screens, and they can be used in combination with products such as 3M's Vikuiti film to put eye-catching digital signage in spaces where screens cannot easily go, including directly on windows or high overhead in atriums. A final advantage of short-throw projection systems over display screens is that by simply turning off a projector a digital sign can temporarily "disappear" if it is in the way of a special event or maintenance activity.

## *Administration of Digital Signage*

Unless a digital signage system consists entirely of stand-alone displays, a system administrator must oversee the larger technological aspects of the system, most notably the server that sends data to individual displays. While the amount of work required of a system administrator will vary according to the size and complexity of the digital signage system, in most library settings this will not be a full-time job or anything close to it. The role of the digital signage system administrator will most likely represent a small part of the duties of a member of the library's information technology staff. Deciding what content belongs on the digital signage system and scheduling when and where it will appear is the job of digital signage content managers. Just about any member of the library staff could serve as a content manager, and with digital signage software that allows web login, it is possible to have multiple content managers working from their individual desktops. It is likely that content managers will also serve as content creators, but anyone on staff who is capable of using presentation software, graphic art software, or video production tools could create content for digital signage. However, digital signage should not be a license to engage in a signage free-for-all. Every signage decision, static or digital, should be given careful thought and be part of an overall communication strategy.

Once digital signage is in place, the library will need to set some standards for content. The easiest standards to establish are technical, such as supported file formats, aspect ratios, and so on. Obviously, content that does not conform to the technical standards of the digital signage system cannot be displayed. More tricky to set are standards that relate to subject matter and appropriateness, especially if library users will be allowed to post messages on the library's digital signage system. Before implementing any digital signage system, library administrators should first establish a clear, succinct, and workable policy for digital signage, quite possibly basing this new policy on existing policies regarding message posting in the library.

## Conclusion

There is no single, simple solution for creating a library space that allows users to successfully find their way. Signage—traditional, digital, or a combination of the two—cannot do it all. Eliminating obstacles to wayfinding cannot do it all. A building designed with wayfinding in mind is a great asset, but even that cannot win the battle all by itself. All of these elements need to be combined and harmoniously tuned to allow successful wayfinding. As with any musical instrument, tuning is not something you can do once and forget. As library operations change, as the way people use the library changes, the wayfinding elements need to be retuned to keep up with those changes. Finally, even in the best-tuned building, some users will still need, from time to time, human help to find their way.

## References

Berger, Craig. 2005. *Wayfinding: Designing and Implementing Graphic Navigational Systems.* Crans-Près-Céligny; Hove: RotoVision.

Bosman, Ellen. 2010. "Creating a User Friendly Library with Signage: Selected Bibliography." LibrarySupportStaff.com. Accessed March 9. http://www.librarysupportstaff.com/libsigns .html.

Branscomb, Harvie. 1940. *Teaching with Books: A Study of College Libraries.* Chicago: American Association of Colleges, American Library Association.

Fischetti, Mark. 2007. "Psst…Hey You." *Scientific American* 296, no. 5: 96–97. http://web .ebscohost.com/ehost/pdf?vid=9&hid=119&sid=d1dd7c1d-4998-49c7-a93a-66d34338f9 23%40sessionmgr108.

LibrarySupportStaff.com. 2010. "Library Signs and Displays." LibrarySupportStaff.com. Accessed November 5. http://www.librarysupportstaff.com/libsigns.html.

Nielsen, Jakob. 2004. "Jakob Nielsen's Alertbox: The Need for Web Design Standards." UseIt.com. http://www.useit.com/alertbox/20040913.html.

# III

# Maintaining an Existing Library Building

# 7

# Library Security and Safety in Building Design and Construction

When they took their first library jobs or started taking library courses, most people entering the library profession understood that their job would, to one extent or another, involve ensuring the security of library collections. Few budding library professionals, however, are likely to have understood from their first day on the job that library security involves far more than keeping books from disappearing or that, even more drastically, their jobs might involve taking responsibility for the safety of those who work in and use libraries. Expected or not, like it or not, security and safety are responsibilities that inevitably fall to those who work in and manage libraries.

For the purposes of this chapter, *security* refers to maintaining the integrity of library property, including collections, furniture, fixtures, equipment, and buildings; *safety*, on the other hand, refers to preventing injury and death. In addressing issues of security and safety, this chapter first considers how library building design and systems can be used to enhance security and safety and then examines the special security and safety concerns associated with library building projects.

## Security and Safety as a Function of Library Building Design and Systems

If a building is not well designed to enhance security and safety, or if it fails to incorporate appropriate security and safety systems, then maintaining security and safety will be an ongoing drain on library staff and resources; indeed, in the worst cases, maintaining security and safety becomes impossible regardless of the amount of staff resources library management throws at the problem. On the other hand, properly designed buildings with well-integrated security and safety systems can be managed at the lowest possible staffing costs and with the lowest possible levels of stress for both staff and users. Nobody wants to visit or work in a library that feels unsafe, nor does anyone want to visit or work in a library that functions more like a high-security prison than as a place to read, relax, and learn; any library that manages to achieve security and safety while still maintaining a relaxed and friendly atmosphere is going to be a more comfortable, more welcoming place for all concerned. Though it may not be apparent in the planning stages of a library building project, investing early on in security and safety will return huge payoffs in both dollars and human contentment over the life of a building.

## The Human Factor

In the day-to-day running of any library or, indeed, the running of any public building, the main threat to security and safety is *Homo sapiens sapiens*. At their worst, these dangerous and destructive creatures are capable of stealing anything from books to bricks; of causing property damage ranging from minor vandalism to the total destruction of a building; and, in the extreme, of harassing, injuring, or even killing their fellow creatures. Libraries face an especially difficult problem because they are among the only public buildings in the modern world in which any human being can spend as much time as he or she wants without spending any money and without needing any particular reason to be there. In the library, loitering is not a crime; it is a right. Because many libraries (including virtually all public libraries) cannot "reserve the right to refuse service to anyone," those who manage libraries must work in conjunction with those who design library buildings to create library spaces that make it as difficult as possible for the dreaded *Homo sapiens sapiens* to act on their worst impulses.

### Visibility

The single greatest deterrent to bad human behavior is visibility. When individuals with the potential to do wrong know they can be readily seen, whether by library staff or by other library users, they are more likely to toe the line or at least take their bad behavior elsewhere; concealment, on the other hand, is practically an invitation to do wrong. Libraries suffer from a serious handicap in that erecting seven-foot-tall book stacks and packing them solid with books creates row upon row of concealed spaces. While there is not much that can be done about the concealing nature of library book stacks, there are steps to take, and mistakes to avoid, to make library interiors safer and more secure by enhancing visibility within them:

- Advocate for building designs that incorporate lots of open spaces and maintain good sight lines.
- Avoid building designs that include blind spots—such as tucked-away nooks and alcoves—in which people can operate unobserved. Especially dangerous are secluded blind spots into which an assailant can lure or drag a potential victim.
- Avoid furniture designs that block users from sight. A classic example of this is the type of tall study carrel which extends several feet above the table top, thereby providing ideal cover for monkey (or, more correctly, primate) business of all sorts.
- All study and meeting rooms must have clear glass panels in their doors or alongside their doors so that passersby can readily see what is going on in every room. Persons using such rooms should never be allowed to cover the windows with any opaque material (such as paper), and the room lights should be designed so that they cannot be entirely turned off while the rooms are occupied.

- Should library users be able to lock the doors of study and meeting rooms from the inside? Those arguing in the negative hold that library users could take advantage of lockable doors to barricade themselves inside a room. Those arguing in the affirmative hold that doors should lock from inside because a lockable door is a good defense in the unlikely event of a violent rampage occurring inside a library building. (Unlikely, but not unprecedented. A number of the deaths and injuries at Columbine High School in 1999 occurred in the school library.) Besides, the latter argument goes, library staff should have master keys with which to override any attempt to barricade the room by locking a door from the inside.

- Library storage spaces, mechanical rooms, janitors' closets, and the like must have secure deadbolt locks and must *always* remain locked when not in use. If someone with bad intentions gets access to a closed-off, totally concealed space in the library, the results can be disastrous.

- While on the subject of lights, it is worth noting that good lighting is a component of visibility. A well-lighted environment with few dark corners discourages undesirable behaviors ranging from theft to vandalism to illicit sexual activity and assaults. Dark areas invite trouble.

- Exterior windows on the ground floor of any building increase visibility. The fact that anyone passing by outside can look in and see what is going on inside will help deter undesirable activity. Allowing landscaping to grow to the point where

---

### Privacy, Security, and Safety in the Library

As a whole, people who work in libraries tend to value and protect the privacy of people who use libraries. The American Library Association's (2010) Library Bill of Rights explicitly states, "Privacy is essential to the exercise of free speech, free thought, and free association." One of the questions this statement raises is where libraries can draw the line—or, more accurately, follow the twisty path—between the kind of privacy that sustains free speech, thought, and association and the kind that sustains theft, vandalism, harassment, and violence. Are security cameras in a library an invasion of privacy? Can library staff ask to search someone's bag? Are radio frequency identification (RFID) security tags a threat to basic freedoms? Within the library profession, some contend that these questions do not have any easy answers, while others counter that they have three very easy answers, respectively: Yes. No. Yes.

Whatever one's personal or professional take on privacy and its limits (or absence thereof), from a strictly legal point of view U.S. courts have ruled time and again that there is virtually no expectation of privacy when one is in a public place, such as a library, and this judicial trend has become even more pronounced in recent years as fears of terrorism have escalated. This means that when people are seated at a library table it is assumed that others will be able to see what they are reading, writing, or viewing. If bags or belongings are left unattended, it is legal and appropriate for staff members to search bags and retrieve items for safekeeping. If the security alarm goes off as a library user passes through, it is legal and appropriate for a library staff member to ask to look into that person's bag. If that person refuses to allow a search, however, then further action should be left to sworn police officers who have search authority and appropriate training.

it partially or fully obscures ground-floor windows will, of course, negate their security benefit.

- Ideally, staffed library service points will be positioned so that library staff can clearly see as much library space, and as many library users, as possible. At the very least, every library entrance/exit point must be clearly visible from a staffed service point.
- Having library staff routinely walk the building makes it clear that someone is watching and that the library staff are alert to potential problems. In libraries where misbehavior—if not full-blown crime—is a serious problem, such patrols are best performed by well-trained, uniformed security guards rather than rank-and-file library staff.
- The concealing effect of isolated areas can be somewhat offset by wall-mounted convex mirrors. Not the most aesthetic solution, perhaps, but effective.
- Security cameras have a strong deterrent effect on misbehavior. See the Privacy, Security, and Safety in the Library sidebar for more detailed information on this topic.

### Other Threats to Security and Safety

Besides the direct actions of the human beings who use libraries, the other major threats to security and safety in the library are animals, natural disasters, and engineering mistakes.

### Animals

While few libraries are located where the presence of large predatory animals is a problem, threats resulting from swarms of insects (book devouring or otherwise), rabies-carrying mammals (e.g., bats), aggressive domestic animals, rodents, and the occasional poisonous snake are not out of the realm of possibility, even in urban settings. The best defense against animal problems is a building design that does not invite unwanted creatures to nest or seek refuge under eaves, on rooftops, or beneath decks and raised foundations. During the design stage of any new building, it is best if the architects take local animal concerns into consideration as part of the total design mix. When animals do create safety or security problems, it is important that everyone gives the animal or animals a wide berth and that animal-control professionals be called in to deal with the problem.

Although not exactly a security or safety issue, building designs that invite birds to nest create maintenance problems in the form of messy nesting materials and bird droppings. Peregrine falcons, for example, are particularly fond of nesting on tall buildings, though they are relatively shy when humans are near. Swallows and pigeons, on the other hand, are not shy at all, arriving in flocks to make a huge mess wherever they decide to nest. Because many bird species are protected by the Migratory Bird Treaty Act (United States, Canada, and Mexico), the Endangered Species Act (United States), or the Species at Risk Act (Canada), it is important to consult federal regulations before attempting to control avian pests. If the library's parent organization has an environmental specialist, always consult with that person. If no such resource is available in house, seek guidance from the appropriate state or provincial agency, the U.S. Fish and Wildlife Service, or Environment Canada. Do not expect local pest-control firms to be experts in the laws governing treatment of wild birds or other pests, as it is unlikely that small local firms will have the legal resources to maintain current, complete knowledge of so complex an array of laws and regulations. Another option when dealing with nonpredatory birds is to hire a falconer. Used by many airports to control pigeons on runways and around terminals, trained raptors under the control of a falconer generally do not attack and kill other birds; instead, they simply fly around and give chase to the point that the locale becomes undesirable for nesting and feeding. In the United States, falconers must hold both state and federal licenses; in Canada they must hold only a provincial license. The best way to contact a local falconer is to check with a statewide, provincial, or regional falconers' association.

Rodents present yet another common and persistent animal problem for libraries. Rodents are voracious eaters who do not limit themselves to what humans consider edible food. Mice, for example, crave wiring insulation, and most rodents like to collect paper waste and small bits of wood for lining their nests. Construction projects that drive rodents out of their outdoor habitat, open gaps that allow rodents to enter a building, or do both simultaneously can worsen an existing rodent problem or create one where none previously existed. In many cases the only thing that can be done about rodents during construction or renovation is to keep trash contained in rodent-proof containers and to seal all access points to the existing structure as tightly as possible. Building project or not, when rodents become an intolerable problem the best option is to hire a reputable pest-control firm.

### Natural Disasters

Because no one can stop natural disasters, there are only two things human beings can do to ameliorate the damage that may be inflicted when they occur. The first is to be well prepared. The second is to construct buildings capable of withstanding the local brands of natural disaster. Preparing a library for natural disasters means having in place procedures for what to do in the event of a natural disaster, training staff on how and when to follow those procedures, and having plans for recovering from a natural disaster. Two useful resources to consult in order to be prepared for natural disasters and their aftermaths include:

California Preservation Program. 2010. *Emergency Preparedness & Response.* CalPreservation.org. http://calpreservation.org/disasters.

Halsted, Deborah H., Richard P. Jasper, and Felicia M. Little. 2005. *Disaster Planning: A How-to-Do-It Manual for Librarians.* New York: Neal-Schuman.

Constructing a building to withstand natural disasters is largely a matter of adhering to local building codes. Because every area is prone to its own particular mix of natural disasters, local building codes vary in terms of the standards they impose. Along the Gulf Coast, for example, building codes emphasize a building's capacity to survive hurricanes, while in California earthquakes are the disaster of greatest concern. Though it is certainly not the responsibility of librarians to make sure that buildings are built to withstand natural disasters, being aware of the relationship between building codes and the local forces of nature provides one with a better overall understanding of the design process and the limitations within which architects and engineers must work.

### Engineering Mistakes

Engineering mistakes may be the result of bad design, bad construction practices, or a combination of the two. While librarians bear no responsibility for engineering mistakes, they have to live with them. Fortunately, most engineering mistakes are rather minor. For example, designers might call for a type of window that is not sufficiently insulated for the local climate, or perhaps the designers call for the right kind of windows but construction crews do not install them properly. While the results of such a mistake would not be catastrophic, the occupants of the building in question must endure cold drafts, minor rain leaks, and excessive energy consumption. Major engineering mistakes, while rare, can be extremely catastrophic. One notorious example of such a mistake was the July 17, 1981, collapse of the atrium walkway in the Kansas City Hyatt Regency which killed 114 and injured more than 200. Resolving engineering mistakes, whether major or minor, is often a contentious and costly business in which the parties involved attempt to place the blame on one another and often end up airing their differences in a court of law. When engineering disputes reach such extreme levels, they have clearly exited the realm in which librarians operate and entered the land of lawyers and expert witnesses.

## Staff Training for Security and Safety

Even when a building is flawlessly designed in terms of promoting security and safety, all that good design will go to waste if the library staff is not well trained in how to maintain security and safety and how to respond to any threats to security and safety. Besides being trained in the daily routines of maintaining security and safety (opening and closing procedures, remaining vigilant to potential problems, conducting regular building walk-throughs, etc.), all library staff should be trained on what to do in the following situations:

- Violations of library rules governing user conduct
- The occurrence of a nonviolent crime (misdemeanor or felony)
- The occurrence of an act of violence or the threat of violence
- Fire
- Building system emergencies (leaking pipes, elevator stoppages, power failures, etc.)
- Medical emergencies
- Natural disasters (earthquakes, tornados, floods, etc.)

For just one example, consider the minimum that library staff should know in the event of a fire:

- Emergency exit routes and where to assemble after leaving the building
- Locations of fire alarm boxes and fire extinguishers

- How to contact emergency dispatch
- How and when to use a fire extinguisher (and when not to use one)

This list is merely the minimum that library staff should know in the event of fire. Every situation is different, so each library will likely have at least an item or two to add to the basic list. Because similar lists can be developed for every type of emergency that may occur in a library, the training load is significant; on the other hand, the payoff in terms of the potential savings of life, limb, and property is huge.

As important as knowing what to do in an emergency is knowing what *not* to do. Library staff, with rare exceptions, are not certified emergency medical technicians, trained firefighters, or sworn police officers. Whatever the emergency, library staff should never undertake any emergency action for which they are not properly trained and equipped. Among other bad outcomes, staff overreaching their capabilities can result in lawsuits against the library as well as injury or death to members of the public and library staff.

### Libraries and First Responders

Establishing good relationships between the library and local first responders (police, fire, and EMT services) is an excellent, cost-effective way to improve security and safety. For starters, first responders are often willing to provide staff training in their areas of expertise. Local firefighters might be happy to train the library staff in the hands-on use of fire extinguishers, while a city police officer might be quite willing to talk to staff about personal safety. Library frontline supervisors (especially night-shift supervisors) should get to know local police, discuss with police the library's main security and safety concerns, and make it clear to local officers that they are more than welcome to drop by the library whenever they are in the area. Observing police officers dropping by the library at random times will have a significant chilling effect on the petty thief who might otherwise consider the library a good place to grab an unattended purse or laptop. Along the same lines, meeting with local firefighters to discuss the library's particular needs and concerns will pay off in the event of an actual emergency. If firefighters enter a smoky library understanding in advance that, as far as books are concerned, water is as damaging as fire, their plan of attack might produce a more satisfactory result than if they come in with nozzles wide open.

## Security and Safety Systems

Building security and safety systems may serve either to prevent problems before they happen or to alert library staff and first responders to the fact that there is a problem.

### Security Cameras

As mentioned, the presence of security cameras will deter unwanted behavior. They also create a forensic record for the prosecution of anyone careless enough to commit their misdeeds in front of a camera lens. Simple computer-based, closed-circuit cameras are not prohibitively expensive, especially if they are planned into the design of a new building or a major renovation. Security cameras do create management issues such as determining from where the cameras will be monitored, who will do the monitoring, and how closely the cameras will be monitored: Every second the library is open? Every five minutes? Whenever the circulation supervisor is not too busy doing something else?

If funds are not available for working security cameras, dummy security cameras can be almost as effective a deterrent as the real thing. Realistic-looking dummy security cameras (complete with battery-powered lights that contribute a convincing glow) can be purchased from retail electronics stores or via the Internet for around $20. One of the authors of this book worked in a library that used dummy security cameras, and on more than one occasion staff discovered that library users had put gum over the lens to prevent the camera from recording whatever it was they did not want to be seen doing. Of course, that behavior demonstrates not only that dummy cameras can be convincing but also that people can come up with ingenious ways of defeating security systems.

There is a widespread assumption that fake cameras and unmonitored cameras are a liability for an institution because they create a false sense of security. The authors of this book have been unable to find a single litigated case in which an institution was held liable for using either dummy or unmonitored security cameras. Furthermore, from all appearances, the bulk of the dire warnings about liability and dummy security cameras are the products of companies that sell working security cameras. The truth is that many public entities either employ dummy security cameras or install far more real security cameras than they can possibly monitor. Because unmonitored security cameras purely serve to create after-the-fact records that can be used forensically and do not alert emergency dispatchers to crimes in progress, one could argue that they are as guilty as dummy security cameras of providing a false sense of security. However, if that argument could prevail in court, then how is it that tens of thousands of ATMs include unmonitored security cameras as part of their basic configuration with no resultant liability problems?

### Fire Alarms

Required by code in public buildings, modern fire alarms operate both automatically and manually. Operating automatically, fire alarms activate when any of their heat, light, or smoke sensors detect combustion. Alternatively, fire alarms can be activated when a person pulls the alarm. Most fire alarms serve the dual purpose of alerting building occupants (through a combination of sound and flashing lights) and automatically contacting local emergency dispatchers. Sophisticated fire alarm systems are often part of total building monitoring systems that incorporate fire, water, and intrusion alarms into a single interconnected system.

### Sprinkler Systems

Discussed in detail in Chapter 2, "Overview of Building System Basics," sprinkler systems are required by code in large buildings but are optional in smaller buildings.

### Burglar (Intrusion) Alarms

Burglar alarms (also known as *intrusion alarms*) detect unauthorized presence in a number of ways, typically by detecting motion, the breaking of glass, or the opening of alarmed doors or windows. The simplest alarms may do no more than emit noise and light in hopes of scaring away intruders, while more sophisticated alarms automatically notify police dispatchers. One drawback of such alarm systems is that false alarms (which are quite common) are so wasteful of police resources that many cash-strapped jurisdictions have taken to charging home and building owners for the cost of responding to false alarms.

### Water Alarms

Water alarms alert responders to leaks from such sources as pipes and roofs before the water is able to damage collections, furnishings, or equipment. Where water pipes run above library collections, catch pans incorporating water alarms can be suspended below the pipes. If a pipe begins to leak, the water collects in the catch pan, activating the alarm. Water alarms can also be placed on basement and ground-floor levels to detect water entering the building from outside.

### Weather Radios

Available for well under $100, weather radios sound an alarm and provide information whenever there is a weather-related emergency. In the United States, the source of such warnings is the National Oceanic and Atmospheric Administration (NOAA) Weather Radio All Hazards (NWR), while in Canada such warnings are issued by Weatheradio Canada. Weather radios provide a big payoff for a small investment, especially in areas that experience severe, fast-changing weather.

### Public Address Systems

Public address systems allow library staff to provide directions to building occupants in the event of an emergency. For example, if the library's weather radio announces a tornado warning, library staff can then use the public address system to warn everyone in the building to move away from windows and take shelter in the most protected areas of the building until the danger has passed.

### Theft Detection Systems

Common in all but the smallest of libraries, library theft detection systems work by sounding an alarm when a book or other library item containing either a magnetic or electronic tag passes through a security gate without having been properly checked out and desensitized. Because security gates are costly and require the presence of staff to respond to alarms, it is most cost-effective to minimize the exit points from the library's security perimeter, with the ideal number of exit points being one. Because there are a number of ways to defeat theft detection systems, they are not effective at stopping a determined thief with some knowledge of how such systems work. They do, however, serve to keep the honest person honest and deter unsophisticated thieves.

### Emergency Caches

Though not technically a system, a well-maintained cache of emergency supplies is worth its weight in gold in the event of an emergency. Typical supplies found in an emergency cache include flashlights (with extra batteries), cleaning supplies (especially paper towels), trash bags, plastic sheeting, rubber gloves, plastic aprons, dust masks, a list of emergency contacts (with phone numbers), and so on. Each of the two disaster-preparedness resources listed in the Natural Disasters section in this chapter provides complete lists of supplies that a library should stock in its emergency cache.

### Enhanced Security Areas

Areas of the library that house especially valuable or unique materials are candidates for enhanced security measures. Library special collections and archives are the most obvious examples of areas that deserve enhanced security, but other candidates include areas where data backups or confidential personnel records are stored. A simple measure to enhance security in a specific area is to issue only a limited number of keys for the locks that provide access to the area. A more sophisticated approach is to install a keycard lock system which strictly limits who can enter a space while also keeping an exact log of whose card opened which door and when. Caged areas are routinely used to provide extra security for especially valuable library treasures, though fireproof safes provide an even greater level of security. As mentioned, surveillance cameras will enhance security in any area where they are used. Perhaps the ultimate security measure is to employ around-the-clock security guards to watch over library treasures, but the cost of this measure is prohibitive for most libraries.

### Locks and Keys

The proper management of locks and keys is a basic component of library security. Libraries may employ traditional metal lock-and-key systems, electronic keycard lock systems, or a combination of the two. Keycard systems, though a more expensive option, provide some advantages over traditional locks. Keycard systems:

- keep a record of whose card opened any given door and when it did so;
- provide complete flexibility in assigning access privileges, including at what times a given card can open a given door; and
- allow rapid, low-cost "rekeying" in the event that a card is lost or stolen.

Keycard systems offer the feature of automatically locking/unlocking specific doors at specific times, though systems that do not use keycards may also offer this same feature.

Good key management is a must when using traditional lock-and-key systems. Those charged with managing keys need to keep exact records of which keys have been assigned to which employees and to ensure that employees return keys upon separation from the library or its parent institution. Most traditional key systems operate on a master-keying model in which different keys provide different levels of access:

- *Change keys* open only one specific lock.
- *Submaster keys* open multiple locks.
- *Master keys* open all, or nearly all, locks in a building.

One of the drawbacks of traditional master-key systems is that the loss or theft of a submaster or, worse, a master key requires expensive rekeying of multiple locks. In a large building, the loss of a master key can result in rekeying costs running into the tens of thousands of dollars.

### Entrances and Exits

In the interest of safety, library entrance/exit areas, as well as all approaches to those areas, should be clearly marked, well lit, and free of lurking places. (The classic library front-door lurking place is the walk-up book drop that requires anyone returning a book to step into a blind spot that cannot be seen from either inside or outside the building.) Glass doors and/or large windows around an entrance/exit allow interior lighting to illuminate the area immediately outside while further enhancing security by allowing those inside the building to clearly see the building's entrance and approaches. Land-scape designers love to place blooming trees and leafy shrubs near building entrances, but if doing so provides a handy spot for an assailant to hide or drag a victim into, it is better to stick with low-growing flowers or ground cover.

A library's security perimeter is typically defined by theft detection security gates, staffed service/security points, or some combination of the two. The entrance to a library building need not necessarily also be the entrance to its security perimeter, and it is usually best when the two are separated by a lobby or some other intermediate area that is inside the library building but outside the library security perimeter. The ideal arrangement for library security includes a single security-perimeter entrance/exit, a single building entrance/exit, and a staffed service point from which both the security perimeter and building entrance/exit points can be monitored. Maintaining a single "front-door" service point:

- reduces the number of security gates which are not only costly in and of themselves but which also require costly wiring;
- reduces staffing costs in comparison to multiple service points, especially in libraries which employ security guards or which routinely check bags and back-packs as part of their security process;
- lends itself to the efficient use of security cameras in libraries where cameras are part of the security mix; and
- allows staff to get a look at everyone who enters the library, a circumstance which will discourage many criminals and troublemakers.

Besides all the above advantages, the presence of friendly (if also alert and observant) library staff at the entrance is a welcoming sight, especially to uncertain library users who enter a building on the lookout for someone to assist them in navigating the library or its collections.

Should a library have one entrance for library users and a separate entrance for library staff? There are pros and cons to both arrangements, and security is only one of several factors (including library traditions, workplace culture, and labor contracts) that should be considered in making a decision one way or another. In libraries where dealing with difficult patrons is commonplace or where food, drink, backpacks, or other personal items are prohibited in public spaces but allowed in staff areas, a separate staff entrance can foster a more comfortable work environment for staff. On the other hand, requiring staff to use the public entrance/exit point can foster staff-user interactions outside of a formal customer-service setting while, at the same time, requiring staff to pass through the library security perimeter just as library users do.

### Emergency Exits

Emergency exits are perfect examples of how security and safety can conflict. Required by building codes, emergency exits are an absolute must for safety while, at the same time, an absolute bust for security. Of course, each emergency exit should be alarmed and outfitted with appropriate ALARM WILL SOUND! signage. An observant thief, however, will soon discover that, in most libraries, staff response time to such alarms is far too slow to catch someone in the act, especially when emergency exits are far removed from staffed service points. In large library buildings, it is common for staff to first learn that an emergency exit alarm has sounded when a library user shows up at a service desk to complain about the ongoing noise. Emergency exits—especially those with a known history of misuse—are excellent locations for security cameras.

### Library Restrooms

Library restrooms present special security and safety problems for two main reasons:

- Of necessity, restrooms provide concealment.
- Unlike other library spaces, there is at least some expectation of privacy in a restroom.

There are no easy solutions to the security and safety problems posed by library restrooms. One good design practice is to choose sturdy, vandalism-resistant restroom furniture and fixtures. Another design practice that many libraries (and other public buildings) have adopted is the doorless, zigzag type of restroom entrance that provides privacy without providing the sense of concealment created by solid doors that close shut. A reasonable staff-based solution is to have library staff (males in the men's room; females in the women's room) pop in to restrooms when they do building walk-throughs. Of course none of these practices is an ironclad solution and, short of hiring full-time restroom attendants/guards, the fact remains that bad behavior is going to take place in library restrooms. And vandalism is not the worst of it. Running the search "library restrooms sex" through any Internet search engine will give some idea of the shocking extent of the problems libraries face. It is not unheard of for a specific library restroom to develop a widespread reputation as a favored location for sexual trysts, drawing to the library visitors with no interest in using the library, or its restrooms, for legitimate purposes.

## Security and Safety during a Building Project

Even the smallest libraries have at least some accommodations for security, though it amounts to nothing more than securely locked doors and, with luck, a theft detection system. All libraries, regardless of size, should have plans for what to do in emergencies, including evacuation plans for getting everyone safely out of the building in case of fire or other emergency. A major building project, however, can dramatically alter library security systems and evacuation plans, as well as introduce new threats to security and safety. Careful analysis and planning are necessary to ensure that security and safety are not compromised during construction. In addition, the construction site itself needs to be secure so that unauthorized personnel do not enter, intentionally or inadvertently, into areas where they may be injured or help themselves to building supplies or equipment.

## Public Safety

When it comes to the public, the first priority during any building project must be safety. While the safety of the public is primarily the responsibility of the general contractor, library staff need to fully support worksite safety practices, even to the extent of pointing out (through proper channels) unsafe conditions or practices which might escape the general contractor's notice. When constructing an entirely new library building, keeping the public safe is fairly straightforward—the general contractor should fence off the construction site and tightly control access. Construction sites are extremely dangerous places for those unfamiliar with their many hazards, not properly trained on construction safety, or unsupplied with adequate safety clothing and equipment. Crane collapses provide an excellent and dramatic illustration of the dangers lurking on construction sites. From 1997 to 2006, the United States suffered 818 crane-related occupational fatalities (Bureau of Labor Statistics, 2008). A single 2008 crane collapse in Manhattan left seven dead, including six construction workers and an area resident (Neuman and Bagli, 2008).

While the most basic security begins with the general contractor erecting secure fencing around the entire construction site, additional security enhancements may incorporate such measures as camera-based surveillance systems, access control devices (locks and keys), and around-the-clock security guards. The extent of construction site security will depend upon the locality, the likelihood of crime, the funding available for crime prevention, and the size and duration of the project.

Maintaining public safety during an addition, renovation, or remodel (ARR) project is even more challenging than during a new-building project because the public may come in close proximity to construction work as well as to construction vehicles negotiating the same roads and parking lots used by the public. Signage and barriers are the minimum requirement for public safety. Contractors may need to take even greater measures such as erecting secure covers over walkways to protect pedestrians from falling objects, employing flaggers to manage traffic flow, or providing full-time guards to keep the public a safe distance from any danger. During major ARR projects there may be times when the only way to keep the public safe is to temporarily close the library until the most potentially dangerous work has been completed.

## Construction Site Crime

Estimates of the total cost of construction-related crime in the United States range from hundreds of millions to billions of dollars annually. The reason for such high dollar figures is that construction sites present a cornucopia of opportunities for an industrious thief. Heavy machinery, ranging from large towed generators to backhoes, are popular targets for well-organized and well-equipped thieves. On the other end of the scale, a casual worksite trespasser can easily grab a cordless drill or other power tool that will bring enough at the local pawn shop to buy a hit or two of the thief's street drug of choice. But not all construction site crimes are committed by trespassers to the worksite. A major element of construction site crime involves contractors stealing from other contractors or employees stealing from their own employers. Whatever the source of theft, it serves to increase the cost of construction—a cost that is ultimately paid by customers, libraries included.

Besides equipment, construction site thieves will steal building materials such as wood, steel, glass, brick, and concrete. Metals are especially desirable targets for thieves. Whenever the price of scrap metal rises, most metropolitan areas quickly develop robust black markets at which one can exchange metal for cash, no questions asked. Besides stealing intrinsically valuable metals—copper is a favorite target—from construction sites, scrap metal thieves can also do costly damage as they have no compunction about destroying drywall, studs, or other in-place building materials in order to make off with electrical cables, copper pipes, and other metallic treasures.

Crime on construction sites is so common and so prevalent that many municipalities have created construction site crime awareness and prevention programs. In addition to programs managed by local law enforcement agencies, several crime prevention organizations track construction crime and work with contractors to prevent crime on construction sites. Crime prevention organizations such as the National Crime Prevention Council (NCPC) and the Crime Prevention Coalition of America (CPCA) provide training and support to prevent crime, including construction site crime, and help further the efforts of local and regional crime prevention organizations. The construction industry has several organizations dedicated to tracking, quantifying, and deterring construction site crime. The Construction Industry Crime Prevention Program (CICPP) is one example. Founded in 1971, the CICPP has chapters throughout the western United States. Each CICPP chapter has its own website, and the national organization holds annual meetings, issues publications, and coordinates with other construction-related organizations.

As mentioned, construction site security is usually the responsibility of the contractor, not the library. However, when thieves see a library in the midst of an ARR project, they do not see a library; they see a construction site ripe for the picking. And once thieves have gained access to that construction site, nothing prevents their path of theft and destruction from extending beyond those areas that are the contractor's responsibility and into areas that are solely the library's responsibility. A scrap metal thief who is looting the worksite of an addition to an existing library might well decide that ripping wire out of the existing library building is just as profitable as taking wire out of the part that is under construction.

The important point is that the library should not assume it is totally insulated from construction site crime or that it need not do all it can to aid the general contractor in preventing theft and related damage.

## Theft of Collections and Equipment

Theft of collection materials and equipment is a concern when any combination of the public, library staff, or construction workers can exit the building without passing through the library's normal security perimeter or when library security devices are simply out of commission as a result of work being done in the building. This often occurs during ARR projects, including at the end of a project when books and equipment are back in place but the formal handoff from contractor to tenant has not yet occurred. Of course honest contractors do not want their employees stealing from their clients, but it never hurts to reemphasize the importance of collection and equipment security with the general contractor before the start of a project. Another good step to take prior to the start of a project is to make sure all library equipment (computers spring to mind) has been properly property-tagged with serial numbers recorded. In extreme cases, it may be necessary to establish staffed security checkpoints to discourage theft. Especially valuable or desirable collection materials and equipment may need to be locked away, possibly off-site, until the library building is fully commissioned and secure.

Though not always possible, it is best if normal security measures remain in place during a building project. If the library maintains a single exit point with a theft detection system or a security guard, these measures should be maintained during construction, if not augmented to compensate for any security holes—some quite literal—resulting from construction activities. For example, if a remodeling project requires the library to temporarily establish an alternate exit, and if it is too costly to relocate the security gates, then it is prudent to hire a security guard and adjust policies to accommodate bag checks or other controls against theft. When security gates are not available or out of commission due to construction, a simple yet effective trick is to record the usual security gate alarm sound, play it randomly a few times per day, and go through the motions of verifying that items are properly checked out. Even without the presence of visible security gates, most users will assume that normal security measures are operating normally.

## Accidental Damage to Collections and Equipment

During an ARR project the likeliest accidental threats to existing collections and equipment are dirt and dampness, both common by-products of construction. Less common but more serious threats can arise from such construction-related disasters as fires, burst pipes, errant bulldozers, and everything else that can go terribly wrong on a worksite. Of special concern to human safety is off-gassing from such building products as adhesives, floor coverings, paint, and treated wood. Preventing and responding to construction-related threats is largely an exercise in common sense coupled with sound emergency planning and training.

For building projects of short duration where the risk of anything more than a little dust is remote, covering collections and vulnerable equipment (including carpet and furniture) with plastic may be sufficient; for larger or more complicated projects, collections and equipment may need to be moved to parts of the building unaffected by construction or removed from the building entirely. (Moving collections and materials out of the library building is discussed in detail in Chapter 9, "Running a Library during an Addition, Renovation, or Remodeling.") Beyond the obvious example of books in the stacks, some library equipment (again, computers spring to mind) may require special measures to keep safe from damage or theft. Construction zones can sometimes be sealed off by covering doorways and corridors with heavy-duty plastic sheeting. In more extreme cases, as when a new addition ties into an existing structure, it may be necessary to use wood panels or other heavy-duty construction materials to properly seal off the construction area (and seal out inclement weather) for the several months it may take before the new structure can be fully tied in to the existing structure.

The physical stresses and strains imposed on an existing building by activities undertaken as part of an ARR project can often cause systems in the existing building to fail. As just one example, it is common for fire sprinkler systems and other piping to develop at their joints small amounts of corrosion that actually help keep the system sealed and prevent leaks. As the building is bumped and vibrated from site preparation and other construction activity, these small rusty spots can break loose, exposing a leak that a bit of rust may have been holding in check for decades. Although over the course of an ARR project there is little that can be done to predict or prevent such occurrences, frequent inspections by building managers and other trained facilities personnel can sometimes identify potential problems before they occur, thereby averting costly disasters. In the end, the best that library staff can do is be extra vigilant and fully prepared to respond quickly and effectively when problems reveal themselves. The two most basic yet essential preparation steps include staging emergency supplies throughout any areas that might be affected and training staff on what to do when the worst happens. Practice drills that include such activities as throwing sheet plastic over bookshelves and furniture will prove worth the effort (and then some) when water unexpectedly begins gushing from the ceiling tiles.

### Safety for Animals

It may seem somewhat odd to include a discussion on the safety of animals during building projects, but it is a legitimate concern. Many wild animals have adapted well to urban life and need to be protected from their own curiosity. For example, raccoons, a familiar urban interloper, are highly adaptive, curious, and potentially dangerous visitors to construction sites. Largely nocturnal, raccoons rarely venture onto a construction site during daylight working hours; however, it takes only a few lunchbox leftovers or a dumpster with some uneaten scraps to attract raccoons and other feral creatures onto a potentially dangerous construction site.

The authors of this book were involved in a library construction project which saw a semiferal animal in the form of a stray dachshund mix running frantic circles through various parts of a partially completed library building. While the dog's antics were more than a little amusing (and best seen to be appreciated), his wild circuits of the building had him repeatedly skittering across two incomplete concrete bridges suspended 20 feet above the floor below. Fortunately, before the dog suffered a potentially fatal fall, he was caught and placed in a good home where, as of this writing, he enjoys life as a thriving, loved, and pampered house pet.

As metropolitan areas grow and encroach on wild lands, animals far more wild than a stray dachshund come into contact with humans and their buildings. One such case involved a mountain lion that took up residence in a partially constructed building during a particularly violent storm. If her mere presence in the building was not problem enough, the lioness promptly gave birth to a litter of kittens. Although local animal control personnel were able to capture the adult female and move the whole family to a safe location, construction came to a complete halt for two days while the situation was resolved, and during those two days armed security personnel had to remain on hand to ensure that those working nearby were kept safe from the lioness. While few would argue against the need to protect human life in such a situation, a terribly tragedy would have nonetheless played out had security personnel been forced to kill a mother whose prime motivation was to protect her newborn cubs. Such tragedies can be averted by entering a project with a good knowledge of what local animals may be endangered by the project, erecting fencing capable of keeping *all* local animals (not just *Homo sapiens sapiens*) from entering the construction site, and following good practices for preventing food and other attractants from luring animals into danger.

### Building Evacuations

During an ARR project, the likelihood of building emergency alarms going off is far higher than during periods of normal library operations. Everything from technicians reconnecting wires to dust from a carpenter's saw can set off emergency alarms. Whatever the cause of an emergency alarm, and no matter how frequent and annoying the emergency alarms become, everyone must remember that every emergency alarm is *always* real even if the cause turns out to be no threat to life and safety. The very phrase *false alarm* is so misleading, inaccurate, and potentially life threatening that it should never be used by library managers; its use by library staff should also be discouraged. Because every alarm is real, when the emergency alarm sounds everyone must evacuate the building and not return until someone with the proper authority to do so—firefighter, fire marshal, or police officer—gives the all clear. It is very important to remember that neither contractors nor their employees have the authority to allow anyone to reenter a building after an emergency alarm has sounded. Even if a construction worker firmly believes that something he or she did caused the emergency alarm to go off and that there is no danger, that worker has no business telling people it is safe to reenter the building.

Prior to any ARR project, it is essential that the library review its safety procedures so that everyone on the staff knows exactly what to do when the emergency alarm sounds. Some organizations follow a policy in which all staff are required to leave the building immediately. In other organizations, selected staff members have assignments that call for them to help clear the building, if it is safe to do so. Whatever the policy, each staff member must know what he or she is expected to do and how to do it in the safest possible way. Everyone on the staff needs to be familiar with the following information: (1) the location of the mandatory staff assembly point and (2) that when there is an emergency alarm all staff must report to *and remain at* the mandatory assembly point until the all clear is given. (Staff with emergency assignments should report as soon as those assignments are completed.)

The staff assembly point must be located far enough from the building to provide safety and so that staff do not hinder emergency vehicles trying to get to the building. Requiring all staff to report to and remain at the mandatory assembly point is the only way to know whether any staff are still in the building should the "false alarm" turn out to be a genuine emergency. It is not acceptable for staff to show up at the assembly point and then go to lunch because it is five minutes to noon. Everyone must remain assembled until the all clear is given. Conducting an unannounced fire drill (with the cooperation of the local fire marshal) a week or so before the start of an ARR project is an excellent way to stress test building evacuation procedures and correct any deficiencies.

### Postconstruction

After construction is complete, be sure to conduct a careful examination and evaluation of emergency pathways and exits. While architects adhere to codes and try to employ basic common sense, what may appear to be perfectly reasonable on a blueprint may, in fact, turn out to be a recipe for disaster in a real emergency. Poorly lighted hallways are one common design flaw that may remain hidden until after a project is completed, but there are others. It is good practice to stage a postconstruction evacuation drill to make sure that emergency alarms sound, the public address system functions, emergency exit doors open freely, exit pathways remain clear, and all other safety features work properly.

In a similar vein, another problem to watch for involves changes caused by small building-improvement projects that may partially block exit pathways or create trip hazards. For example, the new drinking fountain installed for the convenience of those using the children's area may unfortunately prove to be a major obstacle for wheelchair users during an emergency.

## Conclusion

A well-designed library building that incorporates adequate security and safety features is not, by itself, going to keep everything secure and everyone safe. However, it is a great start. Matching such a building to staff that understand not only how to respond to emergencies but also how to identify threats to security and safety before they have a chance to unfold will bring a library as close to security and safety perfection as it is possible to be.

## References

American Library Association. 2010. "Library Bill of Rights." American Library Association. http://www.ala.org/ala/issuesadvocacy/intfreedom/librarybill/index.cfm.
Bureau of Labor Statistics. 2008. *Crane-Related Occupational Fatalities: Fact Sheet.* BLS.gov, July. http://www.bls.gov/iif/oshwc/osh/os/osh_crane_2006.pdf.
Neuman, William, and Charles V. Bagli. 2008. "Fall of Six-Ton Support Caused Crane to Topple." *New York Times*, March 17. http://www.nytimes.com/2008/03/17/nyregion/17 building.html.

# 8

# Green Libraries

Since the turn of the twenty-first century it seems to have become impossible for anyone to launch a library building project without some measure of public boasting about the project's green features: energy efficiency, water conservation, small carbon footprint, green building materials, recycling programs, and on and on. This focus on greenness is due in part to the fact that people who work in libraries, by and large, care about the environment and truly want their workplaces to be part of the solution, not part of the problem. At the same time, the green library is also a no-lose public-relations strategy. It is very unlikely, after all, that someone is going to write a scathing letter to the editor blasting a library for going green. To the socially conscious, a green building says the library cares about its impact on people and the environment; to budget hawks, a green building spells reduced operating costs through lowered energy and water consumption.

In a growing number of cases, building green is no longer an option. For example, the University of California system recently updated its *Policy on Sustainable Practices and Guidelines*, which mandates green practices in all University of California operations and specifically calls for the incorporation of "the principles of energy efficiency and sustainability in all capital projects, renovation projects, operations and maintenance within budgetary constraints and programmatic requirements" (University of California, Sustainability Steering Committee, 2009: 1). Similarly, in the year 2000 the city of Portland mandated at least LEED Silver Certification for all of its new facilities and in 2008 was pursuing a "High Performance Green Building Policy" (Armstrong, 2008: 3–4).

With claims to greenness becoming, by choice or force, nearly as pro forma as standing up for motherhood and apple pie, it is important to recognize that even when one truly wants to make a building (and the library operations housed within it) green, choosing the greenest path is not always easy. Consider the following examples:

- Leather is a superior upholstery material because there is no off-gassing.
  - But the industrial process of tanning leather can be damaging to the environment, as can the raising of the cattle from which leather is made.
- Reducing, or even banning, the use of disposable plates, cups, and utensils in the staff lounge will make the library greener.

- But what about the water required to wash nondisposables and the energy required to heat that water?
- Steel studs are greener than wood 2x4s because no trees are cut down to make them.
  - But iron ore is mined, steel smelted, and, in most cases, the finished studs shipped over vast distances. None of those processes is very green.
- Electronic books and journals are greener than those printed on tree-destroying paper.
  - But the electronic devices required to serve and access e-books and e-journals consume electricity.
  - But because e-books and e-journals can be accessed from anywhere, they save fuel that would otherwise be used making a trip to the library.
  - But books made on quality paper can be reused time and again over hundreds of years without consuming any additional energy.
  - That is if you do not count the vast amounts of energy required to climate control the spaces in which printed books should be stored if they are to last hundreds of years.
  - But anything made of paper can be recycled at the end of its useful life.

And would you prefer to carry your purchase home in tree-killing paper or ocean-choking plastic? (Neither. You, of course, bring your own reusable cloth bags with you when you go shopping.) The arguments about what path is greenest can go around and around, often fueled by the sometimes spurious claims of business interests that do not let inconvenient truths get in the way when it comes to convincing the world that their product is greener than the competition's. In a world of competing, possibly bogus, claims to greenness, it is crucial to base green decisions on the best available evidence rather than on gut reactions or manufacturers' claims. It is also necessary to factor in local circumstances when thinking green. In an area with water shortages, strong recycling programs, and plenty of space for landfill, using disposable plates, cups, and utensils

---

### The Award for the World's Greenest Library Building: And the Winner Is...

Is the greenest car a hybrid, plug-in, or a fuel-cell vehicle? No. The greenest car is the one you did not drive today because you instead walked, rode a bike, took public transportation, or carpooled.

Similarly, the world's greenest library building is not the one that requires the least energy, consumes the least water, uses the greenest building materials, produces the least waste, or wins the most green-building awards. The greenest library building is the one that was never built. Zero consumption. Zero emissions. Zero environmental impact.

Before any building project gets under way, anyone who truly cares about the environment must honestly ask if the project is necessary and, more to the point, if there is a way to meet the intended goals of the building project without undertaking it in the first place.

*(Continued)*

---

**The Award for the World's Greenest Library Building:**
**And the Winner Is . . . *(Continued)***

Thinking green means asking some cynical questions:

- Is the building project being undertaken chiefly to allow the library to warehouse more books, many of which are rarely used and could be weeded or warehoused off-site?
- Is the building project being undertaken to pump up the egos of alumni, faculty, politicians, or donors?
- Is the building project being undertaken simply because there is money available to do it?
- Is the building project nothing more than empire building?

If the answer to these or similarly cynical questions is *yes*, then the greenest option is to stand up and say *no* to the proposed building project. Few things in this world are more wasteful than building something that is not necessary.

But saying *no* to a new project—especially one that is touted as a paradigm of green building—is hard to do. Suppose a public library needs a new branch. Option #1 is to lease an empty strip-mall storefront that could be turned into a branch library with minimal remodeling. Option #2 is to build a brand-new, state-of-the-art green building tricked out with amazing earth-saving features. Option #1 is not going to generate the enthusiasm and warm congratulations of Option #2, but talk about recycling. Option #1 recycles an entire building, lock, stock, and barrel. Unlike a new building, Option #1 does not burn the hundreds of barrels of fuel required to ship building materials to a worksite and build a structure from the ground up. Because Option #1's strip-mall site already has parking, there is no need to add more pavement to the face of the planet. Maybe Option #1's location is close to the library's user population so there will be less traveling involved to get there? Maybe Option #1 is located along existing public-transport routes so staff and users could use their cars less or not at all? Maybe a few green features could be added to Option #1: a high-efficiency heating, ventilation, and air-conditioning (HVAC) system; an automated lighting-control system that uses high-efficiency bulbs; skylights or clerestory windows to enhance daylighting; low-VOC (volatile organic compounds) carpeting manufactured in part from recycled materials?

Every situation is unique, but that shiny new, Option #2 green building would need to be extraordinarily efficient, and remain in use for a very long time, before it turned out to be greener than reusing an existing building that was somewhat less efficient and a good deal less headline grabbing.

---

may be the greenest option. In an area with ample water but little space for landfills, nondisposables may be the greenest way to go.

## How Much Green Does It Take to Go Green?

*We really want to build green, but we just cannot afford to do so under the current budget realities.*

Does building green really cost more than building with traditional materials and methods? The conventional wisdom is that while the up-front costs of building green are higher than for traditional construction, the long-term savings of going green eventually offset those initially higher costs. What has informed the conventional wisdom on green buildings?

- Green building techniques are likely to be unfamiliar to designers and builders, resulting in higher costs because of the additional research and learning curves new techniques require. For example, in order to make up for the extra time required to complete an unfamiliar task, plumbing contractors who are installing a tankless water heater for the first time are likely to charge more than for installing a traditional water heater of the sort they have installed hundreds of times.
- Some green building materials and products are more expensive because they are inherently more complicated than their nongreen equivalents. A sophisticated lighting control system equipped with light and motion detectors is more complicated and costly than a traditional lighting system operated by manual switches.
- Some green building materials and products are more expensive simply because they are specialty items and so are not produced on as large a scale as nongreen equivalents.

The conventional wisdom, however, may be changing, if not flat-out wrong. For example, studies conducted by architects Lisa Matthiessen and Davis Langdon show essentially no difference in the cost per square foot of LEED-certified laboratory buildings versus non-LEED-certified laboratory buildings (Yudelson, 2007: 122). One reason for this reduction in cost is that, as building green has become more common and its techniques better understood by those in the design and construction trades, initial costs are falling in line with traditional construction practices. At the same time, the increased demand for green building materials has spurred manufacturers to produce them in larger quantities, resulting in economies of scale and transforming green building materials from exotic special-order items into products that can be purchased off the shelf.

On the other side of the cost equation, what are the long-term financial payoffs from going green? The answer to this question is found by calculating the life cycle cost of green versus nongreen options. The life cycle cost (also known as "total cost of ownership") is based on the original purchase cost, energy savings (if any), and lifetime operating and maintenance costs (including final disposal costs at the end of the life cycle). Say, for example a green roof costs 30 percent more than a nongreen roof. However, if that green roof is projected to have a 25 percent longer life span, reduce heating and cooling cost by 30 percent, reduce maintenance costs by 65 percent, and cost 90 percent less to dispose of at the end of its useful life, the numbers could well add up to a lower life cycle cost for the green versus nongreen roof. When calculating life cycle costs, it is important to accurately estimate future (most likely increased) costs for energy, maintenance, and disposal. As another example, suppose that a building is designed to take the fullest advantage of natural daylighting. Such a building will save not only on electricity but also on the labor, material, and disposal costs of replacing burned-out lightbulbs as well as on the costs of repairing or replacing light fixtures that will last longer in a building that takes full advantage of daylighting than they will in a nongreen building that relies heavily on electric lights.

When considering life cycle costs, it is important to play the game honestly, for as much as we might want the green products to come out on top, this is not always the case. The quick conclusion when evaluating the cost of waterless urinals is that they must win the life cycle contest because they do not consume any water. However, waterless urinals require rather expensive filter cartridges that need to be replaced on a regular schedule. Not taking the cost of the cartridges and the labor to replace them into consideration would be as unfair an analysis as not accounting for future increases in energy costs when analyzing the life cycle costs of putting window shades on the south and west sides of a building. (That said, waterless urinals may still come out as money savers, especially in areas where water and sewer costs are high.)

For a real-world example of how building green can pay off, consider the Harvard Green Campus Institute (HGCI), a Harvard University loan fund that finances green building projects across the university. It cost Harvard $1.3 million to run the HGCI for one year; during that same year, the university's HGCI-financed green buildings saved Harvard $6 million in energy and other costs. Says HGCI director Leith Sharp, "We're seeing an ROI [return on investment] of more than 30 percent. Our Loan Fund is presently a better investment now than the Harvard Endowment" (Gould, 2007).

Another real-world example comes from an energy-saving project undertaken in 2008 at the University of California, Davis's 400,710-square-foot Shields Library, the largest building on the UC Davis campus. The project consisted of three measures:

- Ten of the building's 12 air handlers were reconfigured to run for only five of 30 minutes during evening hours instead of running around the clock every day.
- Motion-activated light-control sensors were installed at the end of each aisle of the book stacks so that the lights in an aisle come on only when a sensor detects motion. The lights then shut off after two to five minutes with no detectable motion in the aisle. This is in contrast to the previous practice of keeping all book stack lights on from 6:00 a.m. to midnight.
- After closing, lights come on only in areas where motion sensors detect janitorial night-crew staff at work. Previously, lights were left on around the clock during the school year. This last measure was initially implemented only in the library's east wing but then expanded to the entire library in 2010.

Table 8.1 shows a breakdown of the verified yearly savings resulting from these three energy-saving measures.

Somewhat less easy to put on a ledger are the savings green buildings bring in terms of occupant health and productivity. Such green-building benefits as ample natural light, well-circulated fresh air, and little or no off-gassing contribute to healthier, more productive library workers and users. When library staff are neither missing days nor working at a diminished capacity due to such sick-building-syndrome effects as the allergic reactions caused by carpets, upholstery, or paint, the long-term savings in sick-leave and health-care benefits can prove to be significant, if hard to quantify.

The central problem that anyone pushing for building green faces is that the extra costs of building green—if, indeed, there are extra costs—are in-your-face costs that

### Table 8.1
### Shields Library Energy Savings

| Measure | Kilowatt Hours Saved per Year | Estimated Dollars Saved per Year * |
|---|---|---|
| Night HVAC reduction | 297,500 | 48,726 |
| Aisle motion detectors | 595,101 | 70,909 |
| Nightlighting reduction | 43,600 | 12,383 |
| **Totals** | 936,201 | 132,018 |

*Source:* QuEST 2009: 12.

*These dollar amounts are based on the July 2009 California commercial rate of 16.38 cents per kilowatt hour. Energy Information Administration, "Average Retail Price of Electricity to Ultimate Customers by End-Use Sector, by State." 2009. United States Department of Energy. http://www.eia.doe.gov/cneaf/electricity/epm/table5_6_a.html.

must be paid today in real dollars. The long-term payoffs of going green, conversely, are off in the hazy future and therefore somewhat intangible. Sadly, it can be a challenge to get budget managers, politicians, or campus administrators to care as deeply about payoffs that may not be realized until well after they have retired or left office as they care about getting through the current fiscal year.

### LEED Certification

LEED (Leadership in Energy and Environmental Design) is a standards-based green-building rating and certification system administered by the U.S. Green Building Council (USGBC).* As of 2009, LEED ratings are based on a 100-point scale with extra points available for innovation. The LEED ratings categories break down as follows:

- **Certified**: 40 to 49 points
- **Silver**: 50 to 59 points
- **Gold**: 60 to 79 points
- **Platinum**: 80-plus points

A building can earn LEED points by meeting such USGBC standards as green worksite practices, management of storm water runoff, on-site generation of clean energy, the use of recycled building materials, and so on.

Earning LEED certification can be a public-relations triumph, but, more important, it is a way of ensuring that a building project is truly green. Without a set of standards such as those provided by the USGBC, what makes any particular building green becomes so subjective as to be meaningless. An additional benefit from seeking and earning LEED certification is that a growing number of municipalities and states offer incentives for buildings that earn LEED certification. On the other hand, a building project should never be focused on chasing LEED points. Architects should not call for employee showers merely to get a LEED point; they should do it to encourage bicycle commuting by employees who would otherwise drive.

The biggest disadvantage of seeking LEED certification is that it can add to the cost of the building. In some cases, meeting LEED standards means paying more for green building materials and/or contractor services. In every case the building's owner must pay the cost of having a required commissioning authority verify exactly which LEED standards have been met.

*(Continued)*

**LEED Certification** *(Continued)*

Like all standards created by mere mortals, the LEED standards fall short of perfection. For example, as of 2009 LEED recognizes as sustainable only timber that has been certified by the Forest Stewardship Council even though there are other bodies, such as the Canadian Standards Association, which certify timber as sustainable. In defense of USGBC, LEED standards have evolved as new products and building practices emerge and as environmental concerns shift.

LEED is not just about new buildings, major expansions, remodeling, or renovations. LEED-EB (Existing Buildings) is a program that provides a thorough evaluation of an existing building with the goals of improving green practices within that building and engaging staff in the effort to operate in the greenest way possible.

More information about LEED certification is available on the USGBC website at http://www.usgbc.org.

*In Canada, the Canadian Green Building Council (CaGBC) performs a similar function using a version of the LEED standards adapted to better meet Canada's climate and resource needs.

## What Makes a Building Green?

The U.S. Green Building Council's LEED program identifies five key performance areas for evaluating a building's impact on the environment and sustainability—or, in other words, for evaluating its greenness:

- Sustainable site development
- Water savings
- Energy efficiency
- Materials selection
- Indoor environmental quality (U.S. Green Building Council, 2008: 1)

### Sustainable Site Development

The greenest building in the world is no friend of the environment if it is sited without consideration for its environmental impact. With respect to the lands surrounding it, an ideal green building is sited away from critical wetlands, above any 100-year (or more frequent) floodplains, and in such a way that its untreated stormwater runoff does not drain into fragile waterways or onto farmlands. In addition, though perhaps less critically, the finished building is sited and designed so that its interior and exterior lighting is not a source of light pollution for the surrounding area and the wildlife that occupies it. To save energy and reduce carbon emissions, a green building is sited close to its main user population and to existing transportation infrastructure. Building on reclaimed land, such as a brownfield, is much greener than building on land that has not previously been used for building.

Once a suitable site has been chosen, how that site is prepared has significant environmental implications. Preventing runoff from the construction site, minimizing the compacting of soil, taking measures to leave wildlife undisturbed, and preserving as much natural vegetation and open space as possible are all examples of green site development practices.

Once actual construction begins, what takes place on the worksite can be a major source of pollution and waste if green practices are not followed. Perhaps the most significant worksite measure contractors can take is to recycle construction waste, a practice that is not only green but also saves contractors some of the often-substantial costs of disposing of construction waste in landfills. Other ways that contractors can add to the greenness of a project include maintaining a clean worksite to minimize litter, preventing spills of potentially damaging substances, and using heavy equipment outfitted with modern, clean-burning diesel engines. Green construction practices actively prevent dust and moisture from getting into ductwork or behind sheetrock, thereby providing for a cleaner indoor environment from the first day of occupancy.

To assure your contractors accept the idea that doing their work in the greenest way possible is central to a building project—that it is not just an add-on done for show—green worksite practices should be written into construction bidding documents with points awarded to those contractors who can demonstrate that they are able, and willing, to work green.

### Water Savings

A building's use of water is a two-way green street. On the incoming lane is the total amount of fresh water a building consumes. The less water, the greener the building. Restroom technology, such as waterless urinals, low-flow toilets, and automatic faucets, are proven ways to lower total water consumption. Another significant way to conserve fresh water is to landscape outdoor areas with drought-resistant native plants and waterless features such as gravel beds and rock gardens. High-efficiency irrigation systems—possibly incorporating drip-irrigation components—save water while allowing oxygen-producing trees, shrubs, and flowers to flourish.

On the outgoing lane of the two-way street is the wastewater a building sends into the environment in the forms of sewage and stormwater runoff. Obviously, the less water a building consumes, the less it sends to the sewage treatment plant. In jurisdictions where the practice is allowed, capturing and reusing gray water (storm runoff and nonsewage wastewater) for such purposes as flushing toilets and irrigation reduces both wastewater output as well as consumption of fresh water. On-site wastewater treatment can play a role in any effort to reuse gray water.

### Energy Efficiency

In the United States, buildings consume about 40 percent of all energy used nationwide and, as a direct result, account for about 37 percent of carbon emissions nationwide (Environmental and Energy Study Institute, 2009: 1). Because of the hard-money costs of energy and the environmental costs of carbon emissions, improving a building's overall energy efficiency by reducing the amount of energy it consumes is one green benefit that everyone from treehuggers to bean counters can appreciate.

Mechanical and lighting systems are the big energy eaters in any building, so acquiring, properly commissioning, and performing regular maintenance on high-efficiency HVAC, water-heating, automatic lighting, and other energy-dependent systems is a proven way of enhancing a building's energy efficiency. However, simply plugging energy-efficient systems into a building that was designed without regard for energy efficiency is a bit like sticking a bandage on a gunshot wound. Prior to the widespread adoption of electric lighting and massive central HVAC systems, architects designed buildings to make the most of natural heating, cooling, and lighting. This was not because people were more concerned with energy efficiency back in the old days; they simply had no alternatives for keeping a building comfortable. Once architects came to depend on HVAC and electric lights, they were able to toss out the old rule book and create the kind of energy-dependent buildings epitomized by the slick steel-and-glass tower devoid of operable windows, awnings, transoms, adequate daylighting, and just about any other comfort or lighting benefit nature can provide. Today, concerns about energy consumption and carbon output have spurred an increasing number of architects to turn to the concept of integrated design, in which buildings are made functional and comfortable in part by incorporating high-tech, energy-saving systems and in part by making the most of natural lighting, heating, and cooling.

Green buildings that adhere to the principles of integrated design may:

- Incorporate insulating and reflective building materials. Cool roofs, for example, can reduce building cooling costs as well as the urban heat-island effect that has driven up temperatures in many cities.
- Orient buildings to reduce the heating effect of direct sunlight. In North America, this means orienting the length of a building along an east-west axis.
- Use sunshades to keep direct sunlight off windows.
- Use operable windows where feasible.
- Employ daylighting designs that make the most of natural light. Daylighting designs call for rectangular, rather than square, buildings so that daylight can reach all areas of a building.
- Employ displacement ventilation to allow natural, nonmechanical forces to redistribute air in order to maximize the cooling and circulation of fresh air. Underfloor displacement ventilation systems are especially desirable in libraries because they not only enhance natural airflow but also allow for the easy, low-cost rerouting of power and data cables.

Although not a way to reduce energy consumption per se, a building's carbon footprint can be minimized either through on-site green energy generation or through the purchasing of green energy from the energy grid. Green energy is defined as energy generated from such nonpolluting, sustainable sources as wind, solar, geothermal, and hydro, though some also include nuclear power under the green energy heading.

When energy-efficient equipment, integrated energy-saving design, and on-site green energy production are all successfully employed, it is possible for a building to reach the zenith of energy greenness, the triple-zero building:

- Zero net energy consumption
- Zero waste
- Zero emissions

## Materials Selection

Once considered exotic, green building materials are becoming increasingly common both because of demand and because they are, in some cases, proving to be cheaper and more durable than their traditional counterparts. For one common example, homeowners can now walk into any retail lumber or home improvement store and purchase decking boards made from wood-plastic composite (WPC), an extremely durable building material composed of recovered cellulose-based waste products (chiefly sawdust, but also such waste materials as straw and peanut shells) combined with recycled or virgin plastics.

Because using green building materials is key to the greenness of any building project, and because some manufacturers overstate the greenness of their products, it is important to understand what characteristics qualify any particular building material as green.

### Recycled and Recyclable

Building materials that incorporate recycled content have a green advantage over those made from virgin content, especially when that recycled content consists of materials that would otherwise go into landfills or be spewed into the air or water. Materials such as concrete, drywall, newspapers, and fly ash can be recycled into new building materials. Even greener is the practice of reusing structurally sound salvaged building materials, many of which can be reused without needing to undergo an energy-intensive recycling process.

On the other side of the recycling equation are the green benefits to be had from materials that can themselves easily be recycled at the ends of their useful lives. For example, manufacturers now produce commercial-grade broadloom carpeting that not only includes recycled content but which itself can be eventually recycled into new carpet without intensive, energy-consuming processing. For an example from the furniture arena, 99 percent of the component parts of the Steelcase Think chair can be recycled simply by disassembling the chair with a screwdriver and tossing the parts into standard recycling bins.

### Sustainable

Viable green options to traditional building materials include anything that can be regenerated in less than ten years, such as bamboo, cork, linoleum, and wheatboard composites. Bamboo, which is a grass, can be harvested for use as timber after two to seven years of cultivation, depending on the species. This compares to the decades, or even centuries, that must pass before most hardwood and softwood trees can be harvested. Cork can be stripped from a cork oak tree without harming the tree, linoleum is made largely from linseed oil and wood flour (a waste product), while the main components of wheatboard come from wheat chaff and straw.

Even though they take many years to grow, trees can nonetheless be used in sustainable ways. If lumber from a tree that takes 50 years to mature is used to build a piece of wood furniture that is constructed to last at least 75 years, the process is sustainable on the condition that new trees are planted to replace those harvested.

### Locally Sourced

Building materials originating from within 500 miles of a worksite are considered green because less energy is consumed in transporting them to the worksite in comparison to materials shipped from across the country or the planet.

### Energy-Saving Properties

Building materials that insulate from heat and cold or that reflect direct sunlight include insulation, reflective roofs, and ultraviolet (UV)-filtering windows. Building materials with energy-saving properties are not only green, but also have the potential to, over the life of a building, more than repay their purchase price in reduced energy costs.

### Products Made Using Green Manufacturing Processes

Those UV-filtering windows and low-VOC paints are, of course, all the greener if they are manufactured in plants that themselves strive to reduce energy consumption, minimize contributions to landfills, maximize sustainability, and do not release air or water pollutants into the environment.

## *Indoor Environmental Quality*

In a nutshell, indoor environmental quality involves eliminating or reducing indoor air pollutants that contribute to sick-building syndrome, providing sufficient fresh air to building occupants, and maintaining thermal comfort.

Off-gassing is the process by which building materials and furnishings release pollutants into the air, often in the form of VOCs (volatile organic compounds). VOCs are the components that make paint, coatings, glues, carpets, and new furniture smell and are a major contributor to sick-building syndrome. One of the most common VOCs is urea formaldehyde, a compound found in adhesives, finishes, molded plastics, and medium-density fiberboard. In worst-case scenarios, off-gassing processes can last for years, making building occupants sick all the while.

Off-gassing can be largely eliminated by insisting on low-VOC carpet, carpet pads, paint, varnishes, adhesives, engineered wood/fiber products, and fabrics. The furniture that goes into a building can be a major source of VOCs, so it is worth seeking out furniture supplied by companies that use low-VOC materials in their manufacturing processes. Using green cleaning products is another way to avoid sick-building syndrome, as traditional cleaning products may contain harsh, potentially harmful chemicals.

The healthiest buildings provide high levels of fresh air through the use of code-exceeding mechanical ventilation systems and natural ventilation. Besides reducing sick-building syndrome, proper ventilation reduces the buildup of indoor carbon dioxide. Among its other ill effects, carbon-dioxide buildup is a cause of sleepiness (and thus lower productivity) in workers. When people begin nodding off during a meeting in a crowded, stuffy room, it is more likely due to high carbon dioxide levels than that slide-show presentation on the future of the MARC record 850 field. A healthy building should also provide separate ventilation systems for areas that produce high levels of noxious or irritating air pollutants; examples include paint storage areas, rooms where chemicals are mixed, laboratories, kitchens, large copy rooms, and designated smoking areas.

Maintaining thermal comfort requires controlling temperature and humidity at levels appropriate for indoor activities. Thermal comfort is, to some extent, an example of one green goal that can conflict with a different goal—in this case, saving energy. However, as discussed, coupling efficient mechanical systems with integrated building design makes it possible to maintain thermal comfort without wasting energy. Libraries face a special and, to some extent, unsolvable problem in that the ideal thermal-comfort level for printed books is quite a bit lower than the ideal level for people. Temperatures in the stacks are always a compromise.

Windows play an important roll in indoor environmental quality. Because they are a ready source of natural ventilation, operable windows can bring significant volumes of fresh air into a building. Furthermore, the natural light windows provide is beneficial to workers' happiness and productivity. The U.S. Green Building Council recommends that at least 90 percent of all workspaces include a view of the outdoors (Yudelson, 2007: 18).

---

### Is It *Really* Green?

Doing research on a particular building material to evaluate its greenness is never a bad idea. It also pays to find out if a building material has been certified as green by an independent organization. In the case of wood products, the Forest Stewardship Council and the Canadian Standards Association both provide green certification. The word of a manufacturer that its product is green is not, by itself, sufficient evidence for informed decision making. Also be aware that some ostensibly independent certification authorities are nothing more than fronts for the industries whose products they allegedly certify as green.

It is important to acknowledge that almost no building material can have every green characteristic. The broadloom carpet that is green by virtue of being made locally may not have the recycled content of carpet manufactured on the opposite side of the country. The wonderful low-VOC paint may be manufactured from nonrenewable substances extracted under less than green conditions. Choosing any building material will always involve selecting the best from a number of imperfect options rather than uncovering some ideal product that is green in every possible way.

---

### *Designed to Be Repurposed*

Think of all the buildings you know of that have been repurposed. The old fire station that is now a restaurant. The church converted to art-house cinema. The old Main Street five-and-dime morphed into a trendy hair salon. Even easier, think of all the building interiors you know of that have been repurposed. The children's bedroom turned home office. The circa-1960 open-floor-plan office space carved up into private offices and cubicles. The library print-index area that is now a computer lab. The fact is that most buildings are used for a variety of purposes during the courses of their existence and virtually all interior spaces are routinely reconfigured to meet changing needs. The inevitability of all this change means that it is very green to design buildings so that they can be repurposed with a minimum of work and waste products. Buildings designed without load-bearing interior walls are remarkably easy to repurpose. Creating private offices out of modular components makes it possible not only to remove those offices but to also reuse their components for new offices rather than haul broken studs and drywall to the landfill. Even the much despised office cubicle is a green option because it is simple to reconfigure and reuse.

## Green Library Operations

Once a green library building project is completed, the way the library is operated can either carry on the project's green legacy or render it close to meaningless. Library operations that successfully conserve resources (chiefly energy and water) while reducing waste require buy-in from people who may be mystified by green practices or simply skeptical of the whole concept. Waterless urinals, for example, may seem weird to some members of the public, and so an explanation of why these unfamiliar devices have been installed is in order. The University of California, Santa Barbara's exceptionally green Bren Hall (LEED-certified platinum) handles this very communication through permanent restroom signage informing visitors that each waterless urinal saves an estimated (and astonishing) 45,000 gallons of water each year.

Explaining green practices to the library staff can be just as important as explaining them to the public. In a green library operation, custodial staff may be asked to stop using the effective, but not at all green, cleaning products with which they are familiar and to start using unfamiliar, but greener, products. Explaining both why this change is necessary as well as the benefits the new products bring to both the health of the planet and the health of the people using the products will go a long way toward winning acceptance from the custodial staff. Of course it also helps if the new green cleaning products work as well as the products they are replacing.

### Recycling

Most libraries already practice recycling and many have been doing so for years. Providing convenient recycling bins for both library staff and users and encouraging recycling are good for both the environment and the library budget. However, it is worth remembering that even the most efficient recycling process does not hold a candle to the green benefits of not having used the thing going to recycling in the first place. Not printing that important e-mail to a sheet of paper is far greener than printing and, later, recycling the paper. Taking a drink from the water fountain is far greener (and cheaper) than drinking water from a plastic bottle that eventually goes into the recycling.

### Green Transportation

Any library that considers itself green must take into consideration how staff and users transport themselves to the library. Imagine a library staff of 20, each of whom uses a private automobile to commute to work an average of 30 miles round trip per day. This adds up to 3,000 automobile miles traveled per five-day week. The energy consumed and carbon generated by all that travel is a load on the environment that is not going to be offset by the library's pledge to recycle copier paper and reset the thermostats a few energy-saving degrees. Encouraging both staff and the public to use either nonpolluting (biking, walking, skating) or less polluting (bus, train, carpool) transportation is an easy solution. Too easy. Anybody can stand on the sidelines and be a cheerleader for green transportation alternatives. The real question is what tangible incentives the organization is willing to tender so that leaving the gas-burner in the garage becomes an attractive and feasible alternative. Rather than just encourage, the organization could provide the following:

- Secure and convenient bicycle storage
  - Security and convenience are important. Joe Clerk is not riding his expensive road bike only to have it stolen or vandalized while he is working.
- Showers and changing rooms for staff who bike to work
  - There should be one shower for every ten bicycle commuters (Yudelson, 2007: 32).
- Free or discounted bus/train passes to employees who use public transport
- Incentives for staff who carpool
  - A reserved parking spot adjacent to the building is a huge incentive for carpoolers.
- Incentives for staff who do not park a car at work
  - As with a free lunch, there is no such thing as free parking. One hundred parking spots require nearly three-quarters of an acre of land. Staff who do not take up parking spaces deserve some tangible reward in return.
- Green vehicles
  - The library should replace any vehicles it operates with hybrid or other green vehicles. At the same time, the library could offer incentives for staff who use low-emission or high-mileage vehicles to commute to work.
- A management culture that is accepting of the uncertainties of alternative transportation
  - Janie Shelver will hesitate to use alternative transportation if she knows her boss is going to write her up for being late because the 7:45 bus did not arrive until 8:00 or her bike blew a tire halfway between work and home.
- A guaranteed ride home for staff who use alternative transportation
  - Catherine Cataloger would love to take the bus to work, but what is she supposed to do if she gets a call from the school saying her daughter is running a fever and needs to go home? Providing a solution to this dilemma—guaranteeing her a ride home—makes alternative transportation possible for a larger pool of employees.
- Opportunities for telecommuting
  - Telecommuting does not work for everyone. It does not work all the time. Implementing a telecommuting policy often involves taking on entrenched institutional employment policies that, too often, are based on antiquated models of employment and compensation. Even so, telecommuting policies that allow at least some staff to telecommute as little as one day a week have a big green impact and often result in happier, more productive employees.

---

**Recommended Reading: *Green Building A to Z***

Jerry Yudelson's *Green Building A to Z: Understanding the Language of Green Building* provides a highly readable introduction to the subject. In his definition of the term *sustainable design*, Yudelson provides something of a 13 commandments for building green:

- High levels of resource efficiency overall, including transportation and energy use in building materials, construction, and building operations
- Energy-efficient building systems
- Renewable energy use
- Water conservation and gray water reuse
- Habitat preservation and restoration
- Use of natural energies for building heating and cooling
- Rainwater capture, reuse, and recycling
- Natural stormwater management
- Use of recycled-content, nontoxic, salvaged, and local materials
- Healthy and productive indoor environments for people
- Durability of building materials and design
- Flexibility for building use to change over time
- Access to alternative transit modes (Yudelson, 2007: 165)

---

## Conclusion

Although building green has long been viewed as an added extra that drives up building costs, as green-building practices and materials have become more commonplace, and as energy and waste-disposal costs have risen, building green is increasingly proving to be more economical than traditional building, particularly when the long-term costs of ownership are calculated in fair and honest ways. While this is good news for those who want greener libraries, the fact remains that building and running a green library means much more than selecting the most environmentally friendly materials and gadgets. How a library is managed, including the accommodations it makes for its employees and users, has a huge influence on its overall impact on the environment. Making the truly green choice is rarely clear-cut, and library managers must carefully analyze products, library policies, and local circumstances to ensure that the choices they make are the right ones for the environment as well as the people who use and work in their libraries.

## References

Armstrong, Michael. 2008. "Portland's Proposed Green Building Policy." Sustainable Portland.org. http://www.sustainableportland.org/bps/index.cfm?c=41664&a=215279.
Energy Information Administration. 2009. "Average Retail Price of Electricity to Ultimate Customers by End-Use Sector, by State." United States Department of Energy. http://www.eia.doe.gov/cneaf/electricity/epm/table5_6_a.html.

Environmental and Energy Study Institute. 2009. "Building Energy Codes: An Important Component of Climate Policy." EESI.org. Environmental and Energy Study Institute. http://www.eesi.org/ 062209_codes.

Gould, Kira. 2007. "Beyond the Building: Making the Case for Institutional Change." *COTEnotes: Newsletter of the Committee on the Environment* (Spring). http://info.aia.org/ nwsltr_cote.cfm?pagename=cote_a_0703_harvard.

QuEST. 2009. "Shields Library_HVAC and Lighting Control Report." Report. Berkeley, CA: QuEST.

University of California, Sustainability Steering Committee. 2009. *Policy on Sustainable Practices and Guidelines*. Policy Statement. University of California, Office of the President.

U.S. Green Building Council. 2008. "LEED Rating Systems." USGBC.org. http://www.usgbc .org/DisplayPage.aspx?CMSPageID=298.

Yudelson, Jerry. 2007. *Green Building A to Z: Understanding the Language of Green Building*. Gabriola, BC: New Society Publishers.

# 9

# Running a Library during an Addition, Renovation, or Remodeling

There is an old joke about the surgeon who goes to the local garage to have his car repaired. While he is checking out the surgeon's car, the mechanic says, "Our jobs aren't that different. We open them up, look inside, and fix what's wrong." The surgeon thinks about this for a moment, then says, "True, but I have to keep the engine running while I'm making my repairs." Along the same lines, undertaking a building project while simultaneously keeping a library running substantially complicates both processes.

In general, constructing an entirely new library building will not hinder ongoing operations at existing library facilities, though there are some exceptions to this rule. A new building erected in close proximity to an existing library building may bring noise, traffic, and dust that impact library operations. A new-building project may consume some amount of the time and energy of library staff who would be otherwise fully involved in normal library operations. Finally, if all or parts of the library's collections are moved from existing library buildings into a new building, there will be some impact on operations.

On the other hand, a major addition, renovation, or remodeling (ARR) project will almost certainly impact operations in an existing library building, often in ways that frustrate library users and staff. Anticipating possible problems and effectively communicating with the public, library staff, and contractors are the keys to smoothing over the rough patches that come with almost every ARR project.

## Anticipating Problems: Things Will Go Wrong

If there have been library building projects during which everything went exactly according to plan, such creatures are rarer than Gutenberg Bibles. On almost every project, things will go wrong. Whether you consider it pessimism or realism, being prepared for things to go wrong is the best way to minimize, or even avoid, the worst consequences of good plans gone bad.

## Schedules

From the smallest do-it-yourself home improvement job to the erection of a massive skyscraper, it is far more common for a project to take longer than expected rather than to finish ahead of schedule or even on time. Bad weather, material shortages, labor problems, mistakes, accidents—a whole laundry list of phenomena can conspire to slow down the progress of a project. It is more than wise to assume that a project is going to fall behind schedule and beyond foolish to behave as if a projected completion date is written in stone. Construction contracts do require contractors to complete a project by a specific date or suffer financial penalties, but various extenuating circumstances allow contractors to avoid late fees. Notably, actions taken by the contractor's employer (e.g., the library or its parent organization) that delay construction remove the contractor's obligation to finish by the contracted date. So just because a project is scheduled to be completed in exactly 180 days, it is not a safe bet to go ahead and schedule your grand-opening celebration to take place in exactly 181 days. If you do, the grand-opening speakers may find it difficult to make themselves heard over the beeping of back-up horns and the screaming of power saws.

## Conflict

It is possible to simultaneously hold a flower show and a rodeo on the same patch of ground; it is not, however, possible to do so without conflict. When contractors are doing construction where library staff are trying to run a library, there is going to be conflict not only between library staff and contractors but also among library staff who find themselves stressed by the extra demands of doing their jobs in difficult circumstances.

> "It is bad enough we have to live with all that dust and noise, but now those idiots from ILL are parking their book trucks where they block the aisles."

It is the role of library management, and in particular of the library's project liaison, to be prepared to deal with construction-related conflicts before they blow up into major internecine battles, the scars of which may not heal (if they ever heal) until years after the project itself has been completed.

The most important thing to remember when dealing with such conflicts is that, in most instances, it is not a case of anyone behaving badly. The contractors are just trying to do their jobs. The idiots in interlibrary loan (ILL) are just trying to do their jobs. The library staff who are put out by the dust and noise and illegally parked book trucks are just trying to do their jobs. Because there is nobody to blame and nobody to reprimand, assigning blame and handing out reprimands will only make the situation worse. What works is helping the parties in conflict understand one another's perspective, finding workarounds, and fostering compromises, remembering, always, that all construction-related workarounds and compromises are, in the end, temporary. When dealing with the most intransigent conflicts, it is sometimes necessary for management to step in and simply eliminate the work demand that is the source of the conflict: "If we can't have book trucks blocking the aisle, and if we can't do ILL without a place to put book trucks, then we will just have to stop doing ILL for the two days it will take for the work on the ILL offices to be finished. Case closed."

## The Relocation Option

When the circumstances of an ARR project make it too risky to keep collections, equipment, or staff in their normal locations, or when those circumstances simply make all or part of the library building unusable by staff or the public, temporary relocation is the only option short of suspending access and/or services. Relocation, in whatever form it takes, must be planned in anticipation of disruptions to come; it should never be undertaken as an unplanned reaction to a situation that has spiraled out of control. Rather than undertake an unplanned relocation, it is almost always better to instead suspend library operations until the worst of the disruptions are over.

### *Temporary Relocation Scenarios*

In the event of an especially disruptive ARR project, libraries may find themselves facing any, or some combination of, the following temporary relocation scenarios:

- **Temporarily relocating non-public-service staff**
  - Because much of their work can be accomplished remotely, it is possible to temporarily relocate non-public-service staff almost anywhere, even to buildings located quite distant from the permanent library building.
  - The location to which non-public-service staff are relocated must have adequate technological infrastructure to support the staff's information technology needs, up to and possibly including a server room to house any servers that must be temporarily relocated.
- **Temporarily relocating public-service staff**
  - Assuming that some level of public service will be provided during the course of an ARR project, public-service staff must be staged where they are available to interact with the public. In most cases, this means that public-service staff need to be relocated adjacent to the permanent library building.
  - Options include relocating public-services staff to a nearby building, relocating them to a part of the library building not affected by the ARR project, or arranging for the erection of a temporary public-services facility (trailer, modular building, tent) adjacent to the library building.
  - As with non-public-service staff, public-service staff will require adequate information technology infrastructure to do their jobs.
  - Of course it is possible and desirable to relocate both non-public-service and public-service staff to a single facility located adjacent to the permanent library building. However, the relative portability of non-public-service staff provides an option if adjacent relocation space is not sufficient to house the entire staff.
- **Temporarily relocating collections or equipment to a closed facility**
  - A closed facility is the simplest solution for relocating library collections or equipment because once collections or equipment have been relocated, they

remain undisturbed until they are returned to the permanent library building at the completion of the ARR project.

- Because raw warehouse space can be used for a closed facility, this is often the least expensive relocation option.
- The downside of this option is that the collections and equipment remain inaccessible for the entire time they are relocated. In addition, raw warehouse space is not suitable for materials that need highly controlled environments, such as special collections and archival materials.

■ **Temporarily relocating collections to a paging facility**
  - Giving library users the ability to page collection materials from a temporary relocation facility provides a high level of service.
  - The paging option comes with costs that include:
    □ Transporting paged materials from and back to the facility.
    □ Staff time spent retrieving materials when they are paged and reshelving them once they have been returned by users.
    □ Implementing a storage solution that allows library staff to readily locate paged materials.

■ **Temporarily relocating collections, equipment, and services to an open facility**
  - This option provides the highest level of service in that all or most library collections, equipment, and services remain available to the public for the duration of the ARR project.
  - The cost of temporarily relocating an entire library and supplying full access and services is the most expensive relocation option.

## Facility Options for Temporary Relocation

If a library facing a major ARR project chooses to temporarily relocate collections, staff, or equipment, there are several options for the type of facility in which to relocate.

### Existing Surplus Facilities

When the library's parent organization has existing surplus facilities in which to temporarily relocate library staff, collections, or equipment, such spaces are typically available rent free. This is a big advantage that, in many cases, will override other considerations. However, making use of whatever excess facilities happen to be available is often a beggars-can't-be-choosers proposition. The available space may be less than ideally located, too small, poorly laid out for library operations, or otherwise undesirable.

### Leased Facilities

Leasing a facility gives the library some choice over the space to which it relocates, though finding a space that is the right size, suitably located, and generally well suited to meet the library's needs will usually limit the number of choices. Of course, a leased facility comes with the expense of rent payments. In addition, it is likely that the cost of any necessary improvements to, or customization of, a leased space will be borne by the library, not the owner of the facility; this, coupled with the fact that the cost per day of occupancy will be higher for shorter leases than for longer ones, means that leasing is often a prohibitively expensive option for all but the longest relocations.

### Temporary Structures

If there is sufficient open space adjacent to a library building undergoing an ARR project, relocating to one or more temporary structures is a viable alternative, especially if the project is highly disruptive and of long duration. While acquiring (through lease or purchase), siting, and readying temporary structures to serve as a temporary library facility is a costly proposition, this option can be worth the cost and effort when suitable leased facilities are too expensive, too distant, or simply not available. Trailers are usually the least costly and most easily configured type of temporary structure, but the amount of space trailers provide is limited. When more space is necessary, modular buildings or large rigid tents are feasible, though potentially expensive, options. For one example, in 1992 UCLA's entire undergraduate library moved into a two-story, 36,000-square-foot

---

**The Full Cost of Temporary Relocation**

There are many costs associated with temporarily relocating, some of which are easy to overlook when calculating the total cost of a relocation. Relocation costs to watch out for include:

- Transporting collections, staff, and equipment to the relocation site and, at the end of the ARR project, transporting them back to the permanent library building are the most basic costs involved in such a move.
- Relocating some types of equipment (book stacks are a notable example) incurs not only round-trip transportation costs but also round-trip disassembly and reassembly costs.
- Because loaded library book stacks can be erected only on floors capable of supporting the weight of books, the average building can accommodate book stacks on the ground floor only. This may make it necessary to secure more square feet, or more costly square feet, of space than would be necessary were book stacks not included in the relocation.
- Staff time expended as a result of the relocation, including both time spent working on the relocation as well as relocation-related staff downtime, can add up to a considerable expense.
- Relocation will impose the additional technical services workload of inventorying relocated materials and updating their catalog location information (and, possibly, availability) when the materials are relocated, as well as when they are moved back to their permanent location.
- The library may find itself responsible for bills that it is not normally required to pay at its permanent location, including bills for electricity, gas, water, sewer, and trash collection.
- Depending on the temporary facility, sufficient parking for staff (and possibly the public) may incur an additional expense beyond the basic cost of the lease.
- Configuring a temporary space so that it meets the needs of the library can be hugely expensive. Configuration costs may include:
  - Upgrading network, telecommunication, and other technology infrastructure
  - Supplying furniture for office and/or public spaces
  - Meeting human comfort needs in a warehouse or other raw space that may lack or be deficient in restrooms, staff break rooms, HVAC, and so on
  - Providing interior and exterior signage

tent and remained there for the duration of a two-year project to bring the circa-1927 Powell Library building up to modern fire-code and seismic standards. This solution was so successful that the temporary structure won an American Institute of Architects/ American Library Association Building Award. Readying the site, erecting the tent, and preparing the tent's interior space took one month and cost $2 million ("UCLA's Powell Library Moves into Tent during Rehab," 1991: 441).

### Evaluating a Temporary Facility

When temporarily moving library collections, equipment, or staff out of a library facility, it is important to carefully evaluate the safety and security of the facility to which those resources are being moved. First, it goes without saying that if staff are relocated to a temporary facility, the facility must meet their needs for comfort and safety. For collections and equipment, there is no sense in moving these to a facility where they will be no better protected than if they were still smack in the middle of a construction project. For this reason, it is necessary to obtain a thorough, professional evaluation of a prospective relocation facility well in advance of signing a lease. Features to look for in temporary facilities include:

- Floors capable of bearing the weight of loaded book stacks (150 pounds per square foot)
- Ceiling height sufficient to allow the erection of book stacks
- Secure doors and windows
- Good key-management practices on the part of facility managers
- Alarm systems (burglar, fire, and water)
- Adequate temperature and humidity control (HVAC system)
- Pest control
- Light control (no direct sunlight on collections or equipment)
- Weatherproof (no leaky roofs, windows, doors, etc.)
- No, or at least minimal, overhead water sources: water pipes, storage tanks, evaporative coolers, etc.
- Bonded facility managers and personnel
- Adequate insurance in the event the library needs to make a claim for loss or damage
- Absence of hazardous materials such as insecticides, dangerous chemicals, asbestos, flammables, explosives, or radioactive substances. If a facility has any history of being used to store hazardous materials, it should be professionally tested to ensure that no dangerous trace amounts of any such materials remain on site.

When evaluating a temporary facility, take into account the fact that the longer collections or equipment are to be stored there, the more safe and secure the facility must be. For example, storing 50,000 books in a warehouse without adequate temperature and humidity control might be an acceptable risk for a week or month; however, it becomes a far less acceptable risk to do the same for six months or a year.

Finally, before embarking on any library building project that might in any way endanger library collections, equipment, or staff, it is good practice to check the library's insurance policy to determine if it adequately covers construction- and relocation-related losses; if it does not, investigate the possibility of obtaining a supplemental policy for the duration of the building project.

## Communicating with Contractors and Their Employees

Unless there is an imminent threat to life or property—say, for example, a forklift is about to back over a rare-book cataloger—library staff should never directly tell construction workers what to do or how to behave. If library staff observe construction workers doing anything that creates a problem, the message needs to go to the library's project liaison who can then bring it to the attention of the project manager and the general contractor. From there, whatever remedies are required can go down the general contractor's chain of command to the workers. This is not to say that, in the course of a project, library staff cannot speak to or become friendly with construction workers; but it is important that any problems involving construction workers need to be resolved through the proper channels. A situation in which a bunch of self-appointed construction bosses run around barking orders is a formula for disaster.

Anyone who has worked for long in a library knows that the stereotyped image of the bun-haired, shushing librarian is a far cry from reality. Similarly, anyone who has been around construction workers knows that the stereotyped image of the apelike, wolf-whistling construction worker is just as much a myth. Most construction workers are completely professional in their on-the-job behavior, and so it is a mistake to automatically assume that bringing construction workers into a library will result in bull-in-a-china-shop problems. That said, the best practice during a building project is for the library-project liaison, the project manager, and the general contractor to go over the ground rules before the first worker sets foot in the library. Some worksite rules to consider include:

- Library staff and users have the right to expect respectful and appropriate behavior from construction workers. This means that while on the worksite construction workers should use language that is appropriate for an office-type environment, respect the privacy of library users, and not engage in any type of harassing conduct.
- Construction workers have the right to expect respectful and appropriate behavior from library staff. As mentioned, library staff should not give direct orders to construction workers or criticize their behavior. Any problems library staff may have with construction workers should go through the proper channels.
- Construction workers will, of course, show up dressed to do hard, physical labor; however, they should not report to the worksite wearing clothing that displays blatantly offensive images or language.
- Construction workers must follow the same rules for smoking and tobacco use that apply to library staff and users.

- Construction workers may not bring anything into the library that staff or users are prohibited from bringing, including alcohol, controlled substances, pets, weapons, etc.
- Construction work is almost always noisy, but unnecessary noise should be avoided. The sound of a pneumatic drill is necessary noise. Amplified Van Halen is unnecessary (albeit hard-rocking) noise.
- Construction workers should be respectful of library collections and equipment and do their best to avoid causing any damage to them. Carpenters should not use library study tables as sawhorses; plasterers should not use book stacks as impromptu scaffolding; laborers should not sit on upholstered library furniture while wearing dirty clothing.
- Construction workers should not eat or drink in any library areas where food or drink is not normally allowed.
- Construction workers should not clean tools (paintbrushes, trowels, buckets, etc.) in library sinks, on lawns or sidewalks, or anyplace else where doing so will leave a mess. They should also properly dispose of any trash resulting from their presence in the library.
- Construction workers may be required to park in designated construction parking areas.

In addition to these suggestions, there are always special local considerations to take into account. When remodeling a prison library, for example, construction workers will of course be required to follow a number of rules and procedures unique to a prison setting. Construction workers employed on a school-library or military-library project may be required to undergo background checks. On one library project with which the authors of this book were involved, both construction workers and library staff underwent required training on what to do should they encounter any endangered species on the worksite.

## Communicating with the Public

The construction-related stresses that impact library staff during an ARR project will also impact the public and quite possibly create bad feelings about the library. The Knitting Club's favorite meeting room will be unavailable for two months. The elevators are out of service until Monday. The stacks are closed to browsing and books must be paged. While it is all but impossible to undertake an ARR project that does not result in at least some inconvenience for the public, good communication during such situations can go a long way to prevent, or at least ameliorate, public displeasure caused by a library building project.

### *What to Communicate*

After ensuring public safety during the project, providing acceptable levels of service and access to information (without hindering work on the project) should be the library's biggest concern. Under the often-trying circumstances of construction, good service begins with communicating fully and honestly with the public so that everyone knows what to expect. Communication should begin well before the start of any project and include information that falls under the following broad headings.

## When

The public will want to know when the project will begin and when it will end. While beginning dates are easy, unanticipated schedule delays, as previously discussed, make ending dates trickier. It is good practice to label all ending dates with hedge words like *estimated* or *projected*. It is also not a bad idea to overestimate completion times. Library users are generally delighted when a project finishes a week earlier than they were told it would; just the opposite feelings can set in when a project finishes a month later than its estimated completion date.

The public will also want to know specific dates for temporary building closures, shut-downs of online systems, inaccessibility of all or part of the collection, and interruptions of regularly scheduled library services and programs. The further in advance the public knows a building, service, or resource will not be available, the more able individuals will be to make other accommodations.

## What

Naturally enough, the public wants to know what will be done during the course of a building project: the children's room will be renovated; five new meeting rooms will be created; the heating and air-conditioning system will be updated. When library staff are closely involved in a building project, it is easy to make the mistake of forgetting to share with the public the basic information on what the project will accomplish.

## Why

Explaining why a project is being undertaken goes a long way toward promoting understanding. Instead of focusing on the inconveniences brought about by construction, explaining why focuses on the benefits to come at the end of the process: more space for reading and studying, better technology, more attractive surroundings. A different kind of *why* falls under the rubric of "because we have to," as when a project is undertaken to bring a building up to seismic code or to remediate a health hazard such as asbestos. Even though the "because we have to" whys may not be terribly inspiring, sharing them with the public can nonetheless increase understanding and tolerance in the face of inconvenience.

## Risks

Members of the public should be made aware in advance of any risks to their health and safety that may result from a building project. Even if the chance of any harm is slight, it is better to give fair warning and let members of the public decide for themselves how to respond. For example, when asbestos is properly removed from a building, there is no risk to workers or the public; even so, making it clear that there will be asbestos removal allows those who wish to avoid even the remotest possibility of risk to stay away until after the removal has been completed. Examples of common construction-related risks to the public include:

- Construction-related traffic
- Extremely loud noise
- Dust
- Presence of hazardous substances (asbestos, paints, glues, cleaners, diesel exhaust, etc.)
- Falling objects

**Specific Details**

Besides the broad communication categories previously listed, any building project will include a laundry list of specifics that needs to be communicated. A few of these fall under the broad categories already listed but are worth repeating anyway:

- Building closures
- Limitations on access to printed books and other library materials
- Limitations on service and programs
- Downtime for electronic systems (catalog, databases, full-text information resources, computer lab)
- Anticipated noise or other annoyances that may interfere with normal use of library facilities
- Traffic and parking issues
- Lists of alternative resources such as other area libraries and online information sources unaffected by construction
- Information about the architect and general contractor
- Financial information (cost of the project, how it is being paid for, who is paying)
- Work completion timeline (with updates as the timeline shifts)

## *How to Communicate*

Once a library has decided what needs to be communicated to the public, staff may use any of the means of communication the library normally employs to get the message out:

- Print-format publications (flyers, bookmarks, brochures, newsletters)
- Webpages
- Telephone hotlines (live and/or recorded information)
- Signage
- Press releases and advertisements (newspapers, radio, television, billboards, websites)
- Social networking tools (Facebook, Flickr, Twitter, blogs, etc.)
- In-person meetings (town halls, brown bags, guest speakers, etc.)
- Special events (parties to celebrate construction milestones, story times that relate to construction, etc.)

A particularly effective way to communicate information about building projects is via architectural renderings and models. Design architects are normally required by contract to provide renderings and models, so these visual artifacts should be available to share with the public via static displays. Renderings and models also can be scanned or photographed and thereby made available to the public in digital formats. Note that architectural models are astoundingly expensive to produce, so it is unusual to see more than one per project.

### Involving the Public in the Process

Allowing the public to feel like part of the process is a time-honored way of helping everyone feel better about the inconveniences brought on by a project and focusing attention on the benefits to come. Public participation is arguably most important for public libraries, but academic, school, and even special libraries may reap benefits from finding ways for those they serve to participate. If nothing else, the sound and fury of a building project draws attention to the library, and this attention can be used to increase general awareness of the library and its services. Involving representatives of the public in the early planning process of a project (see Chapter 1, "Getting Familiar with the Process: The Stages of a Building Project") is a good start. Once work begins, public celebrations of project milestones—groundbreaking, topping out, grand opening—are great opportunities for involving the public and, at the same time, communicating good news about a project. Any effort to involve the public in actual work—such as moving books into a finished building—will more than likely be symbolic rather than functional. Like it or not, the safety and liability risks of allowing volunteers from the public to engage in anything more than symbolic work far outweigh any good that might result. Finally, when planning any public event related to a building project it is essential to work closely with the general contractor so that the event does not hinder progress or, even worse, endanger any member of the public.

### Public Services and Access during Construction

Providing public services and access during construction requires planning, creativity, and flexibility. The planning starts with determining to the fullest possible extent what services and resources are going to be made unavailable by the construction, when they will become unavailable, and for how long. When the impact is small, the actions taken by the library need not be extreme. For example, if the collection is going to be made unavailable for two days but will otherwise be accessible as usual, the library may do nothing more than inform the public and encourage everyone to check out any materials they want in advance of the two blackout days. If the collection is going to be unavailable for six months, more drastic measures are in order, up to and including the extreme (and costly) expedient of running the library out of a temporary facility.

Creativity and flexibility come into play when, for example, the reference desk ends up wrapped in protective plastic and covered with a good inch of plaster dust. Is the solution laptops, wireless, and a folding table in the front foyer? Roving reference librarians prowling the stacks with laptops in hand? An all-e-mail-and-telephone reference service? Whatever the solution may be, it will certainly not involve sitting at the reference desk conducting business as usual.

It is in a library's best interest to provide the highest possible level of service and access in spite of construction, but there are times when construction is so disruptive that providing service and access becomes either impossible or counterproductive. Obviously, if construction reaches a point where it presents a danger to library staff or the public, there can be no access to, or services provided within, that building until the danger has passed. There may also be times when libraries are faced with the question of whether it is better to entirely close for a day or two so that some major part of a project can be finished without anybody getting in the way or, instead, to keep the library open while the contractor spends days trying to work around the complicating presence of library staff and the public.

### *Do Not Forget Library Staff*

Providing library services during a major ARR project can be tough on library staff. They may find themselves struggling to keep the library going while simultaneously dealing with the stress of relocation, the gripes of extra-cranky library users, or job assignments they never dreamed of when they read the phrase "and other duties as assigned" on their job descriptions. As with the public, library staff will feel more involved if they are given a voice in the early design phase of the project, informed in advance about what to expect, and kept well briefed as the project unfolds. Library managers should encourage staff to find creative solutions to the inevitable problems that pop up during a project. Managers must also be understanding when a chaotic situation prevents staff from performing at their peak or saps their morale. The library staffer who spent two days packing offices for a temporary relocation or a week putting up with the noise of a jackhammer on the other side of her wall should not get managerial grief because she fell behind on her copy cataloging quota or made a mistake processing an ILL request. Anything library management can do to recognize what staff have been going through as a result of the construction work or to thank them for their efforts can help staff hang in through tough times. Even simple gestures like the occasional pizza lunch, catered coffee break, or commemorative I SURVIVED THE REMODELING T-shirts can mean a lot to library staff.

## Conclusion

Closing down an existing library for several months in order to carry out a major ARR project is a luxury that few, if any, library managers will ever enjoy. Providing access and service during a project brings challenges and frustrations—and the bigger the project, the bigger the challenges and frustrations. However, library managers can minimize the pain if they do their best to anticipate problems before they materialize and communicate effectively with the public, library staff, and contractors. Finally, when anticipating and communicating are just not enough, library managers need to have the wisdom and courage to admit that—for however many days, weeks, or even months it takes—the intensity of the work being done on the building simply prevents the library from providing access and/or services. Suspending library operations may be a bitter pill, but sometimes it is the best medicine.

## Reference

"UCLA's Powell Library Moves into Tent during Rehab." 1991. *College & Research Libraries News*, 52, no. 7 (July/August): 441.

# 10

# Building Maintenance

A robust building maintenance program is critical to extending the life span of a library building and everything it contains, including mechanical systems, furniture, fixtures, equipment, and collections. At the same time, proper maintenance keeps a building safe, healthy, and serviceable for its occupants. Employing good maintenance practices to extend a library building's life span not only wrings the maximum amount of value out of every construction dollar spent, it is also an extremely green practice by virtue of saving the natural resources, energy, and landfill space that would otherwise be consumed in prematurely building a replacement structure. In cases where, for the foreseeable future, a replacement for an aging building is not in the plans, building maintenance shifts from best practice to basic survival strategy.

Building maintenance is valuable and necessary, and like most valuable and necessary things, it comes with a price tag—a high one. Consider this: The cost of properly maintaining a building for 50 years is greater than the cost of constructing the building in the first place. This means that building maintenance must be professionally and thoughtfully managed in order to get the most value out of every maintenance expenditure. Badly managed building maintenance will not only destroy a building; it will destroy a budget as well.

## Routine Building Maintenance

Routine building maintenance is hardly exciting stuff. It may seem to just happen, often at night when library staff and users are not around to see the work being done. Of course, routine building maintenance does not just happen; it requires people, supplies, equipment, and money to carry out. More important, boring, old routine maintenance is the backbone of any building maintenance program.

### Interior Cleaning

At first glance, routine interior cleaning seems like something done in the name of keeping up appearances and basic sanitation; however, it is actually an important element of extending the service life of valuable building components. Regularly vacuuming carpets, for example, not only removes germs and allergens while keeping building interiors looking spruce, it also removes dirt and grit that will, over time, send carpeting to an early grave. Also, carpets and other building components that are not properly cleaned may impact other parts of a library building: a single soda bottle spilled on carpet can, without prompt and proper cleaning, produce a mold bloom with the potential to devastate an entire library collection and force the library building to be closed for weeks of mold remediation.

Just as regularly cleaned floors and carpets last much longer than floors that are allowed to go dirty, the same is true for window treatments, furniture, mechanical and electronic equipment, and even books. There is always a danger that, in tight budget times, cleaning services will be reduced to save on salaries. While cutbacks in cleaning services will produce short-term savings, the long-term effects will be increased expenses as furniture, fixtures, equipment, and building components deteriorate prematurely.

Routine cleaning must be supplemented when a library hosts an event that brings more than the usual number of visitors into the building. When planning a major event, the cost of extra cleaning services and supplies (especially for restrooms) should be included in the budget. Extra cleaning services are also necessary during most remodeling, renovation, and expansion projects, as these activities introduce high levels of dirt and dust into a building. Similarly, allowing food and drink into the library will require more cleaning than if food and drink are completely banned (and the ban is effectively enforced). All of which is not to say that either special events or relaxed food-and-drink policies are bad things, but that the need for increased cleaning needs to be considered as part of any decision-making process.

As discussed in more detail in Chapter 8, "Green Libraries," the use of green, low-VOC (volatile organic compounds) cleaning products provides many benefits and is worth discussing with those who manage a building's cleaning services.

### Exterior Cleaning

Exterior cleaning includes the cleaning of windows, stonework, decorative metal, concrete, and cladding, as well as the removal of graffiti. Of all of the forms of exterior cleaning, window cleaning is the most familiar, as it tends to occur more often than other forms of exterior cleaning. For a multistory building, the cost of cleaning window exteriors can easily run to tens of thousands of dollars. Therefore, exterior window cleaning is not an everyday occurrence, and it may not be an every year occurrence. For a large organization, such as a university campus, window cleaning is often performed on a rotating schedule under which each building's windows are cleaned only once every few years. Cleaning of other exterior surfaces (bricks, concrete, siding, etc.) may happen even less often or not at all. Graffiti removal, however, should occur on an as-needed basis, as graffiti that is allowed to remain on a building will attract even more graffiti.

### Painting

Like cleaning, painting may seem more like a cosmetic procedure than a maintenance practice, but this is not the case. Metal or wood that is exposed to the elements, excessive moisture, high heat, or caustic substances needs to be protected by paint or, for some woods, stain in order to last as long as possible. Even interior drywall and plaster will gain some measure of protection from proper painting.

Painting schedules, common in large organizations, call for interior repainting to take place once every *n* years, while exterior painting takes place every *y* years. The actual numbers that take the place of *n* and *y* will vary depending on building materials, climate, organizational culture, and budgets. As with cleaning, scheduled painting is often put off during tight budget times, much to the detriment of the buildings involved.

### Pest Control

Pests can spread disease and seriously damage library collections and furnishings. Regular cleaning of building interiors and proper trash management are the best pest-control measures. Library staff should always be on the lookout for signs of infestations, including insect eggs, bird nests or droppings, rodent spoor, pest-damaged items, and actual sightings of pests themselves. Pest problems are more likely to surface during renovation, remodeling, or expansion projects as the work creates new pathways into an existing structure or drives pests indoors by disturbing their habitat. When a pest problem surfaces, the best option is to bring in a professional pest-control company. Many pest-control companies offer green and/or humane options for pest control, but in some cases there is no choice other than employing the entire arsenal of traps and industrial-strength poisons.

### Grounds Maintenance

The tasks that comprise grounds maintenance will vary from region to region, but typically include mowing, leaf raking, pavement sweeping, trimming and pruning, planting and cultivation, watering, snow and ice removal, and pest control. Allowing grounds to become overgrown is not only unattractive; it attracts pests and can damage buildings, as is the case when tree branches rub against rooftops or painted surfaces. Failing to manage snow and ice accumulations not only damages buildings but can lead to injuries and possibly lawsuits.

---

**Who Is Responsible for Building Maintenance?**

In libraries that are part of larger parent organizations, it is possible that all maintenance of the library building is the responsibility of some external-to-the-library department—such as Facilities, Physical Plant, or Buildings and Grounds—that operates with almost compete independence from the library organization. Under such an arrangement, the library is placed in the role of a tenant with no responsibility for building maintenance and little to no direct control over maintenance operations. To make the role of tenant work to library's advantage, it is crucial that the library administration have an effective working relationship with the maintenance department. Ideally, the maintenance department will be represented by a designated building manager with responsibility for the library building in his or her portfolio and with whom the library administration can establish a mutually satisfactory working relationship. For a very large

*(Continued)*

---

**Who Is Responsible for Building Maintenance?** *(Continued)*

library building, 100 percent of the building manager's time may be devoted to managing the library building; for smaller library buildings, the building manager's time may be divided among several buildings in addition to the library. The keystones to a library working effectively with a building manager, or a maintenance department at large, are mutual understanding of each other's operations and effective communications. The best practice is to have one person on the library staff who serves as the designated liaison to the maintenance department and through whom all building-maintenance matters should be channeled. Such an arrangement allows the liaison to develop a good working relationship with the maintenance department while preventing a chaotic state of affairs in which individual library staff members drive maintenance staff to distraction with uncoordinated, possibly uninformed, barrages of questions, problems, and complaints. It does no good at all for library staff to demand a level of service that no maintenance department could hope to provide. Nor is it reasonable for library staff to assume that those charged with maintaining the library building somehow intuitively understand all the needs of a library operation. Indeed, a major justification for this chapter is that it will help library staff understand enough of the essentials of building maintenance to communicate effectively with building managers and maintenance staff. Turning librarians into professional building managers is beyond the scope of both this chapter and this book.

Especially in smaller or independent libraries, it is possible for building maintenance to be integrated into the library's organizational structure. While having the virtue of allowing library administration to exert direct control over maintenance operations, such an arrangement brings with it the requirement that either (1) someone within the library administration possess strong working knowledge of building maintenance or (2) the library must have on staff a professional building manager to oversee building maintenance.

In any library, large or small, there is always the temptation for library staff to take building maintenance into their own hands either as a matter of expedience or out of frustration with slow or nonresponse from those charged with maintaining the library building. Certainly there is no problem with library staff performing small maintenance chores such as picking up a piece of paper that did not make it into a trashcan or, in the absence of custodians, mopping up a spilled drink before it runs off the table and onto the carpet. Problems arise, however, when library staff begin taking on maintenance tasks that are well beyond the scope of their job descriptions or training. Library staff should not be unclogging toilets, painting office walls, or climbing ladders to clean out gutters. The questions library staff members should ask before taking on any building maintenance task are:

- Is it safe for me to do this?
- Will my doing this violate any laws, codes, or union agreements?
- Can this maintenance task wait until a professional is available to do the work?
- Do I really know what I am doing?
- Do I have the proper tools and equipment to do this job?

In almost all cases, library staff are better off avoiding temptation by leaving building maintenance to the professionals, no matter how annoying the wait may be.

---

## Maintenance Frequency and Scheduling

The elements that together comprise building maintenance can be sorted in several ways, with one of the most significant of these being frequency of occurrence. At one end of the frequency scale are the maintenance tasks that take place at daily, or nearly so, intervals. Examples include sweeping, cleaning restrooms, emptying trash cans, and most other cleaning functions. Next come the weekly to monthly to semimonthly tasks that can range from carpet cleaning, to cleaning out roof gutters and drains, to inspecting the relief valves on boilers. Then there are maintenance tasks that may take place on (roughly) an annual basis, such as washing exterior windows, dusting book stacks, and inspecting and adjusting mechanical systems (elevators, HVAC, electrical systems, plumbing). Finally come the maintenance tasks that take place at greater-than-annual intervals. As mentioned, window cleaning may be on a schedule that calls for several years to pass between each cleaning. Repainting may occur at intervals of five, ten, or more years. Toward the far end of the maintenance timeline are tasks such as repointing exterior bricks, a bit of maintenance that needs to be done at intervals of 30 or 40 years, depending on the quality of the original mortar, the skill of the brick masons, and the local climate. Some infrequent building maintenance tasks, such as replacing a worn-out roof, are closer in nature to renovation projects than what is typically thought of as maintenance.

A professional building manager should maintain a written building maintenance schedule that lists all building maintenance tasks, shows when each task must be performed, and provides a historical record of when each building maintenance task (including inspections) was performed and by whom. Paper-based building maintenance schedules are traditional, but several commercial maintenance scheduling software programs are available for purchase. Besides saving time and paper, maintenance scheduling software can be programmed to send electronic reminders so that upcoming maintenance tasks are not overlooked. While it is unlikely that anyone other than a building manager or other maintenance professional will be involved in establishing and maintaining a building maintenance schedule, library administrators can benefit from at least passing familiarity with the maintenance schedule so that they remain aware of when major, possibly disruptive, maintenance is scheduled to take place. For example, if you know that in six months the entire library interior is due for its ten-year repainting, you might want to hold off on doing that mural on the wall of the children's room.

## Preventive, Condition-Based, and Emergency Maintenance

Most building maintenance tasks can be sorted into the categories of *preventive maintenance, condition-based maintenance*, or *emergency maintenance*. While all three types of maintenance are, of necessity, part of the total building maintenance package, close attention to the first two categories of maintenance will avoid having to resort to the latter.

### Preventive Maintenance

Preventive maintenance involves routinely and properly caring for facilities, fixtures, and equipment; conducting regular building inspections; and detecting and responding to any emerging problems discovered during either inspections or the day-to-day use of a building. The concept of preventive maintenance will be familiar to any automobile owner who regularly changes the oil and keeps tires at the recommended pressure in the hope that a small amount of up-front effort combined with relatively small maintenance expenditures today will help avoid costly repairs and major inconveniences tomorrow. In a library building, preventive maintenance may be performed by in-house maintenance staff, such as custodians or facilities staff; it can be outsourced, as when a company is on contract to perform regular maintenance and inspection of a major mechanical system within the library building; or it can be managed by a combination of the two, with the latter being by far the most common solution. The phrase *planned preventive maintenance* is used to describe preventive maintenance that involves scheduled service visits from a trained professional, often an employee or authorized representative of the manufacturer of the equipment or system being maintained. Under planned preventive maintenance the scheduling of service visits is based on either passage of time (every six months, every two years, etc.) or amount of use (the number of hours a piece of equipment has run). While preventive maintenance (planned or not) comes with associated costs, the idea is that preventive maintenance will save money in the long run by extending the service life of systems and equipment, by reducing the need for costly emergency repairs, and by avoiding unscheduled downtime.

### Condition-Based Maintenance

Condition-based maintenance involves providing maintenance as systems or equipment begin to show age or wear. Using the automobile analogy once again, condition-based maintenance means taking your car to the shop when the left front wheel starts making a funny noise rather than ignoring the noise until the wheel falls off at 70 miles per hour. In a library building, it may be the HVAC blower that begins making the funny noise, but the concept of getting it serviced before something really bad happens is the same as with an automobile. For automobiles or buildings, the trick to successful condition-based maintenance is to detect potential problems and take action to ameliorate them before they turn into costly emergencies. The Achilles' heel of condition-based maintenance (and the reason that planned preventive maintenance is so important) is that some systems can fail (at times catastrophically) with no prior warning.

### Emergency Maintenance

While preventive and condition-based maintenance come with a cost, emergency maintenance is the most expensive maintenance of all. First of all, resorting to emergency maintenance often means paying overtime to facilities staff or outside contractors as well as paying a premium to rush-order parts and other supplies. Second, emergency maintenance often results in costly downtime while repairs are being made. Third, when a maintenance problem becomes an emergency, it may result in damage to more than just the system that has failed. For example, if a roof suddenly begins to leak, there is not only the cost of repairing or replacing the roof but also the cost of rectifying the damage caused by any water that enters the building. Potentially even more catastrophic is the situation in which the sudden failure of a building system results in a fire or explosion. While no amount of preventive and condition-based maintenance can head off all maintenance emergencies, failing to carry out good maintenance practices all but ensures that emergency maintenance will be an ongoing problem—and expense—for a library building.

## The Role of Inspection in Library Building Maintenance

Regular inspection is key to keeping a building running well and avoiding building emergencies. The library building manager should arrange for a thorough, buildingwide maintenance inspection at least annually. The annual inspection should include, but not be limited to, the following:

- Structure
  - Roof
  - Foundation
  - Walls
  - Ceilings
  - Floors
  - Entrances/exits
  - Glazing (e.g., windows and structural glass)
  - Cladding (e.g., siding, brickwork, exterior metal)
- Mechanical systems
  - Electrical
  - Plumbing
  - HVAC
  - Elevators
  - Lighting
  - Data Networking
- Furniture, fixtures, and equipment
  - Book stacks
  - Compact storage areas
  - Office and public spaces
- Exterior spaces and ground
  - Sidewalks
  - Parking lots
  - Exterior lighting
  - Landscaping
  - Irrigation system

Keep in mind that the phrase "annual inspection" can be interpreted loosely, as inspections may need to take place more often than annually, especially as a building ages. Even the best-built library building will see components and systems fail over the years, while library buildings that suffer from poor design, shoddy construction work, and low-quality materials will see age-related problems surface sooner and more frequently.

In either case, aging buildings benefit from a higher frequency of inspection than might have been necessary when that same building was new.

Many components and systems found in a library building require inspection more frequently than once a year in order to identify wear and tear, damage, or deterioration. Manufacturers may recommend inspection periods shorter than one year, and in some cases adhering to an inspection schedule is necessary to keep a component or system under manufacturer's warranty. All inspections should be included in the building maintenance schedule so that none are overlooked in the daily grind of keeping a library building running. For some critical building systems, such as elevators and boilers, local codes require inspection by a licensed inspector at prescribed intervals. Even when the law does not mandate a licensed inspector, the best practice is for inspections to be conducted by qualified building maintenance professionals. That said, library staff can still be on the alert for potential building problems, as it is always a good practice to have the maximum number of eyes regularly looking to spot small problems before they become major ones.

### Spotting Structural Problems

Because structural problems are so potentially costly and, in extreme cases, dangerous, being alert to signs of structural problems should not be limited to annual inspections. Depending upon geographic region and building type, structural problems in a library building may be caused by one or more of the following:

- Moisture-related ground shifting
- Earthquakes
- Insects and other pests
- Extreme weather conditions, including:
  - Severe rainstorms
  - Hurricanes
  - Tornadoes
  - Snowfall
  - Freezing/ice
  - Flooding
  - Extreme heat
- Aging

An experienced building maintenance technician or inspector will know how to spot the signs of damage or potential damage from these threats. However, there are a number of signs for which anyone can be on the lookout. It is worth encouraging library staff and other building occupants to notice and report (through proper channels) anything regarding the library building's structure that looks odd or questionable. This includes, but is not limited to, the following:

- Cracks in interior walls (concrete, plaster, or drywall)
- Fractures in concrete on (or adjacent to) the building (e.g., walls, sidewalks, stairs)
- Moisture or moisture stains

- Bulges or depressions in walls or floors
- Bowing or cracking of overhead beams
- Doors that do not open and close properly (often indicative of shifting floors, walls, ceilings, or foundations)
- Windows that do not seal or are cracked
- Any signs of problems with the building's roof (wet spots on the ceiling, finding pieces of roofing material on the ground, roofing material that appears to be loose)
- Insects entering or leaving the building
- Wildlife in or near the building
- Unusual odors

## Maintenance Supplies

One of the keys to a good building maintenance program is maintaining adequate stocks of basic spare parts and materials. These can range from custodial supplies like mops and cleaning products to air system filters and lightbulbs. Unfortunately, in tight budget times spare parts and materials are areas where cash-strapped maintenance departments and building managers will cut corners to keep down costs. This is a poor stewardship tactic, one that often costs more in the long run due to such unintended consequences as high rush-shipping costs, lost productivity, and costly damage to building components or systems that are not being properly maintained due to lack of supplies. It is more than obvious that destroying thousands of dollars worth of HVAC equipment for want of a $10 air filter is pennywise and pound foolish, but such avoidable calamities can happen all too easily in a budget-slashing climate. Similarly, it is poor stewardship if the library has to request frequently used items such as lightbulbs or packages of paper towels in tiny quantities and then do without while waiting for the requested items to be delivered piecemeal from a central facilities warehouse. Dollar costs aside, scrimping on basic spare parts and materials will lead to dissatisfaction among library users and employees. By themselves such annoyances as burned-out lightbulbs, nondraining drinking fountains, and empty soap dispensers are trivial, but cumulatively, and over a long enough period of time, they send a message of a library on the downslide. Though all possible needs for spare parts and maintenance materials cannot be foreseen, and though some items are simply too expensive or bulky to maintain in stock, a well-managed maintenance department should keep sufficient supplies of appropriate, frequently used items on hand.

## The Basics of Maintaining Building Systems

As discussed in Chapter 3, building systems are essential to make a structure habitable for its human occupants. When these systems do not function properly or fail entirely, a building will quickly become uncomfortable and potentially unsafe for occupation. While the following sections do not go into great depth, they provided enough understanding of the basics of maintaining building systems to allow library staff to effectively communicate with building maintenance professionals when the need to do so arises.

## HVAC Systems

Of all building systems, the HVAC (heating, ventilation, and air conditioning) system is the most important for making a building habitable for human beings and a suitable home for collections. If air is not circulating properly in a library, it is impossible to maintain the constant humidity and temperature that are optimal for library collections. Because human beings have different temperature preferences depending on race, gender, and age (with age being the most significant factor), some percentage of a building's occupants will be uncomfortable even when the HVAC system is functioning properly. When the HVAC system fails, the percentage of building occupants who feel uncomfortable will rapidly increase.

Because HVAC systems are complicated and incorporate many moving parts, they have a high potential for failure even when properly maintained. When HVAC systems do not receive regular routine maintenance, catastrophic failures are inevitable. Blowers—the fans that move air around a building—are critical pieces of machinery in any HVAC system, yet they are quite prone to failure. For example, fan belts in blowers break frequently, especially when exposed to extreme cold or heat. Good maintenance practice calls for replacing all blower belts at the interval specified by the system's manufacturer and keeping spare belts on hand for the occasional failure. Strange noises coming from heating/cooling vents are often warning signs that an HVAC blower will soon fail without proper maintenance. Besides blowers, other parts of an HVAC system that may fail without regular inspection and maintenance include chillers, filters, vents and dampers, and mechanical parts of the system other than the blowers. Building expansion, renovation, and remodeling projects can play havoc with existing HVAC systems, principally by forcing them to work extra hard to heat or cool the building. It is good practice to keep new and existing HVAC systems separate until the new system has been fully tested and commissioned.

While not always visible or audible to the casual observer, signs of problems with an HVAC system include these:

- Excessive icing on HVAC equipment
- Dripping water or wet spots beneath HVAC equipment
- Blowers that never stop running
- Excessive electrical consumption
- Inability to adequately heat or cool the building
- Unusual noises
- Insufficient or excessive airflow
- Odors

## Electrical Systems

Modern building electrical systems are relatively robust and stable. However, there are electrical-system maintenance tasks that should be performed periodically. In most instances, these should be performed only by qualified electricians or by building maintenance personnel who have been trained by an electrician.

Floor receptacles are one of the most vulnerable parts of any electrical system because their location leaves them subject to accumulating dirt and debris even when properly covered. If floor receptacles are located in an area where spills are possible, they should be either ground fault interrupter (GFI) outlets or on a GFI circuit equipped with appropriate breakers. Inspecting floor receptacles for debris, moisture, and broken or missing covers should be a regular part of the building maintenance routine.

The most common lighting system failure is the burning out of bulbs and (for fluorescent lights) ballasts. (A *ballast* is a device that regulates the amount of current flowing into a fluorescent bulb's electrical circuit. When a ballast begins to fail, it gives off a strong burning smell.) To avoid a gradual descent into darkness, every library building should be on a scheduled bulb and ballast replacement cycle supplemented by the replacement of individual bulbs and ballasts on an as-needed basis.

Even with a modern electrical system, it is possible to trigger a system failure by overloading an electrical circuit. Overloading occurs when the demand for electricity (by such devices as computers, photocopiers, fans, microwave ovens, etc.) exceeds the capacity of the circuit into which the devices are plugged. Before adding electrical devices to a circuit, it is essential to consult with a trained professional to ensure that adding those devices will not overload the circuit.

Typical indicators of problems with an electrical system include these:

- Tripping of circuit breakers (including surge protectors)
- Dimming of lights
- Excessive power consumption
- Burning odors
- Electrical sparking

### Plumbing Systems

Besides regular cleaning, there are a number of routine maintenance tasks that will keep plumbing systems working properly.

Plumbing systems employ traps and seals that rely on moisture to function properly. For example, if a floor drain trap is allowed to dry out, odors can escape and spread throughout a building. To keep traps moist and prevent gases from escaping, maintenance staff should pour approximately one quart of water into each trap once a week, regardless of whether the trap has been used. Dried-out traps are most likely to occur during slow times, such as winter and summer holiday periods when plumbing systems get little or no use.

Another common plumbing problem is mold buildup around fixtures. Besides being unsightly, mold can have health implications for building occupants, particularly people with such upper respiratory problems as asthma and allergies. Regular, thorough cleaning is usually enough to keep mold under control in a public building, but adequate ventilation and humidity control play a major role in mold abatement as well. Besides harming people, mold has the potential to spread to library collections with potentially devastating consequences.

Water and steampipes can be sources of damaging leaks. Because pipes are often concealed from sight, it is easy for leaks to go undetected until considerable damage has already been done. Pipes most often leak at joints, usually because a joint (1) has become loose over time, (2) was never properly tightened and sealed, or (3) has failed with age. Banging pipes should receive immediate attention from a professional plumber as this can be a sign of either a water hammer or steam hammer, conditions which can cause pipes to burst—in rare cases with enough force to injure or kill building occupants.

Water heaters may be subject to a number of problems, including excessive pressure, unsafe water temperatures, sediment buildup, improper venting, and any situation which allows a water heater to run dry while its heating elements remain hot. Regular inspection by a professional plumber is essential to ensure that water heaters operate safely for the full term of their intended service lives.

The signs of plumbing problems, though somewhat obvious, include:

- Banging pipes
- Lack of hot water or excessively hot water
- Leaks or drips
- Fixtures that have come loose (even slightly) from the floor or wall
- Corrosion (rust)
- Clogs (drains that back up, toilets that do not flush properly)
- Low water pressure
- Mold growth
- Odors

## Conclusion

As stated from the outset, reading this chapter will not make anyone into a building maintenance professional. At the very least, having read this chapter should make anyone who works in a library aware that building maintenance is an important, complex, and expensive component of running a library, even if the complexity and expense are not the direct responsibility of library professionals. For those who want to learn more about building maintenance, the best tactic is getting to know the building manager for your library and spending some time with that person to learn the ins and outs of your particular building. Accompanying your building manager on inspection tours is the best way to learn a great deal in a short time. Asking to occasionally sit in on meetings of building maintenance managers is another good way to learn (especially if you do more listening than talking). In addition to learning from your local professionals, following are two books that go into the subject in considerable detail:

Payant, Richard P., and Bernard T. Lewis, eds. 2007. *Facility Manager's Maintenance Handbook*, Second Edition. New York: McGraw-Hill.

This thorough handbook is divided into the following major parts: "Organizing for Maintenance Operations," "Facility Operations and Maintenance Plans," "Equipment and Systems Operations and Maintenance Procedures," "Facilities Emergency Preparedness," and "Capital Investment."

Wood, Brian. 2009. *Building Maintenance*. Chichester, UK: Wiley-Blackwell.

Although Wood's book has a U.K. focus, its 300-plus pages provide an excellent short course on the subject of building maintenance.

# 11

# The End of the Job: Building for the Future

To some extent, every library building project is the same in that the desired outcomes of every such project is a library building that is attractive, safe, efficient, comfortable, durable, and designed to support the needs of those who use the library as well as the needs of those who work in it. In other ways, every library building project is unique because a host of local circumstances—climate, zoning, codes, funding sources, population, topography, transportation, architectural traditions, building customs, and materials (not to mention local library traditions and culture)—combine to make themselves felt during the course of the project and to leave their mark on the final result. Due to the unique forces shaping every library building project, no architect, builder, librarian, electronic discussion list, article, or book (this one very much included) can totally prepare you for every surprise that will surface during the course of a project. A building project with no surprises would be a surprise indeed.

We, the authors of this book, have called on our experience and education in an attempt to introduce library professionals to most of what typically goes into, and goes on during, a library building project. Some of the things we have written about will not apply to certain projects, and of course we cannot anticipate every possible surprise. So what then, are the main concepts we hope readers will take away from this book, incomplete though it may be?

1. Appreciate the importance of the programming process:
   - Involve a wide spectrum of stakeholders early in the process.
   - Use effective group processes to get the most out of programming efforts.
2. Strive for the best possible design outcomes:
   - Make sure that outcomes support the needs of both users and staff.
   - Take into account current needs (based on actual data) while allowing flexibility for future needs.
3. Accept the realities of design and construction:
   - Do not try to assume the role of architect, contractor, or construction worker.

- Take the time to learn about building codes, building plans, and construction practices and terminology so that you can understand what is taking place and, when necessary, communicate effectively with builders.
- Enter into every library building project knowing that problems, crises, and disappointments are inevitable.

4. Value the importance of preparation:
   - Prepare library staff and users for what is to come.
   - In advance of the project, take the necessary steps to safeguard people, collections, and equipment for the duration of the building project.

Most important of all, however, is understanding that all library building projects must be undertaken with the future in mind. No library building project should be any one individual's private playground; nor should it be the private playground of the current day, year, or decade. Though no one with feet planted in the present day can guess with complete accuracy how libraries will be used decades into the future, creating a library building that will serve the future as well as the present is far more likely if the project is undertaken with the humbling knowledge that today's library users and library workers are no more than the temporary occupants and custodians of a structure that will, with any luck, be passed on to others who will benefit, it is hoped, from the foresightful choices made by those who preceded them. This is true whether it is your privilege to see a brand-new building through to completion or to shepherd a renovation, remodeling, or expansion of a building erected before your parents were born.

# APPENDIX

# The Art of the Request for Proposal

While the following section (based in part on a library furniture RFP issued by the University of California, Merced, in 2004) focuses on a request for proposal (RFP) for furniture, it can also be a guide for writing other types of RFPs, including those for fixtures and equipment.

To begin with, a good part of any RFP will consist of institutional boilerplate devoted to contractual details that are much more the purview of purchasing officers than of library staff. However, if a furniture RFP is left entirely to purchasing officers and, perhaps, facilities staff, the suitability of the furniture that comes through the door is going to be anyone's guess. The concerns of purchasing officers and facilities staff, while valid and worthy of consideration, are not the same as those of the library staff who must live with the result. Library staff who understand the programmatic needs of the library and, ideally, the needs of library users, must be involved in the RFP process—in particular, with the specifications section of the RFP—to ensure a successful outcome. Taking this one step further, there are also benefits to be gained from having library users involved in the RFP process (assuming the purchasing rules allow it).

## Specifications

When writing specifications for an RFP, the general idea is to balance openness with specificity. Openness is good because it allows bidders to offer creative solutions that those issuing the RFP might not have considered. Specificity is good because it ensures that the library gets what it needs. Examples:

**Too open:**  "All library study chairs shall be manufactured of wood."

  - This wide-open specification allows a low-budget manufacturer to enter fly-apart, pressed-wood chairs into the competition.

**Too specific:**  "All library study chairs shall be manufactured of oak."

  - This specification eliminates the manufacturer of an excellent, competitively priced library chair that happens to be made of ash.

A further problem with excessive specificity is that it can result in manufacturers being forced to build custom furniture to meet the very detailed conditions called for in an RFP. Custom furniture is far more expensive than furniture that is part of an existing product line.

Besides this need for balance, good furniture specifications should address the following:

- Pieces, Quantities, and Dimensions
- Design
- Durability
- Code Compliance
- Service
- Delivery and Installation

## Pieces, Quantities, and Dimensions

The RFP must detail what pieces of furniture are wanted (e.g., traditional library tables and chairs, upholstered armchairs and sofas, occasional tables, study carrels, stacking chairs, lamps, etc.) and indicate how many of each piece is needed (e.g., ten eight-person library tables, 80 study chairs, six sofas, etc.). Because an RFP and a final contract are two distinct (though related) documents, the exact number of pieces to be delivered is subject to some adjustment in the drafting of the final contract; that said, it is bad practice to ask bidders to deliver one thing in the RFP and something wildly different in the final contract.

How much furniture to purchase is a question that regularly comes up during major building projects. Stuffing a space with too much furniture will make it feel crowded and may actually violate fire codes and/or Americans with Disabilities Act (ADA) regulations. Too little furniture will make a space feel empty and result in a shortage of places for library users to sit and work. Project architects typically submit drawings showing proposed furniture layouts, but very often these are not reliable guides as the architect's layouts have little to do with the realities of library programs or actual furniture, fixtures, and equipment (FF&E) budgets. A professional interior designer can be a great help for both determining how much furniture is the right amount for a given space as well as for deciding how the furniture might best be laid out. The easiest mistake to make is to put furniture too close together. This is especially true with traditional library tables, where there must be not only space for the tables, but also for chairs. The passageways between the tables—which should be measured from the backs of the occupied chairs, not the edges of the tables—must be wide enough for people in wheelchairs to navigate. A rule of thumb is that a wheelchair needs the same space as two people walking side by side (36 inches minimum, 48 inches ideal). Before the furniture actually arrives, you must have an accurate furniture-layout diagram that the installers can consult as they move the pieces into place. A useful trick is to use blue painter's tape to lay out the shapes of full-sized tables and other furniture pieces on the floor to envision various furniture layouts and come up with a useful diagram.

With or without professional advice, too often the amount of furniture that goes into a building is driven by the limits of the FF&E budget instead of by the programmatic needs of the library. When the FF&E budget provides only so much money for furniture, the question often becomes, "Should we buy more furniture of lower quality or less furniture of higher quality?" In the long run, it is best to opt for less furniture of higher quality because the total cost over time will actually turn out to be lower. That said, the realities of needing to provide enough places for people to sit and work can result in compromises between quantity and quality.

The RFP can provide dimensions for furniture pieces, but it should allow reasonable flexibility in order to take advantage of the cost savings that come with ordering from existing product lines as opposed to calling for custom furniture. Requiring custom 30.75-inch-high tables instead of allowing the use of noncustom 30-inch-high tables can end up costing thousands of dollars extra.

## Design

The RFP should address furniture design, a concept that encompasses both aesthetics and functionality. Of course it does no good to provide only a general requirement in an RFP, such as, "The furniture must be aesthetically pleasing and functional." Most furniture manufacturers believe that everything they make is aesthetically pleasing and functional. However, an RFP can describe what effect the library is trying to achieve with a particular type of furniture in a particular space while, at the same time, explain what function the furniture is expected to fulfill. For example, for library study chairs the RFP might specify:

> Library study chairs should be comfortable for users who may spend several hours at a time occupying these chairs for reading, studying, or using notebook computers. Library study chairs should have the look of classic library furniture.
>
> Keywords for library study chairs: *Classic. Traditional. Timeless. Clean.*

For the leisure-reading-room furniture the RFP might specify:

> Furniture for the leisure-reading room should invite users to relax while they enjoy a magazine, newspaper, novel, or other reading-for-pleasure item.
>
> Keywords for leisure-reading-room furniture: *Relaxing. Comfortable. Homey. Casual.*

By thinking carefully about the design qualities you want and stating them in an RFP, the job of evaluating bidder responses is made easier because there is something more than "I like it" or "I think it's ugly" on which to base aesthetic judgments.

In addition to providing the just-described function and keyword specifications, the design section of a furniture RFP may ask each bidder to:

- Describe how its furniture will accommodate technology.
- Supply photographs of furniture pieces the bidder is proposing, a list of any design awards the bidder may have won, and a list of libraries or similar institutions currently using the bidder's products.

- Provide specifications that address ergonomic issues.
- Provide a brief statement describing how the design of the bidder's products is appropriate for the project in question.
- Provide any other information or statements that speak to the design of the bidder's products.

## Durability

Bidders should be asked to submit documented evidence that its products can endure years of hard use in a library environment. Types of evidence that a bidder may submit include, but are not limited to, the following:

- Product data for each type of product, including materials, construction, and finishing materials and processes
- Shop drawings that:
  - show large-scale details, attachment devices, and other components;
  - show connection details for all members;
  - show locations and sizes of members;
  - distinguish between solid lumber and veneered components;
  - identify wood species of components;
  - show locations and sizes of cutouts and holes (if any) for accessories (including furniture/technology interfaces); and
  - show grain direction, identifying flat and edge grain surfaces
- Samples of exposed hardware and accessories
- Samples of internal hardware
- Samples of upholstery
- Full-sized furniture samples (provided only upon request following initial proposal evaluations)
- Complete product warranty information, including policy on replacement of parts, including labor
- Description of all owner maintenance that is either required as part of any warranty or recommended by the bidder
- Information on the bidder's ability to provide extended warranties, if required

## Code Compliance

The RFP should ask bidders to submit documents showing that their products are in compliance with various national, state, and, in some cases, local codes. In particular, bidders should submit documents:

- verifying that each model of furniture proposed in response to the RFP meets ANSI/BIFMA (American National Standards Institute/Business and Institutional Furniture Manufacturer's Association) standards;

- verifying that each model of furniture proposed in response to the RFP meets appropriate state and/or local fire safety codes; and
- specifying which of its products comply with ADA (Americans with Disabilities Act) requirements.

## Service

The service portion of the RFP asks each bidder to describe how it will handle such matters as returns, damaged products, manufacturing defects, order cancellation, and customer-requested delays. This section will also ask bidders to elaborate on any no-cost, value-added services the bidder can provide as well as on the geographical location of the staff and facilities that will support installation and ongoing service if the bidder is successful.

The service section of the RFP is a good place to specify that the bidder must provide compact discs containing complete CAD engineering drawings of the furniture manufactured as part of the bid within 30 days of delivery. These drawings provide a detailed record of the dimensions and other specifications of the furniture and components ordered so that the library can order identical furniture in the future.

## Delivery and Installation

Delivery and installation are an important part of any furniture installation; if mismanaged, the result will be delays and extra costs. The RFP should require each bidder to provide a detailed plan for how it will handle delivery and installation of the finished products. To avoid unpleasant surprises, the RFP should clearly state that the fees charged for installation must include prepaid delivery. Other delivery and installation specifications should include the following items. The bidder:

- must coordinate dates for delivery, staging, and final installation of its products;
- must deliver all furniture to the final building destination, including movement to and from any staging area;
- must install all units so that they are plumb, aligned properly with adjacent units, and in accordance with layout provided;
- will leave the premises in clean condition; all packing materials and debris will be removed and all items will be free of dust and lint;
- will be responsible for immediate minor repairs, paint touch-up, or replacement of any damaged items; and
- will instruct the client in the operation or adjustment of any items installed.

## Other

This section of the RFP is a grab bag of issues not covered in other sections. Examples of the specifications called for in this section include, but are not limited to, the following:

- An overview of how discontinued products are supported during the life cycle of the product
- A description of the bidder's proposed plan for managing the account being bid, including descriptions of the roles and organization of the bidder's dedicated account support team, along with descriptions of its technical-support system, response, and problem-resolution procedures
- A description of the bidder's order-entry system and its method for confirming orders and coordinating all service components to ensure accuracy and on-time delivery
- A description of the bidder's back-order procedure and delivery guarantee for any items that are not delivered on time
- Information regarding the resources, expertise of personnel, training, and stability of staff that will service the account being bid
- A description of the bidder's environmental stewardship and the environmental sustainability of the products proposed, including information related to Greenguard certification and Forest Stewardship Council–certified products

## Parceling

Within a single RFP it is possible to divide the bid into different parcels and allow bidders to bid on any or all parcels. For example, soft seating might be one parcel, library study tables and chairs another parcel, carrels another, and lamps another. Or parcels might be based on spaces in the library: the main reading-room parcel, the leisure-reading-room parcel, the computer-lab parcel, the children's-room parcel, and so on. Parceling out a bid creates the possibility of selecting more than one vendor and, by so doing, cherry-picking from the strengths of each bidder. Bidder A might be very strong on library study tables and chairs, while Bidder B provides more quality and variety when it comes to soft seating. Choosing multiple bidders does complicate purchasing and installation, but the benefits in terms of lowered costs and higher quality can make such complications worth the trouble.

## Bidder Questions

Bidders are allowed to ask questions about an RFP before they submit a final bid. In most cases, these questions must go to the institutional purchasing officer, who then solicits answers from those involved in the RFP and, in the interest of fairness, presents the questions and answers to all bidders. It is important to note that a bidder can be disqualified for contacting anyone other than the designated purchasing officer once an RFP has been released. If you are involved in an RFP, be sure your purchasing officer briefs you on all the rules before you get started; in extreme cases, failing to follow purchasing rules can cost you your job or result in criminal charges.

## Issuing the RFP

Once an RFP has been completed, the institution's purchasing office is responsible for issuing it. There are standard conduits for issuing RFPs, but the library can suggest to purchasing officers the names and contact information of potential bidders. A number of companies specialize in library furniture; of course these companies should be notified. However, companies that do not specialize in library furniture may be able to bid on all or some parcels of an RFP and should not be overlooked when the RFP is issued. The more companies that bid on an RFP, the more likely the library will be able to get the furniture it wants at the best possible price. Every RFP will include a strict deadline for responses from bidders. That deadline should be far enough in the future to give a bidder time to make a thoughtful response while still allowing enough time for the responses to be evaluated, contracts drawn, and the furniture built, delivered, and installed on time.

## Evaluating Responses to an RFP

Once the responses to an RFP have been received, the winner of the bid is determined through an analysis of the quality points awarded combined with the price quoted by the bidder. When done properly, this method of awarding a contract prevents the RFP from simply being awarded to a low bidder regardless of how unsatisfactory its products may be. Analyzing the price quote in relation to quality points is the business of purchasing officers; however, library staff should be involved in actually awarding the quality points.

The best way to award quality points is to devise a scoring sheet that lists scoring criteria along with the maximum number of points that can be awarded for any one criterion. The scoring criteria absolutely must be derived from what is called for in the RFP. For example, if the RFP asks bidders to address the durability of their products, the scoring sheet should have a criterion that allows points to be awarded for durability. On the other hand, points can never be awarded for something that is not in the RFP. Thus, if the RFP does not ask bidders to provide information about the greenness of their products, the scoring sheet cannot have a criterion in which points are awarded for greenness. It is also important to think carefully about how much weight any single criterion is given. If 80 percent of the total points awarded are for durability, the end result could be unpadded steel seats of the type normally seen in prison mess halls.

Once the scoring sheets have been developed, a good practice is to distribute copies to those who will do the scoring (again, library staff must be represented in this group) and allow the scorers to independently review the bidder responses and assign scores. This approach prevents powerful or persuasive members of the committee from unduly influencing others. The scores can than be submitted to the chair of the committee, tabulated (anonymously, if necessary), presented to the committee, and then discussed (see Sample Furniture RFP Scoring Sheet sidebar).

| Sample Furniture RFP Scoring Sheet | | | | |
|---|---|---|---|---|
| Quality Point Assessment | Maximum points | Bidder A | Bidder B | Bidder C |
| Design | 225 | | | |
|   1. Aesthetics | | | | |
|     ■ Appropriate to parcel | | | | |
|   2. Functionality | | | | |
|     ■ Ergonomics | | | | |
|     ■ Technology interface | | | | |
| Durability | 500 | | | |
|   1. Sample quality | | | | |
|   2. Warranty | | | | |
|   3. Required maintenance | | | | |
| Code Compliance | 25 | | | |
|   1. Fire | | | | |
|   2. Structural | | | | |
|   3. ADA | | | | |
| Service | 100 | | | |
| Delivery and Installation | 100 | | | |
| Overall Bid: Completeness, Creativity, Responsiveness | 50 | | | |
| TOTAL | 1,000 | | | |

An important point to remember is that the total number of points awarded is arbitrary. There is nothing magical about 100 or 1,000 or any other times-10 number of points, though scorers familiar with traditional school grading may find factors of 10 easier to work with. Also, the fact that one person may give low scores or another issues high scores does not matter once the scores are averaged. The most important thing is for each scorer to be as consistent as possible from one bidder to the next. The best way to achieve consistency is to begin with a solidly written RFP and for the scorers to base, as much as humanly possible, their scoring on what the RFP calls for rather than on any personal likes or dislikes.

# Index

Page numbers followed by the letter "f" indicate figures; those followed by the letter "t" indicate tables.

# About the Authors

## Donald A. Barclay

After graduating from the University of California, Berkeley, School of Library and Information Studies, in 1990, I began my library career at New Mexico State University. I later worked at the libraries of the University of Houston and Houston Academy of Medicine–Texas Medical Center before taking a position at the nascent University of California, Merced, where I am now the Deputy University Librarian. When I began work at UC Merced in 2002, there were no students, faculty, or buildings. Helping to raise a university, a campus, a library, and a library building from a cow pasture was a once-in-a-lifetime experience and still remains the most satisfying adventure of my professional life.

*The Library Renovation, Maintenance, and Construction Handbook* is my fifth book for Neal-Schuman Publishers, a great group of professionals with whom it is always a pleasure to work. I have also published in the field of Western American Literature, an area of study which has always fascinated and amused me. When I'm not working or writing, I enjoy spending time with my delightful daughter, Tess; rooting for the San Francisco Giants baseball club; and obeying the orders of our three family dogs: Maggie, Chica, and Luna (aka "You Little Monster").

## Eric D. Scott

I have worked in University of California libraries for more than 15 years, and I have been involved with large and small construction and renovation projects. The largest of these is the UC Merced Library, where I currently wear the dual hats of Director of Administrative Services and Head of Access Services. After earning a bachelor's degree in history and geography at the University of California, Los Angeles, I worked in libraries for several years before pursuing an MLIS at San Jose State University. Prior to my work in libraries, I was a journeyman carpenter for small contractors working primarily in residential remodeling and residential and light commercial construction. I also spent several years in U.S. Army Special Forces and served on a U.S. Department of Energy Special Response Team.

When I'm not running the day-to-day operations of the library so my esteemed coauthor can focus on his prolific publishing, I enjoy spending time with my wonderful wife, Claudia Lange, and enjoying our five cats (aka "The Pride") led by an affectionate but willful 18-pound male Maine Coon named Viggen (Thunderbolt). I am also an advisor for the Sports Shooting Club at UC Merced and regularly teach firearms safety and personal defense to members of the public.